Born in Eastbourne in 1957 and educated at Brighton and Cambridge, Joe Bennett taught English in a variety of countries before becoming a newspaper columnist and writer of travel books. He lives in Lyttelton, New Zealand.

Also by Joe Bennett

Bedside Goats and Other Lovers
Fun Run and Other Oxymorons
A Land of Two Halves
Mustn't Grumble
Love, Death, Washing-Up, etc.

Where Underpants Come From

From Checkout to Cotton Field –
Travels Through the New China

JOE BENNETT

POCKET
BOOKS

LONDON • SYDNEY • NEW YORK • TORONTO

First published in Great Britain in 2008 by Simon & Schuster UK Ltd
This edition published by Pocket Books, 2009
An imprint of Simon & Schuster UK Ltd
A CBS COMPANY

1 3 5 7 9 10 8 6 4 2

Simon & Schuster UK Ltd
1st Floor
222 Gray's Inn Road
London WC1X 8HB

www.simonandschuster.co.uk

Simon & Schuster Australia
Sydney

A CIP catalogue for this book is available
from the British Library.

ISBN: 978-1-84739-001-1

Typeset in Palatino by M Rules
Printed by CPI Cox & Wyman, Reading, Berkshire RG1 8EX

Contents

Contents

For Spencer

Introduction

There are 6.5 billion people in the world. Line them up as on a parade ground, then inspect them like a commander in chief. Roughly every hundredth person you pass will be British. Every fifteen-hundredth or so will be a New Zealander. Every fifth will be Chinese.

Officially China has 1.3 billion citizens. Actually it has rather more, perhaps as many as 1.6 billion. That's as near as makes no difference a quarter of the world's population. It's also five times as many people as America's got.

Having gone to the trouble of gathering 6.5 billion people into one place, do another little exercise. Ask all the farmers to step forward, the people who make their living by tilling soil or tending livestock. Of those, one in three will be Chinese.

Dismiss the people and line up the world's pigs. I have no statistics on British or Kiwi pigs, but every second pig in your line will be Chinese. China produces 49 per cent of the world's pork and eats the lot. The figure for ducks is even more impressive, but they're harder to line up.

To put it simply, China is unimaginably big. And China is booming. That boom has only just begun. Most Chinese people

1

remain poor but are keen to do whatever it takes to become rich. So China looks set to dominate the twenty-first century. And once it has gained domination there seems no reason why it shouldn't retain it for however many centuries are left to our species. China is just too big to argue with. Only India could put up much of a fight and it probably won't.

Already most of us are clothed by China, shod by China, supplied with hardware by China, effectively in debt to China. And yet most of us know very little about China. My experience is typical. I left university thirty years ago, ostensibly educated. My knowledge of China was nil.

Such ignorance has precedents. Until the thirteenth century, when Marco Polo got banged up in a Genoese prison and passed the time by telling tall stories to his cell mate, very few people in the West knew anything much about China. Back then, travel was more difficult and ignorance more understandable. Today China is only a day in a plane from anywhere else, and yet for most of us China remains mysterious. The reasons lie in China itself.

In the Chinese language two characters represent the country. The first is a rectangle with a vertical stroke through it. It means middle. The second looks like a malformed Christmas tree in a box. It means people. China sees itself and has always seen itself as the centre of the world. To the Chinese, China is all. It is the Middle Kingdom with the mandate of heaven. And the non-Chinese bits of the world have never mattered much.

For a couple of millennia China led the world in technology and pretty much everything else. Only since the eighteenth century has the West collectively caught up with China and then overtaken it. But the West's triumph looks like proving brief. China has rejoined the race and is coming up fast on the rails. It will get its nose ahead soon. Then it will streak away. Again.

This book recounts my first experience of China. There are plenty of better-informed books about China, but I suspect this is the only one to begin with a pair of underpants.

1

Becoming Sherlock

Within living memory, men's underpants were simple. They were white and capacious. When eventually discarded they were more capacious, but less white. Today they are less simple. The displays in The Warehouse in a Christchurch shopping mall hold perhaps a hundred varieties of underpants, from satin boxer shorts with scarlet hearts, to hugging hipsters with pictures of racing cars.

I buy six pairs. Five come rolled in a clear plastic pouch and they cost me NZ$8.59. They are the simplest, plainest briefs for daily wear. The sixth pair is for special occasions. They are black with a grey waistband into which the word 'Authentic' is embroidered. There is no vent in the front, but there are two stickers where a vent would be. One says 'stretch' and illustrates the verb with arrows going in all directions. The other says 'double front'. In other words, these pants will accommodate an erection and absorb accidents.

Underpants ought to be a swift purchase because the only

consideration is practicality, but it takes me a minute or two to settle on the Authentics. What delays me is vanity. I want the pants to flatter me a little. It is a ridiculous concern. No one will ever see these underpants except my dogs and perhaps the occasional sexual partner. The dogs will take no interest, and if a sexual partner and I reach the underpant stage, then, frankly, it's a done deal. It would take more than pictures of racing cars to halt the momentum. Nevertheless I am clearly not alone in taking aesthetic considerations into account, otherwise there would not be a hundred different varieties of underpants.

The waistband tells me that my Authentics were made in China from cotton and elastane. Another label says 'CLASS' in capital letters, and on the reverse, 'Mens Lifestyle Underwear combines fashion styling with functional features for all-day comfort.' Despite the word 'lifestyle', the euphemisms, the needless capitalization and the missing apostrophe, I have to acknowledge that the label reflects my reasons for choosing these pants. They are conventional and sturdy, which is more or less how I am, but with a hint of elegance, which is how I'm not. But it is how I would like to be. These pants are aspirational. They cost NZ$5.99.

On the way home, with my pants in a bag on the seat beside me, it strikes me as remarkable that underpants can be made in China and transported to New Zealand, passing through the hands of, and making a profit for, I don't know how many middle men, and still be sold to me for just NZ$5.99. And as for the pack of five pairs for NZ$8.59, well, the economics of it is beyond me.

It also strikes me that I have effectively no idea how to make a pair of underpants. I know that cotton grows on bushes in rabbit-tail tufts, but not how those tufts become thread, or the thread cloth. Is the spinning jenny involved? And what about the waistband? I suspect the involvement of elastic, and that presumably means rubber, but what is the relationship between rubber, elastic and elastane?

My ignorance of underpants is representative of a far wider ignorance. In forty-nine years I have learned next to nothing about the commercial and industrial processes on which my easy existence depends. If some cataclysm were to reduce society to a few survivors, I'd be the one sitting on a heap of rubble with his head in his hands and no idea how to start again.

Back home my dogs follow me to the bedroom, where I pose before the mirror in my Authentics. The dogs display every bit as much interest in the pants as you would expect. But I have become interested in the pants, so interested that I send an email to my agent in London. 'Jim,' it says, 'I've got this idea for a book and I need someone to tell me it's a crap idea.'

I explain that I want to find out everything I can about a single pair of Chinese-made underpants, to trace them all the way back, if possible, to the source of their raw materials. In the process I hope to discover everything I can about the commercial world on which we all depend but about which I know so little. At the same time I want to learn something about that ever-growing giant called China. And it seems such a fine idea to me that without waiting for a reply I set about the research.

'Welcome to The Warehouse customer service. You're talking with Kim.'

'Kim,' I say, 'I've got a bizarre request', and I sense her steel a little on the phone. 'I'd like to talk to the person who buys your underwear. Not *your* underwear, of course, but, well, you know what I mean.'

Kim laughs. 'I'll put you through to the girls in Clothing,' she says.

I don't get the girls in Clothing. I get Sue in Gardening. I explain that I am after underwear. 'I'll put you through to the girls in Clothing,' says Sue. After a brief interlude of tinny rap music I get Kim again.

'Didn't anyone pick up the phone?' she says.

I explain about Gardening Sue. Kim asks what exactly I want to know, and then suggests that I try The Warehouse head office in Auckland. And I realize, suddenly, and much to my surprise, that I'm enjoying myself.

The head office answerphone offers four options, none of which bears any relevance to my request. I press Customer Service and get Kelly. I explain my purpose, conscious that I am refining the line already in the hope of kindling a flame of interest. When I say that I hope to track these pants all the way back to source, Kelly becomes gratifyingly intrigued.

'The bloke you want is Nick Tuck,' she says. 'He travels to China a lot.' She gives me his extension number. Her last words are 'Good luck.'

Nick Tuck's out of the office but his answerphone promises to return my call as soon as possible. It also gives his mobile number. I leave a message, then dial the mobile. As it starts to ring I picture Nick Tuck in an Auckland traffic jam or in a waiting room or a lift. And if, as Kelly suggests, he is the man I really need to talk to, the man who can set this quest properly in motion, the man with contacts in the great unknown of China, then I want to talk to him in more propitious circumstances than a traffic jam. I put the phone down.

The following morning I get an email from my agent. 'Joe,' it says, 'it's a crap idea. Best, Jim.' Well now, Jim knows his stuff. But I persevere, partly because it's costing me nothing, partly because I am enjoying feeling like Sherlock Holmes, but mainly because I am genuinely curious. I want to find out about these pants, and I also, just as strongly, want to find out what finding out about these pants will be like. How far will I get? And will I be allowed to see the mysteries?

Over the next few days I ring Nick Tuck's land line several

times but get no answer and I don't leave the same message again for fear of seeming demanding. Eventually I ring head office again.

'Welcome to Customer Service. You are talking with Tracy.'

When I tell Tracy that my research may eventually turn into a book, she too becomes intrigued.

'The guy you want to talk to,' she says, 'is Nick Tuck.'

I say that I have tried to talk to Nick Tuck.

'Then let's try Pam Hadlee,' says Tracy. 'She's lovely. She's away today but she will definitely return your call. I'll tell her all about you.'

I leave a message for Pam Hadlee. Two days later, she rings back. 'The person you want to talk to,' she says, 'is Nick Tuck.'

There's nothing for it. I ring Nick Tuck's mobile. Nick Tuck is in a traffic jam.

'Joe, yes,' he says, and I think I detect a wariness in his tone. 'I got your message. Sorry I haven't got back to you. Hold on while I put you on speakerphone. Now, what was it you wanted again?'

I explain, adapting my tale a little once more in a bid to assuage that wariness. I stress what good publicity this could be for The Warehouse.

'Email me the bar code,' he says, 'and we'll go from there.'

The bar code is 9401011304278. His reply is prompt and it reeks of relief. He explains that The Warehouse sources most of its underpants directly from factories in China, but it also sells a few lines imported into New Zealand by other outfits. My Authentics belong in the latter category. He gives me the number of the importers and a name to ask for, and he wishes me all the best.

Shortly afterwards I get an email from agent Jim. 'Joe, on second thoughts, your idea may not be as crap as all that. Can you send me a slightly fuller proposal? Best Jim.'

I send him a slightly fuller proposal. And I resist the urge to crow.

The bloke who answers the phone at the importers does not

tell me his name or say, 'Welcome to Customer Service.' He says 'Yeah?' then he pages the boss.

The boss's voice is purringly educated. I plump up my own accent a notch or two, a chameleon habit I acquired growing up in the English class system, and explain that I am eager to trace a pair of his underpants back to source.

'Why?' he says.

I start to explain that the underpants are not so much under-pants as a vehicle through which I can discover a little about the world of global commerce and particularly about the growing industrialization of China and its relationship to the West, but the purringly educated voice soon stops saying 'Ah-ha' or 'I see' or even 'Why?'

'Would it be easier if I sent you an email?' I ask.

'Yes.'

So I do. As follows:

Thanks for being open to my idea. The underpants I'm studying are a pair of men's Authentics. They're black with a grey waistband. My mission is to trace all the constituent parts of the underpants to source. I want to discover how they got from China to here, where they were made in China, where the constituents originated from. In short, I want to know everything that it is possible to know about this par-ticular pair of underpants . . .

I am NOT looking to uncover scandal or to do any sort of hatchet job. I will respect anything that you may wish to keep confidential – name of factory, price paid per item or whatever.

Here are some questions that I would be grateful for any answers to:

Where are the pants made?

Do you deal directly with the factory or through an agent?

Who organizes the shipping?

Which company actually does the shipping?

Where do the ships sail from and to?

Can you give me the name of someone I could contact in China regarding a visit? (He or she will have to speak English, I'm afraid.)

Is there anything else I ought to know but obviously don't?

Gratefully

Joe Bennett

At which point providence steps in, disguised, as always, as random chance.

I used to teach. The kids I taught in New Zealand are now in their twenties or thirties, and being Kiwis they have scattered all over the world. One, I now discover, has gone to Japan where he has made friends with an expatriate Kiwi art dealer. This art dealer is trying to get a book published in New Zealand. My former pupil suggested that I might be able to help, so the art dealer calls me. His name is Michael Gorman.

I offer Michael what advice I can, then I ask whether perhaps he might be able to give me some. Briefly I explain my mission. Michael loves the idea. His enthusiasm encourages me. I ask whether he has any contacts in China. And yes, he says, he has abundant contacts, and in particular the invaluable Ning Ning.

Whenever Michael visits China on business, Ning Ning acts as his researcher, guide, interpreter and factotum. Michael insists that I make use of her and that she will make everything easy for me.

Immediately my mental image of China changes. Until now China has been a vast unknown, a daunting impenetrability. But suddenly I have a name, and with it comes a sense of China being simply a country full of people like anywhere else.

Ning Ning replies immediately to my email. She is too busy to take me on. But the good news is that she has a friend Ruth, who, she assures me, speaks English every bit as good as hers and who, she also assures me, will be delighted to help.

Ruth, too, replies immediately to my email, and she is indeed delighted to help. I ring her to say that I'll come to see her and China in a couple of months. I say it glibly, but when I put the phone down I realize with a mild lurch that I'm now committed. It is all going to happen. I'm going to China. I rather expected to die without ever going to China.

Then I get this:

HI JOE
SORRY BUT I DO NOT HAVE GOOD NEWS FOR YOU.
I INCLUDE BELOW A REPLY FROM MY HK PARTNERS MAN-
AGING DIRECTOR.

> Alicia forwarded this mail of yours to me.
>
> The whole project sounds very interesting. If we are semi retired we should be able to show him around.
>
> However, all of us are just too busy to handle the case.
> There are so many areas involved that even ourselves are unable to cover.
>
> Although through contracts we will be able to penetrate into the depth of the aspects, the efforts put in will be enormous.
>
> Then your orders and production can be neglected . . .
> I don't think we will take up the mission.
>
> Kind regards.
> Ricky

THESE PEOPLE AR THE HONG KONG AGENTS THAT WE USE WHO HAVE ALL THE FACTORY CONTACTS. THEY SURPER-VISE ALL OUR PRODUCTION FORM ORDER TO SHIPMENT TIME.

AT THE FACTORY NOT EVEN I CAN COMMUNICATE

WITHOUT THESE PEOPLE ALONG SIDE TO TRANSLATE JOE
AND I HAVE BEEN DOING THIS FOR YEARS.

SORRY JOE BUT WE ARE UNABLE TO ASSIST IN YOUR
REQUEST.

GOOD LUCK

REGARDS

I reply:

Thanks for taking the trouble.

I don't want to seem a pest, but all I need is the name and address
of the factory where these underpants are made. The rest I can do for
myself and I'll leave you alone.

Is there any chance of just that single piece of information?

Regards

Joe

The reply is prompt and it reads like a door closing

HI JOE

SORRY I DON'T HOLD THIS INFO.

CHEERS

At which point Jim writes to tell me that my publisher is keen.

I decide to attack from both ends. I ask Ruth to contact any
Chinese underpant manufacturers she can find. She is to pretend that I am a prospective buyer from New Zealand. I feel
uneasy about the lie, but Ruth seems to have no such qualms.

Meanwhile I buy myself another pair of pants and start again.
My new pair are called Underdaks. They are grey with a black
waistband and have an agreeably soft and stretchy feel to them,
as they should at NZ$12.99. Though made in China, they are
marketed by Pacific Brands who have a factory on Brougham
Street in Christchurch.

11

When I ring the factory, I am swiftly transferred to head office in Auckland and a woman called Paula.

Paula listens, thinks the idea fascinating, is sure they can help, and promises to get back to me. Reasonably soon, she does.

Hi there Joe

    I apologize for the delay in coming back to you regarding your query. Unfortunately I have found that company policy is not to provide information on our supply sources — and so we are unable to help you with your project.

    I wish you well with the assignment.

Kind regards

Paula

Ruth, however, has met with success. Within days she has assembled a list of Chinese pant-makers who are terribly keen to meet me. But I still want, if possible, to follow a single pair of locally bought pants. It turns out that providence wants it too. On a brief trip to London, providence serves up Tim Coles.

I went to university with Tim. While we are having a coffee in Great Portland Street he asks me what I am writing at the moment and I tell him about my underpant plans. I mention The Warehouse.

'The Warehouse?' says Tim. 'I know the boss.'

The boss is Ian Morrice, a Scot recruited a few years ago to come to New Zealand and take over the company. I've heard him on the radio. Tim and he, it seems, worked alongside each other for a while at, I think, Tesco.

Dear Mr Morrice

    My name's Joe Bennett. I'm an author and newspaper columnist. I also happen to be a friend of Tim Coles, with whom you used to work in the UK. He suggested I get in touch with you.

    I have a commission from a London publisher to write a book

called 'Where Underpants Come From'. The mission is to trace a pair of Chinese underpants from the supermarket shelves back to source. This would mean finding how they're transported here, seeing where they're made, then following the materials from which they're made right back to cotton bush and rubber tree.

I started with a pair of Warehouse underpants. I eventually reached your buyer who told me they were bought from a third party importer. I got in touch with that importer but they refused to help.

What I would like is for you to give me clearance to follow a pair of underpants that you yourselves import, back to the factory where they're made and so on. The intention is to get to understand and explain the commercial and industrial processes that are a mystery to punters like myself.

I am not looking to uncover scandal. The book will be an honest record of my travels and my discoveries. If there were anything you wished to keep confidential, I would respect your wishes. I am confident that the book could bring you good publicity, especially since the cover photo would be almost certain to feature the pants themselves . . .

Any assistance I receive, will, of course, be acknowledged . . .

Sincerely

Joe Bennett

I never hear back from Mr Morrice. But within three days I get this.

Hi Joe

Ian forwarded me your email re: interest in The Warehouse. Shouldn't be a problem. Give me a call . . .

Rgds

Phil Jamieson

General Manager Strategy and Corporate Affairs

The Warehouse Group Limited

And I'm away. It pays to go to the top.

It rapidly transpires that I simply started with the wrong pants. The ones I should have begun with were the humdrum workaday briefs that I bought for next to nothing in a pack of five. Via its office in Shanghai, The Warehouse orders these pants direct from the factory and imports them itself.

When I apply for a visitor's visa to China, a friend advises me not to use the words 'writer' or 'journalist'. He also suggests that I give myself a bogus title such as 'Dr' or 'Prof'.

'They love a title in China,' he says. 'They've even got a "Department of Foreign Experts".'

I don't give myself a title, but in the section called 'Purpose of Visit' I write 'tourism'. It feels excitingly covert.

The visa is granted. I send an email to Ruth. 'I'm on my way,' it says.

2

Pooh in Shanghai

From the plane Shanghai's invisible. It's smothered by a pall of grey stuff. Not cloud, just grey stuff, tinged with brown.

Shanghai's official population is 17 million. Its actual population is anyone's guess. The only guess that no one makes is less than 17 million. Seventeen million is four New Zealands.

The airport is monolithic, its policemen tiny. In the queue for immigration, surrounded by a language I don't understand and policemen with guns, I feel mildly nervous. But my documents are scrutinized, my passport stamped and I am released into the country quicker than I would be at Heathrow, and infinitely quicker than I would be in Los Angeles.

My taxi is a Volkswagen Santana. So is every other taxi. When I get in beside the driver I unthinkingly reach for the seat belt. The driver lays a dissuading hand on my arm. He grins and mimes discomfort. I grin back. He then drives me into traffic where for the first time in my life I would like to be wearing a seat belt.

The traffic seems Italian but without the theatricality. To the casual observer it appears to be without rules. I am far from being a casual observer.

My driver takes every opportunity to thwart others, nosing into lanes, squirrelling for advantage. So does everyone else. Horns blare. My driver is immune to them. To him they are the equivalent of tyre hiss. He uses his own horn according to a simple pattern: whenever he brakes, he honks. It isn't anger. It's habit. And perhaps a sliver of vestigial hope that sounding a horn in Shanghai might make a difference.

He drops me in central Shanghai on the far side of the road from my hotel. Huaihai Road is three-laned if you discount the contraflow of bikes and motorbikes on either side going in both directions, plus the ones down the middle. I cross the road in comfortably under ten minutes.

A uniformed youth with more teeth than face holds the hotel door open for me, says 'Hellogoodmorningsirhowareyouwelcome', takes my dirty rucksack and leads me to reception where I have the undivided attention of three girls who take my details, photocopy my passport and by pooling their resources speak excellent English.

'May I smoke in my room?'

'Of course,' say the girls in a unison of astonishment.

From my room I ring the Shanghai office of The Warehouse and I am both delighted and surprised to find that they are expecting me. I arrange to meet them in a couple of days, and then I arrange to meet Ruth in a couple of hours. Whereupon I leave my room, take the lift to the lobby, say hello to the girls and step out into a city and a country about which I know effectively nothing.

Huaihai Road is shopping central. It is lined with the chain stores of parodic poshness that you see in airports: Louis Vuitton, Dunhill, Barbour, and tailors with Italian names. But two streets back from the main drag, the international veneer dissolves. Here is territory unmistakably Chinese. Every frontage is devoted to commerce, much of it pitiful. A tiny recess holds five dusty white toilet bowls and one less dusty one that the proprietor is sitting on. He is watching a portable television and using chopsticks to lift noodles as long as my forearm into his mouth. At a restaurant consisting of three formica tables, a single vast saucepan steams on a gas ring. Used plates sit half submerged in a pink plastic bowl of water drawn from a pump. Prices are chalked on a board. No meal costs more than 3 yuan. There are 5 yuan to the NZ dollar.

In an alcove a man squats to hammer the rim of a bike wheel. Next door a cave of stationery is so crammed from floor to ceiling that the removal of anything would threaten the stability of everything. Another shop offers umbrellas, combination underwear, slacks, lemon squeezers, thermometers and dusty plastic fish. And everywhere there are people. People on motorbikes, scooters, pushbikes, foot. The sheer density of humanity is daunting. Pairs of old women go arm in arm, both of them four foot six, wearing trousers and walking in a splay-footed manner suggestive of ancient gynaecological misadventure.

Smells are trapped under a funereal sky, smells of baking, boiling, frying, fish, fruit and drains. Occasional dispirited trees that aren't quite sycamores drop leaves the size of my palm. A pair of what look like larks swing in tiny cages a yard apart singing fiercely at each other.

I meet Ruth in a basement restaurant. She is faultlessly laundered and tiny. Her wrists are twigs. But I sense a strength of purpose about her that belies her size. I ask her to order the sort of food that locals might eat, so I have no right to complain that the bowl of soya porridge that is placed in front of me within seconds looks like wallpaper paste but lacks the flavour.

As I fail for the third time to pick up a spring roll with chopsticks, Ruth's phone rings. An underpant manufacturer wants to know whether the distinguished underpant buyer from New Zealand has arrived in the country yet. If so, would he like to visit their office and talk business?

'You want to go?' asks Ruth, her hand over the phone.

'Why not?' I say, with a sudden onset of apprehension that I conceal by having another go at the spring rolls. This is all happening too fast. As we rise from the table Ruth picks up a spring roll in her fingers and bites it neatly in half.

Two men are waiting at the kerb for taxis. When a car pulls up Ruth beats both men to it, and blithely ignores their protests.

In the taxi Ruth and I invent the details of the fiction we will spin. Or rather I invent the details and Ruth just smiles and nods and says yes. She seems to share none of my nervousness. We agree that I am a middleman specializing in men's underwear. I buy the stuff from importers and I distribute it to market stalls around New Zealand.

'But do I look like an underpant buyer?' I ask. I am wearing knee-pocketed khaki trousers and a short-sleeved cotton shirt, clothes that I put on yesterday in my bedroom several thousand miles south-east of here.

'You look good,' says Ruth. 'Perfect. When did you born?'

'When *was* I born.'

'You are good teacher,' she says, smiling, 'you will be my Uncle Joe. When was you born?'

From her handbag she extracts a folding electronic gizmo and punches my date of birth into it. 'You are rooster,' she says, 'you and I do not get married. No no no. I am rooster too. We are always fighting', and she squeezes my arm.

Outside the underpant offices, a digger is scooping into the road. Men with shovels help on the tricky bits. Traffic edges round the digger. Pedestrians and bikes worm between the digger's monstrous metal claw and the hole it is digging. There are no barriers, no cones, no hi-viz vests, no earmuffs, no hard hats, no safety notices and no apparent problems.

A young man is waiting at the door. He greets me effusively. He is dressed with urban chic in a suede jacket and he has the fingers of a pianist. The three flights of stairs leading up to the office are lined with photographs of young men, all of whom are noticeably European. They are lounging in ruined industrial settings wearing only underpants. They sport the standard sultry pout of the model, a bid to convey brooding sexual intensity that never fails to fail to convince.

Sales director Ivy has spent several years in Holland and you can hear it in her English. The earnest Dutch intonation emerging from her very Chinese face is disconcerting. But both she and the youth with the fingers seem to swallow my tale of being an underpant distributor. And they are very eager to hear my professional opinion of the product displayed on shelves along the office walls. It's high-end stuff, fashionable, stretchy, funky. When I ask what price they sell a typical pair of underpants for in China, Ivy laughs. They don't sell anything in China. Her laugh implies that China isn't that foolish. Yet.

Ivy wants to know which designs would prove popular in New Zealand. 'New Zealand men aren't quite ready for pink,' I say as I apply what I hope looks like an expert pinch to a pair of shiny briefs with a pocket on the hip, 'or for pockets.' Fingers and Ivy look as though they've been stabbed.

'But these would sell,' I say, holding up a pair that are quartered like a rugby jersey. 'Very nice.' And actually I think they would sell. If they'd been on display in The Warehouse I'd have bought them. I pretend to take a keen interest in the stitch quality.

'We go business lunch,' says Ivy.

We pick our way past the digger, do a little dance around the bonnets of slow-moving cars in a manner that only I seem to find perilous, ignore five restaurants all thrumming with lunchers and take a table at an apparently identical sixth restaurant. Business lunch consists of fish soup, bamboo shoots, pork bones, several bottles of beer and a chopstick lesson for me which the whole restaurant enjoys. It seems that you have to align the top stick with your middle finger and cradle the lower stick with your thumb and, anyway, the soup and the beer are excellent.

The underpants are made at a factory somewhere on the outskirts of Shanghai. I say that I'd like to see that factory. Fingers and Ivy look puzzled. I explain that in New Zealand everyone is concerned about Chinese working conditions. I use the word ethical. Fingers and Ivy still look puzzled. Ruth translates, though I don't think she knows what ethical means either. Her words provoke a vigorous discussion. I wonder whether I am being doubted. But ten minutes later the four of us are driving through afternoon Shanghai in an air-conditioned saloon with tinted windows. The company driver looks like a not-very-former bouncer. And he drives like one.

I have less than no idea where we are. I got off the plane eight hours ago and have yet to achieve any orientation in this place. At the same time I feel overwhelmed by the speed of events and by a sense of having little control over them. Striving to achieve the mental equivalent of a shrug and to simply yield to what happens to happen, I sink back in the seat, let the Chinese conversation wash over me and stare out of the window.

Shanghai just goes on going on, sunless and endless. All I can relate of the journey is that to travel from the centre of Shanghai to the periphery is to travel down the income scale and back in time. After three-quarters of an hour of unremitting city we have left modern Shanghai behind and reached a world of potholed roads and far fewer cars and ancient trucks and battered people on iron bicycles that look as old as I am.

From my plush cool seat I see a pageant of work: gangs of men in a yard with welding gear and no protective visors, a team of women sweeping metal shavings into a pile, a bicycle towing a trailer of pig carcases, an electrical components factory ringed with rubble, a non-stop urban world of too many people and grainy air. It feels like an early novel by J. G. Ballard. And it feels a very long way from my life.

In order to reach the factory on the other side of the road, the bouncer performs a U-turn of startling audacity against a set of lights. In doing so he neatly baulks a truck, a fleet of pushbikes and a youth on a Vespa. The youth wears a flared leather jacket and a look of resignation. The look acknowledges our greater economic clout.

A hundred yards back along the road we turn right across the footpath into an alley. I am sitting by the rear passenger door. The youth on the Vespa drives smack into that door. He bounces off the car and is flung across a concrete yard. Ivy screams.

The driver stops the car, opens his door, leaps out, runs round the back of the car and bends over to examine, with intense concern, the damage to the door. He runs his hand over it repeatedly, then pulls his mobile phone from his pocket and is shouting down it within seconds. Also within seconds, fifty cyclists and pedestrians have stopped to gawp. Within a minute they have been joined by the entire workforce of a nearby stone-cutting factory. All of them stand in a delighted semicircle some thirty feet away. Their interest is the posh car and the driver's reaction to the accident. No one has paid the Vespa-rider any attention. Fingers, Ivy, Ruth and I get out.

Everyone in the crowd is smiling, but sheepishly. They are relishing the incident, the conflict, the potential dispute, but are daunted by the car's obvious importance. When a Westerner emerges from the vehicle their relish becomes delight. I hear giggles.

The Vespa-rider gets to his feet. One arm of his leather jacket flaps like a dandy's sleeve. He was not wearing a helmet, and he is clearly shaken, but he seems physically sound. He makes towards the bouncer with obvious intent. The bouncer simply turns his back on him and keeps shouting down his mobile, stooping from time to time to run his hand once again over the dented bodywork. The Vespa-rider fires up his own mobile. So does Fingers. Ivy meanwhile ushers me some distance from the scene.

Shortly afterwards the factory manager arrives on a moped. He completely ignores the accident, smiles like the rising sun and presents me with his business card, offering it with both hands. Then he leads me down the alley of rough concrete slabs beside the stone-cutting factory whose workers are still all out enjoying the drama. Jets of water cool an unmanned electric saw that screams slowly through a block of white stone. The stone is held in clamps over rollers and is the size of a medium bit of Stonehenge.

Twenty hours ago I was in Christchurch airport about to embark on I wasn't sure what, and now I am standing in a Chinese underpant factory. It's a single-storey shed, clean, cool and neon-lit. Perhaps fifty girls are sitting at sewing machines made by Brother or Singer. The place resembles the factory run by the long-serving smoothie in *Coronation Street*, except that the girls are not calling each other luv or m'duck. Nor are they discussing the series of improbable events illustrative of contemporary British social concerns that have taken place with such remarkable compression in their neighbourhood in the last twelve hours. They aren't discussing anything. They are working. In silence. Each girl takes an incomplete garment, makes her contribution to it, sewing the side seam, say, or attaching the waistband, then drops it into a cloth bag on the far side of her sewing machine from which it will be taken to the next girl. Some of the girls glance up at me. Most don't. I have the impression that they have been warned of my arrival.

The girls are young. They come, Ivy tells me, from inland rural provinces. On average they stay for two years. Few return to their home provinces except during the two-week Spring Festival in January. Having come to the city they stay in the city, swelling it. When they leave for other jobs or to get married, they are easily replaced. 'Everyone wants to come to Shanghai,' says Ivy.

In a separate room at one end of the shed a couple of girls check each finished garment under bright lamps. 'QC,' says the manager proudly, pointing, 'QC.' QC seems to be the full extent of his English.

In the cutting room, on a vast table, swathes of cloth are laid out to be sliced with bandsaws.

'We make big brands,' says Ivy. 'Mickey Mouse, Bo.'

'Bo?'

'Bo. Bo the Bear.' She mimes a round stomach.

'Oh Pooh,' I say. 'Winnie the Pooh.'

'Yes,' says Ivy, 'Bo.'

The stockroom is piled with boxes. Many are stamped with the word Disney is the familiar cursive script. It feels odd to see it here in a low-rent room in shambling, industrial, grey-skied Shanghai. I feel I've come backstage on Western culture.

Not culture in the sense of unreadable Arts-Council-sponsored poetry, but culture in the true sense of the word, meaning what people do because it's what people do, stuff that they do unconsciously. In this case it's a chunk of commercial culture, a chunk that began with A. A. Milne drawing a bear to amuse children, a toothless, clawless, plump and affable bear. The bear's omnivorous predation was reduced to an affection for honey. The image was then disseminated by book and cartoon and film and became installed irrevocably in a billion childish skulls, skulls that grew into adult skulls but never discarded the furniture of childhood. And thus, by a process indistinguishable from religious education, Pooh became that priceless thing, a brand. The brand sits in the head like a sleeper cell. Its coochy-coo image touches off instant sentimental associations, and those associations are enough to prompt the purchasing nerve. And so the toothless bear is stamped on to articles entirely unassociated with it – toothbrushes, toy tractors, hats. And here, underpants.

The brand's owners scour the globe for the cheapest labour

force. The result is this unprepossessing shed with its neon light-ing and its plastic chairs and its fifty fine-featured country girls. Had they not got a job here, these girls would probably never have heard of Pooh. I wonder whether they ever stop to wonder. Probably not. They just work ten hours a day making thousands of branded underpants that are then shipped around the world by grown men from distant lands who take Pooh Bear under-pants very seriously because they represent money, and who take themselves even more seriously. The company that orders and sells these pants is colossal. Its name is quoted with rever-ence on the New York Stock Exchange, its fortunes studied by teams of analysts and hedge-fund managers. The fates of pen-sions, governments and a million men in suits are entwined with the image of an imaginary bear that has been planted in our heads for ever.

Pooh is a fake bear. And for all I know this Chinese Pooh may be a fake Pooh, a fake fake bear, one of the rip-offs for which Chinese manufacturers are well known. But this Pooh is impos-sible to distinguish from the real thing since the real thing isn't a real thing. It's just a highly profitable myth, an example of the belief system that lies at the heart of the capitalist world that we all like to live in and that we like to think of as rational. And it starts in places like this.

The girls live on site. Through Ruth I ask to see their quarters. The factory manager is surprised but happy to comply. The girls sleep six to a room on bunks as in a barracks. Above each bunk is another where the girl keeps her few things: clothes, comics, toiletries. The ablutions block is made of undisguised concrete and it is not a thing of beauty, but it is clean. In the communal dining room a much older woman squats in the corner like a refugee. She is shaving vegetables over a blue plastic bucket with a cleaver that would bring gasps from a jury.

'Ni hau?' I say to her, which means literally 'You good?' and is exactly 50 per cent of my Chinese vocabulary. When I speak, Ivy,

Fingers, Ruth and even the taciturn factory manager burst into laughter. I don't know why and Ruth can't or won't tell me. The squatting woman doesn't laugh. She stares up at me in silent wonder. The look on her face is precisely the look with which she would have greeted a Martian. Then she returns to her cleaver work and my first visit to a Chinese underpant factory is over. I am surprised by how unsurprising I found it.

The driver says something soft to me as he opens the car door. The words are a mystery of course, but the tone seems out of keeping with what I've seen of his habitual manner. I shrug and smile. Outside the stone-cutting factory the crowd has dispersed, the Vespa and its driver have gone, and the only evidence of the accident is a few shards of plastic from the Vespa's headlight.

On the long drive back into the town centre, through traffic that thickens and slows with every quarter of a mile, Ivy quizzes me about my business. Where do I source my supplies? Who do I sell to? What quantities do I deal in? I improvise, guess and fudge, and to my own ears sound deeply unconvincing. But Ivy is convinced enough to offer me the exclusive New Zealand agency for their own brand, the pink and pocketed and parti-coloured stuff that I inspected at the office. And I feel like a shit. I have deceived these kind and amiable people who are trying to make a living. And I want to say yes. I want to accept Ivy's offer. Partly this is to shrive my guilt. But it's also because I think I could make money. The markup that Ivy suggests is prodigious.

In the end I tell her I will have to think about it, and that she should send me an email when I am back in New Zealand.

'OK,' she says. 'We do business.'

When we reach the office Ivy insists that the driver takes me back to my hotel. Ivy, Fingers and I part with enthusiastic expressions of joy at the booming profits we will make by introducing New Zealand to modish stretchy underpants.

It's a relief to get away.

'Thanks for lying,' I say to Ruth when we are at last alone in the back of the car. The bouncer clearly doesn't have a word of English.

'Uh?' says Ruth.

'Thanks for pretending I am a businessman,' I say, 'but you're not going to have to do it again. I don't like it. From now on we will tell the truth.'

'Good,' says Ruth, and she snuggles deeper into the comfort of the company car. Though I have the impression that if I had suggested that from now on we were going to pretend that I was David Beckham, she would also have said 'good' and snuggled deeper into the comfort of the company car.

In order to deposit me as close as possible to the door of my hotel, the bouncer drives unhesitatingly on to the pavement. Pedestrians yield; then swarm round us like fish round a reef. He opens the door for me, whispers to Ruth, then urges her to speak to me.

'The driver want that you know,' says Ruth, 'he is very sorry with the accident. You are important businessman.'

'*Shia shia*,' I say, meaning thank you, which is the other 50 per cent of my Chinese vocabulary and though it is not quite the phrase I need, it's nearer the mark than 'You good?'

The bouncer looks suddenly unburdened, like a hit man emerging from an Italian confessional. He expresses his relief by getting back into the car and surging into the traffic without looking, scattering pedestrians like hens, just failing to notch his second Vespa of the day, and leaving my life for ever to a valedictory fanfare of car horns.

3

No Teasing the Shrimps

Jet lag and excitement wake me early. The jet lag was predictable, but the excitement wasn't. One day in this city and I am surprised by my enthusiasm to see more of it. There's an edge here, a fervour, an energy that has quickened my interest. And with no underpant appointments until tomorrow I am eager just to wander the streets and drink the place in. Already I have begun to realize what a slab of unthinking prejudice I have brought with me. Like all prejudice it was born of ignorance.

At school I learned nothing of China. People whispered about Mao's *Little Red Book* as though it were pornography, but we heard little of the Great Leap Forward or the Cultural Revolution, and nothing at all of a couple of thousand years of extraordinary dynastic history. To me and my generation, the Chinese were as remote and mysterious and comically different as they have been for every generation. We told bad jokes about Wings and Wongs, and prefaced sexual puns with the words, 'Confucius he say.'

The subsequent thirty years have done nothing to enlighten me. When the Duke of Edinburgh made his famous 'slitty-eyed' comment, he was speaking for me and my kind.

Overnight Shanghai has been cleaned. The gutters have been rinsed, the roads and pavements swept. Numerous cleaners in drab civic overalls are still at it, wielding besoms of bamboo twigs, some worn to a nub, others still with their leaves on them.

Three women in aprons are swabbing the marble steps of a bookstore in Huaihai Road, supervised by a man in the cheap uniform of a security guard. The one thing uncleaned is the sky. It has shifted from black to grey-brown. The only evidence that the sun has risen is that things have become visible. Traffic is already dense. The city's bicycle herd is up and whirring, pedalling round, through and against the cars, helmetless, vulnerable, the hugely numerous antelope on the predatory vehicular plain.

I wander the streets at random, ingesting the strangeness, pleased to be here, joining a queue for steamed buns, pointing at a startlingly white confection the size of a cricket ball, holding out a handful of change for the seller to pick a few pennies, saying *shia shia* and being stared at with wonder by the vendor and giggled at by the queuers behind me. The bun has the taste and texture of slightly sweetened polystyrene. But the sparrows like it.

The few birds I've seen have been dowdy, as if evolving to merge into their landscape. Shanghai is for people, as an ant colony is for ants. And as with ants there is constant industry. Work is more physically evident here than in any Western city. Walk through London at this hour of the day and most of the people are not doing what they do to earn money. They are on their way to doing it behind closed doors. Here they are doing it in the street, hauling pigs, beating metal, cooking buns, begging, mending, scraping, cleaning, guarding, or preying on big-nose honky Western tourists.

On the main drags predators lurk at every intersection. They descend as I wait for the lights to change, obsessively cheerful young men in leather jackets, or young women whose faces look to have come from distant mountainous provinces. 'You want handbag?' they say. 'You want shoes? You want DVD? First quality. Very good. You come with me.'

I try smiling and saying no thank you. I try not smiling and not saying no thank you. Neither makes any difference. I watch another Westerner raise a hand as the pests descend. 'No,' he booms when they are still five yards away. They back off.

I try it myself. 'No,' I boom at an approaching youth.

'You want handbag, you want shoes?' he says. And then, conspiratorially, bloke to bloke, one hand raised to mask his words, 'You want sexy DVD? I got sexy DVD. Come with me. Very good. First quality.'

As I cross the road he grasps my arm, jokey but insistent, and tries to steer me to his emporium of the fake, the rip-off, the illegal. I feel the sudden swell of honest anger. 'Fuck off,' I say. And he does. A sign in English outside Fuxing Park says:

> Ethic and moral codes should be duly honored. Visitors are expected not to urinate or shit, post ads or posters . . . exposing one's top, lying about, scavenging or begging from others is unallowable . . . mental patients are admitted only under custody . . . Visitors are not supposed to tease, scare or capture bird, cricket, fish and shrimp, or cicada (except those for commercial purpose) . . . The visitor to the park should discipline himself instead of making himself a nuisance to others . . . activities of feudalistic and superstitious nature, gambling and those banned under law are prohibited.

Inside Fuxing Park I find no one scaring the shrimps. But I do find seventy people of all ages, clearly unacquainted with each other, singing. They have gathered in front of an energetic conductor who stands on a dining-room chair. A chunky cassette deck plays the melody and an easel displays the lyrics. The conductor points at the easel with a baton and the people belt the song out with unselfconscious gusto.

When I was a child there was community singing at Wembley before the FA Cup Final. 'Abide with Me' was always one of the songs. How remote it seems now, almost Enid Blytonish, like something from a lost world, a world in which it was simply impossible, unthinkable, that a section of the crowd could sing, in public, 'You're gonna get your fuckin' head kicked in', without being immediately arrested. By a single rosy-cheeked policeman on a bicycle.

Beside a muddy ornamental lake stands a concrete rotunda, where couples are dancing. They, too, have a seventies-style cassette deck. The music is Chinese pop. It has an upbeat cheerfulness, like Dana or the Andrews sisters or American boy bands before Elvis, innocent as apples, but with that alien tonal twang that makes oriental music oriental. The dancers improvise. Seemingly at random they shift from a waltz of sorts with its formal distance between man and woman, to a rock and roll of sorts with the woman twirling under the man's upraised hand. The couples range in age from twenty to ancient. At the edge of the gathering a balding man of forty dances alone, one arm outstretched to clasp the warm little hand of a woman who isn't there, the other curled delicately, decorously, round the small of her absent back.

On a lawn stand statues of Marx and Engels, dressed like European gentlemen in granite frock coats, both with the sort of beards worn by Edwardian royalty. Dotted among them are men and women who could also be taken for statues. They are doing very slow calisthenics that may or may not be t'ai chi. They seem agelessly Chinese. Controlled and flexible, they unfurl like warming reptiles. The essential quality would seem to be balance. The old boy who slowly raises his knee to his face then straightens his foot above his head, does so without once looking like toppling, without once adjusting his single-footed stance. He seems oblivious to the park around him.

In the West I am suspicious of stuff like this. I associate it with personal growth fads, and the search for a quick exotic fix to an unsatisfactory life. But not here. Here it seems of a piece with the bamboo grove, unremarked, unremarkable and free of pretension. Most of its practitioners, I notice, are old. But then again, I suppose that at nine o'clock on a Wednesday morning most people of working age are working.

Beneath the trees old men play a form of chess that I don't understand. And they spit. They spit magnificently. Each spit starts way down below the diaphragm with a noise like a rumble of magma that the proprietor makes no effort to conceal. Indeed, he seems to relish its richness, its bubbling rasp. Up comes the gob as fatly and noisily as possible and then out into the world with a fierce forward movement of the neck and head and a triumphant explosion. It hits the ground with an audible splat. No one pays any attention, not the chess-players, nor the card-players nearby who are preoccupied with making their own noise, flinging down their hands with bellows of triumph, hoots of mockery, whistles of if-only. They, too, are mostly old.

Indeed, the old seem far more in evidence here than in the West. In the streets around this park I have seen women who look a hundred and must be at least eighty working at stalls, washing dishes, sweeping. And other ancients walking arm in arm with far younger women, their granddaughters, I presume, or their great-granddaughters.

My impressions confirm what I've read, which is that the Chinese continue to venerate their old people. The old are just a short, though drastic, hop away from becoming ancestors, and ancestor worship has been central to Chinese superstition for millennia.

In China most old people live with their families. The contrast with the West is stark. In the West respect for the old has dwindled markedly within my lifetime. Since Elvis or thereabouts we have grown ever more obsessed with youth. That obsession has been fostered largely by commerce. Youth is the age of sex and shallowness and ignorance and intense emotion. Sex and shallowness and ignorance and intense emotion are exactly the qualities that advertising likes. So in a commercially driven world, youth has become our principal good.

I taught for twenty years. Increasingly in that time I heard kids referring to their parents as the olds, the fossils, the wrinklies. And the old in turn have gradually bought into this shift of attitudes. They seek to stay young. Gyms, health supplements, Botox, paragliding, sixty is the new forty, all are invoked to stave off the apartheid of the rest home.

As the morning wears on in Fuxing Park the young emerge, the seriously young, toddlers swaddled against the sharp air in bulbous synthetic jackets. Each is attended by one, two or even three adults, a random selection from parents, grandparents and great-grandparents. The child is constantly amused, praised, delighted over, fed, tickled, bounced, indulged. And every child that I see is a singleton. For these are the offspring of the one-child policy that has been officially in place throughout China for almost thirty years. Thirty years means that the first singleton children are now parents. Of singleton children.

There are many ways round the one-child diktat. In some provinces you can buy the right to have more. In many provinces you can bribe your way to it. Party membership can confer it as a privilege. And some of the remotest rural provinces do not enforce the policy as strictly as other provinces. All the same, for the last three decades the average Mr and Mrs Chin has been restricted to a single child, and 300 million Chinese citizens have simply not been born. The population of the United States has been wiped out before it existed.

In a few provinces, parents are allowed a second child if their first is a girl. For reasons of tradition and dynastic succession, every Chinese parent wants a boy. And they get them. Though it is illegal to determine a foetus's sex before birth, it happens everywhere. Girls are aborted. And some infant girls are either abandoned, or put out for foreign adoption, or simply killed. In consequence, there are now approximately 120 young Chinese men to every 100 young Chinese women.

These only children must inevitably receive the affection, the attention and the money that would otherwise have been spread among many. They don't scrap with brothers. They face less adversity. They never feel supplanted. They aren't denied, aren't made to wait their turn. Their distress never goes uncomforted.

And in the newly affluent east coast cities these children are spoilt. I can see them being spoilt now in front of me in Fuxing Park on a grey Wednesday morning. A child of perhaps four in a purple puffa jacket and little woollen bonnet has had a fishing rod rented for him so that he can angle for goldfish. The rod-vendor has baited the hook with a knob of dough. Dad, squatting, embraces the child with his thighs, encircling him, sheltering. Dad has full control of the rod, has flicked the cast among the floating sycamore leaves, is watching the three-piece bob-float. But the child isn't. His attention is already straying. He has one hand on the rod but it is an ineffectual hand. The activity that he ran gurgling towards two minutes ago has lost its appeal. The rod will go back soon, the next gaudy bead will soon be strung on the endless necklace of the child's indulgence.

And when this child is fifty, the father, very possibly, of one, one who may also be the father of one, how will China cope? More particularly how will the child cope? He will be the sole root of a family tree that has become unnaturally inverted. He will have eight great-grandparents, and, unless I've made an error of genealogical mathematics, each of those great-grand-parents will have a single great-grandchild. It will be a strong infant that is not drowned by the torrent of love. And when he grows to man's estate, will all eight great-grandparents be living in his house? If you have cash to invest, I'd suggest a punt on Chinese rest homes.

But I am at ease in Fuxing Park. I spend a couple of pootling hours there, smoking, sitting with weak tea, watching the martial artists, the card-players, the chess-players, a pair of middle-aged women batting a shuttlecock back and forth without a net. There seems more overt pleasure here than in a Western park, more social cohesion, and no misfits, wastrels, mumblers or drunks. The phone booth in the park from which I ring my only other contact in Shanghai is as graffiti-free as the day it was erected.

Compton Tothill is an expat Kiwi and 'an old China hand'. He answers the phone immediately with a gentle old-world formality. When I ask if I could meet him for a chat about things Chinese he suggests tomorrow evening at O'Malley's pub where there's a special Kiwi night. 'There'll probably be about fifty of us,' he says.

Having got to China, I don't much want to spend an evening with fifty compatriots, but I say exactly the opposite.

Most public transport baffles me. Bus timetables are my particular Rosetta Stone. But underneath the streets of Shanghai there runs a system of bright-lit clarity. On the Shanghai metro, public announcements are given in both Chinese and English. The ones in Chinese are about as comprehensible as the ones on the London tube, but the ones in English are beautifully lucid. The platforms are clean and the travel is cheap. A few yuan, a dollar or two, will get you anywhere the metro goes. The only difficulty is spending those yuan. The automated ticket dispensers do not have queues in front of them. They have crowds. The shape adopted by that crowd is dictated by the need to be able to see the front of the machine and move towards it. That shape resembles the head of a cauliflower, each customer a floret. Minor fluctuations as people leave or join the cauliflower make little difference to the cauliflower as a whole. And if you look closely at its heart you can see a single static floret. That's me.

My fellow florets are ordinary Chinese people. They are almost all smaller than I am but they are better at securing tickets. They jostle and elbow and nudge. I yield.

The British passion for queuing is often mocked. It should be revered. A queue is civil. It protects the halt and the lame and the tourist. A cauliflower head does not. Though actually the halt and lame seem to do all right in the quest for tickets. As does a ferocious little woman who is bent at the waist like an angle iron. She joins the mob at the same time as I do but is soon away riding the train to happiness. It's only the tourist who gets nowhere.

The cauliflower is the physical expression of self-interest. And though most of the people around me were brought up sternly communist, and all of them remain nominally communist, they are clearly naturals at the free market. In this insignificant cauliflower are the seeds of Mao's failure.

There comes a time when one sheds one's upbringing. It takes me perhaps ten minutes at the cauliflower's static heart. My conversion begins with a man in a drab raincoat who makes to shuffle in front of me. I give him a chicken-wing block, and brace for a repercussion. None comes. The man accepts my manoeuvre in the same way as one accepts an opponent's chess move. Within a minute I'm a committed thwarter. Old women, pretty girls in postage-stamp skirts, youths in tight jeans, they do not pass. But thwarting is not quite enough. My blocking manoeuvres only permit the flanking florets on the cauliflower to insinuate themselves between me and the machine. I have to step forward and ward them off. So I do. It is mildly thrilling. I pre-empt them, projecting an arm ahead of me like a car-park barrier, clearing my way ahead and filling the putative gap before anyone else. If anyone else tries, I baulk them with calf or hip. No one protests. No one, indeed, shows the least emotion.

A man collects his ticket and I am nearest to the touch-screen. An old dear half my height and a third of my weight reaches towards the slot but I am swifter, stronger and better prepared. She yields and I am there, the machine's proprietor. I press the screen and all instructions turn from Mandarin to English. I press People's Square (complete with apostrophe) and the machine tells me to pay three yuan. I slot the coins, take my ticket and battle out through the fringes of the cauliflower. I feel triumphant to have learned to do what I was trained not to do, and a little disappointed that I can now stop doing it.

A barrier set with automatic gates separates passengers from the tracks. When the train stops its doors align to those gates with millimetric precision. Doors and gates open simultaneously and on the instant two crowds of people, those boarding and those alighting, separated by half a metre of platform, walk straight at each other and mesh. In seconds, the confrontation resolves itself. The two crowds have swapped places. The doors close and I have missed the train.

The next train arrives within a minute. This time I'm in the vanguard of the charge. And despite the welter of people, I board the train without physical contact. I feel culturally re-educated.

The train is as clean as Mrs Beeton's kitchen. On the tube in London you are likely to see kids arrogant with youth, pleased to be louder than the adults around them, undaunted by the waves of dislike that radiate from their elders. Here I see none of that. Just along the carriage a girl of perhaps thirteen and a woman who looks old enough to be, and may indeed be, her great-grandmother are sitting side by side holding hands and gossiping. Everyone else is either using his mobile, or merely staring at it lovingly, as if it were a first-born.

The image is apt, because for most Chinese people their

mobile is their first and only phone. Under Mao almost no one had a phone. In the new China everyone is going mobile. Coverage is excellent, rates are cheap, the phones are made in China, and at present the networks are gaining approximately 5 million new subscribers a month.

Within minutes I am disgorged into People's Square. I have a mental template of anything called People's Square. It is vast and desolate, like Alexanderplatz in the former East Berlin, or whatever the equivalent is in Pyongyang. It is a place for orchestrated rallies of the obedient, a place for missile parades and stone-faced recruits goose-stepping past a podiumful of butchers in uniform. The architecture is monolithically civic.

This People's Square isn't like that. Once it was Shanghai's racetrack and gambling centre. Now it has ornamental gardens and an exhibition hall of civic planning which doesn't tempt me but also doesn't daunt me. The Theatre cum Opera House is a colossal box of glass with a Chinese roof curving up at the brim like the cross section of a saucer. And there's nowhere to hold a missile-parade.

Rain has happened. It isn't falling so much as being squeezed from the grainy air. Umbrellas sprout like a sudden mushroom farm and, in the great tradition of tourists since tourism was invented, I take refuge in the museum. The building was erected in the 1990s and is supposed to resemble a traditional cooking pot. To me it looks more like a reef knot done in concrete, but it's impressively capacious. At the door an attendant mechanically offers me a plastic sheath for the umbrella I haven't got.

Superficially the museum is every large museum I have ever visited. Laid out in galleries round a central hall it seethes with tourists and children. The tourists are quiet. The children are not. Most members of both groups are more drawn by the cafeteria than by the exhibits, but only the children are willing to appear so.

When I read, last month, a single book of Chinese history,

300 pages that took me from the earliest records of human life to the communist revolution of 1949, the first thing I realized was that I knew nothing. The second thing was that I effectively knew everything. The history of China is the history of everywhere. It is the endlessly repeated four-phase story of power: the revolutionary bid for power, the assumption of power, the gradual corruption of power and the loss of power. Each story is an imperial dynasty. Some dynasties lasted a decade, others half a millennium, and their stories are dotted with extraordinary characters and events. But in essence the story of each dynasty is the same. Viewed from a distance Chinese history resembles a pattern of waves.

In the coin section of the museum you can see the dynasties' efforts at financial control over their vast kingdom, with coins dating back a couple of thousand years. Square coins, coins with holes in them, crudely minted, finely minted, cheap alloys, pure silver, all indicative of one common aim which was to unify and control and tax.

More telling for me is another story that the museum recites, which is the story of the arts. That story seems independent of dynastic history. It also seems very different from European art history.

Blindfold someone of moderate education, station them in any room of the National Gallery in London, and remove the blindfold. They should be able to make a reasonable guess at the century on the walls. But here they'd struggle. To my inexpert eye, there is little to distinguish between the style of scrolls, paintings or pots made a thousand years apart. Here, in defiance of the rise and fall of dynasty after dynasty, is extraordinary continuity.

One moment in the museum touches me and will stay with me. It says, I think, a lot about China. In the manuscript gallery two girls perhaps ten years old are standing in front of a letter written during the Northern Song dynasty by a man named

Guang. He died in 1086. One of the girls runs her finger down the glass and reads Guang's letter aloud. She barely hesitates. In the British Museum the equivalent would be to see a youth in a hoodie reading the *Anglo-Saxon Chronicle*.

Writing developed independently in China at roughly the same time as it did in the West. Both systems began with drawings that represented what they recorded – cartoon images of sheaves of rice, say, or a bird in a tree. But whereas all Western systems continued to refine themselves until they had shrunk to alphabets of thirty or so sounds, the Chinese system didn't. It remained as pictures. They became stylized rather than representational but they remained numerous. A keyboard that offered a key for every Chinese character would cover an acre. Even the characters needed to tell a children's story run into the thousands. Thus script stood to one side of the inevitable development of the language.

The system has many disadvantages, the greatest of which is cumbrousness. But it retains one huge advantage. Characters are units used to compose words. They are unaffected by changes of pronunciation or meaning or usage. And they are unaffected by the development of dialects.

Dialects abound in China. The standard dialect is Mandarin, which is modelled on the Chinese spoken in Beijing. Most people above the peasantry understand it because it is disseminated by television and radio. But the Chinese they speak is regional. For example, in Ruth's home town of Wenzhou, a couple of hundred miles south of here, they apparently speak a dialect that is by and large incomprehensible to the Shanghainese. And the Shanghainese dialect is similarly impenetrable to Wenzhovians. But the characters used to transcribe both dialects are the same, just as they have been for aeons. Which is what permits two young girls in urban Shanghai to read a thousand-year-old manuscript without difficulty.

That script has always separated China from the West.

Acknowledging this truth, in 1958 the Chinese officially adopted Pinyin. Pinyin is Mandarin Chinese transliterated into the Western alphabet, more or less. You see it everywhere in Shanghai. Every street sign in the centre of town has the street's name in characters and underneath it the Pinyin version.

But Pinyin has never caught on. Most ordinary Chinese can't read it. And the transliteration is also impressively perverse. The letter q, for instance, represents the sound ch as in cheese. So the Qing dynasty is pronounced Ching. Similarly zh represents a j as in John, and ou the sound of the o in go. As a result, Wenzhou is pronounced Wenjo. In short, Pinyin isn't as helpful as it could have been, and it is tempting to imagine that its vagaries were deliberate. The foreigners could be allowed in only so far.

In a damp street off People's Square I witness my second Chinese traffic accident in twenty-four hours. A bicycle travelling against the flow of three lanes of cars is clipped by a bumper. The rider wobbles, slews crazily, hits a car then falls. Brakes screech. A big green Audi scrunches into the bike. The Audi's grille stops inches short of the prostrate rider.

The middle lane of traffic backs up behind the Audi, horns blaring. The lanes on either side carry on. The driver of the Audi does not get out. He reverses off the bike and nudges the nose of his car into the right-hand lane until another car is obliged to let him in in order to avoid a collision. Behind the Audi, every stalled car is doing the same to right or left.

The cyclist gets to his feet. He and his bike have become a traffic island. His trousers are torn, and the back of his thin cotton jacket is black from the wet road. Dragging his bike, he scampers for the safety of the pavement, provoking a furious chorus of horns. Once safely off the road he examines the damage to his clothes, his skin and then his bike. The handlebars are set at ninety degrees, the back wheel is mangled. He spits, once, and voluminously, then starts the long trudge back in the direction he came from, pushing his ruined bike, the back wheel elliptically lolloping.

Shanghai traffic, like the battle for a metro ticket, is essentially a free market. The rules are minimal. You get away with what you can. Your objective is simply to get ahead and you use every weapon at your disposal to do so. But the horn, the only weapon installed in every car, has become enfeebled by overuse. In the West, a driver who is honked at reacts as if jerked. The honk is an abrupt upbraiding for misbehaviour. But here, as I noticed in the taxi from the airport, a honk has no effect on the honkee.

The reason seems to be that the person doing the honking is behind you. In Shanghai, the rear-view mirror is by and large decorative, because the person behind you is not your concern. You are his concern. Your concern is the person in front of you, whom you are making every effort to get in front of. The rule that operates is the one that got Darwin into such trouble with the theologians.

Pedestrians are weak. To survive they must be constantly alert to danger. For instance, when a pedestrian light turns green it does not mean that you are free to cross the road. It means only that there's been a slight improvement in the odds. If there is any gap in the pedestrians on a crossing, a car will drive hard at it in a bid to widen it. It's a game of chicken. To hesitate is to lose. Alone I always hesitate. So already I have learned to step off the kerb only with a shielding native beside me. Locals are better attuned to the free-for-all. They step fearlessly in front of vehicles, and the vehicles stop. Just.

The afternoon passes fast with the novelty of the world around me, the smells, the markets, the crowds and the beetling skyscrapers. I grow gradually more familiar with the little ways of things. I unconsciously learn how to walk the clogged pavement without baulking or being baulked. My ears become attuned to the whirr of bikes attacking from behind. And I become able to navigate by sense of direction rather than recourse to a map. The skyscrapers help. Each has a different design at its crest. I use one to the north-west of People's Square as a point of reference. It is crowned by four inwardly curved cones, like pincers on a crab.

When darkness falls giant fairy lights cascade down the pincers. And I duck into a restaurant. I'm keener to drink than to eat, but the only pubs I've seen are foreign-styled things, including one place called the Buddha Bar.

Chance has served me up what seems a splendid restaurant. It is three-quarters full and I am the only Westerner. The patrons range in age from six to sixty. They are eating, drinking and smoking with vigour, but above all they are talking, or rather shouting. The place sounds happy.

The maîtresse d' looks the opposite. She is wearing what looks like the uniform of a London parking warden and her hair is tied back in a manner that the Soviet Union's champion woman tractor driver of 1956 would have found just a little severe. Nevertheless we conduct an entirely satisfactory conversation which consists of Chinese on her part and gestures on mine, and which establishes that I want a table for one and a big bottle of local beer, that one over there in the fridge that advertises Budweiser but, fortunately, hasn't got any Budweiser in it.

A waitress brings the beer. '*Shia shia*,' I say and she giggles. It would be nice to know a phrase in English that was so infallibly amusing. Another waitress brings me a bowl, chopsticks, a ceramic spoon and a twenty-page menu listing every part of every beast or fish or bird I've ever eaten plus a hundred I haven't. Many dishes are illustrated with photographs. And every dish is translated into English.

'Braised chicken intestine with satay sauce' looks more tempting than the 'stewed pigs tendons with assorted meats' but I pass on both. I don't choose the pigeon soup either. From the illustrative photo it is impressively clear that pigeon soup means pigeon soup. The soup is a broth with a few vegetable slivers floating on its surface. The pigeon is a pigeon. It lies slumped on its side in the broth. The difference between this pigeon and one in the street is only that this one is dead and plucked. Its claws poke over one side of the bowl, its head flops over another, its eyes and beak are intact, and its skin is the colour of putty.

I order twice-fried pork with cabbage Sichuan-style, stir-fried beef with lemon, a plate of assorted vegetables and a beer to replace the first one which seems to have evaporated.

On the next table a man with glasses a quarter of an inch thick, a roll-neck sweater and a lantern jaw is holding forth. He is the wag of his party. Four men smoke and listen to him, occasionally breaking into throaty, uninhibited laughter. A woman pays equal attention to the wag and to the tattered head of a carp that she is holding in chopsticks while she gnaws at its cheek. The wag notes that I am watching and addresses me loudly. I gesture incomprehension by shoving forth my lower lip and flattening my palms like a waiter carrying a two-foot-wide tray at shoulder-level. Everyone laughs. One of the men raises a glass to me. I raise a glass in response and hit a waitress smack on the forearm with it. Beer flies. The men laugh. The woman drops her fish head. The maîtresse d' scurries over looking as though she's just lost her tractor-driving title, scolds the waitress, summons three others with cloths and addresses me in a manner that clearly indicates that I, who am in every way to blame, am in no way to blame.

If I eat Chinese food in the West I unashamedly ask for a knife and fork, but on the when-in-Rome principle I am determined to master chopsticks. My twice-fried pork with cabbage Sichuan-style turns out to have been coated with Teflon. I manage to move five slivers from the plate to the tablecloth and one from the plate to my crotch. When I finally get a piece of cabbage to my mouth, I do so by a neat last-second flick of the jaw as it falls. Then I wish I hadn't, partly because the man in the roll-neck sweater applauds and partly because the cabbage is off-the-Richter-scale hot.

I have never coped with hot food. Sweat erupts on my forehead in an instant. I gasp and reach for the beer, drink a glass at a single gulp, refill it, drink again, look up and see half the restaurant grinning at me. Red of face, I raise my beer to them all and everyone laughs. I mean everyone. I may never get a job as an interpreter in China but there's a living to be made as an entertainer.

One of the wag's companions comes over to my table. He brings his chopsticks, demonstrates the correct grip, which as far as I can tell is exactly the one I am using, raises a slice of Teflon pork, swings it about for a while as if conducting an orchestra with it, then pops it into his mouth. It is my turn to applaud and again I get a round of laughter.

'Good,' says my chopstick teacher, chewing. He gestures that I should have another go. I use the universal wordless gesture for 'this isn't actually food. This is a hazardous substance as declared by the UN' and it proves a winner with the crowd once again.

My stir-fried beef with lemon arrives. It doesn't look hostile but then neither did the twice-fried pork. I allow the wag's friend to adjust the chopsticks in my fingers, seize beef at the first attempt, lift it unerringly to my mouth and await the burst of heat. It doesn't come, but another bottle of beer does, sent by the wag, and when I look up those who are still looking my way are smiling. And I surprise myself by feeling happy. Just plain buoyant happy. I do not feel that I have pierced to the heart of Chinese society. I do not feel that I have made a clutch of new friends. But I do feel that I have lost, permanently, a previously unacknowledged distrust of China and the Chinese, a prejudice born of ignorance and propaganda. Everything I have ever heard or read about this country stressed its difference. But a few trivial merry minutes in a middle-of-the-road restaurant on a damp Wednesday evening in Shanghai have stressed its similarity. These people are people and I am familiar with people. What's more they are easy-going people, people who like to laugh and people who don't consider a restaurant meal to be an exercise in isolation, formality or social pretension.

My chopstick tutor's English stretches no further than 'good' and 'cheers', though these keep us going nicely for a while. Even after he's gone back to his table, he turns from time to time to check on my chopstick technique. It serves reasonably well with the beef but is challenged by the plate of vegetables. It specifically struggles with some beans that are the colour of egg yolks and so close to spherical that on the polished wooden floor they roll to some remarkably distant parts of the restaurant. No one cares. I order a second plate of beef and a lot more beer. And I reflect that I couldn't imagine a restaurant in England or New Zealand taking such unmalicious collective interest in a solitary monoglot middle-aged Chinaman. Or enjoying such uninhibited fun with him. Or making him feel so plain bloody happy.

When the waitress removes my plates, you can see where they stood, little islands of pure white tablecloth surrounded by shoals and reefs of detritus. The waitress leaves me with an ashtray, four slices of watermelon, a damp towel that I make good use of, and a bill for everything that comes to about NZ$20.

I am farewelled by the wag and my chopstick tutor and their friends, and by the woman with the fish head who has proved the most formidable smoker of all of them, and by two giggling waitresses, and by the tractor-driving champ who is not giggling because she simply can't, but who has permitted herself a sort of rictus that is designed to denote amiability.

When I am twenty yards down the damp street a waitress catches up with me. She tries to give me back my tip.

45

'No, no,' I say, giving up entirely on Chinese, 'for you, for you' and I make shovelling motions in her direction. I leave her on the pavement, clutching a few yuan, stationary amid drizzle, her mouth agape.

4

The Dart on My Gusset

Tony Pendleton, country manager for The Warehouse in China, is a chunky affable Scouser. He's been in the job five days. He's wearing a red fleece vest with The Warehouse logo on the breast, and a red polo shirt also with The Warehouse logo on the breast. Chest hair bristles through the neck of both.

'Where are you staying?' he asks.

'God knows,' I say, gesturing through the window at the vast grey cityscape of Shanghai. 'It took about half an hour to get here, but the taxi seemed to go round in circles.'

'It probably did,' says Tony. 'Which hotel?'

I tell him. 'It did,' he says. 'Now, have you got those pants?'

I hand him a pair from my pouch of five.

'Got the bar code? Perfect. Piece of cake. Hang on a sec. I'll just give these to Jenny', and he disappears down the corridor.

The office occupies the eighteenth floor of an unremarkable building in Xuhui District. Through the window Shanghai stretches for ever before dissolving into a smudge of cloud and smoke and dirt. Everywhere the skyline is spiked by cranes. A few years ago this city was reputedly home to one in five of the cranes on planet earth.

The Warehouse was founded in the eighties as a discount store. Its motto and jingle, known throughout New Zealand, is 'The Warehouse, The Warehouse, where everyone gets a bargain.'

In its early days it acquired a reputation for cheapness, with goods and stores to match. But over twenty years or so it has risen to become the dominant retailer in New Zealand. Its 'red sheds' now cover the country. Its rise has coincided more or less exactly with the growth of industrial China. As China boomed, so did The Warehouse, and as the quality of Chinese exports improved, so did The Warehouse's reputation.

I am surprised to learn that this is its first full-scale procurement office in China. The place has a just-cleaned smell. The shelves and cupboards are empty but the floors are littered with the stuff that will fill them.

Tony sits me down in a small bare meeting room, gives me a bottle of water and teaches me all about the process of acquiring goods from China. A lot of it is business jargon, and a lot of that jargon is acronyms. TWL is The Warehouse Limited. QC is quality control. CNF is carriage and forwarding. FOB is free on board. CBM is cubic metres. TEU is twenty-foot equivalent unit. And CSR is very important.

TWL is big on CSR and Tony is keen that I should know so. CSR is Corporate Social Responsibility. The phrase is an unwieldy mix of PR and PC but the aim of CSR is benevolent. I have little doubt that Tony has been advised to tell me all this stuff for understandable publicity reasons, but I have equally little doubt that it's true.

TWL audits every factory it buys from. The purpose is to ensure that the factory reaches acceptable standards. There is a lengthy accreditation process. The factory is measured against a checklist of virtues. If it fails then it has an agreed period in which to improve before being reaudited. It can fail because of a shortage of fire extinguishers or poor payroll records or other more drastic reasons. The aim is eventually to create an establishment that approaches Western standards of employment and manufacturing practice. TWL does this partly for ethical reasons, partly for commercial reasons and partly because the Chinese government doesn't.

It is clear even from an anodyne paper like the English-language *China Daily* that the Chinese economic miracle is fed by a multitude of shonky enterprises. Shonky can mean barbaric. Mining is especially suspect. Every day, it seems, there's another disaster in some provincial coal mine – an explosion, a flood, a tunnel collapse – and another dozen miners are crushed, trapped, gassed or in other ways killed. The owners flee to avoid prosecution. I have read no reports of such owners being brought to justice.

Scan the Western newspapers and you will regularly see weighty articles about sweatshop working conditions. Throughout China there are enterprises whose employees are effectively prisoners on starvation wages, or on no wages at all. In some enterprises the employees are truly prisoners, political dissidents in remote detention centres who were set to work and then effectively forgotten about by the authorities.

Rogues abound. Anyone trading with China will tell you horror stories of orders that were paid for but that never arrived, or of goods that arrived bearing no resemblance to the ones ordered, or of orders that went fine until the big one was placed, whereupon the company took the cash, shipped a container of rocks and disappeared without trace.

And seemingly every week there is a fresh consumer panic about dangerous Chinese goods. Present dramas concern formaldehyde levels in clothing, and poisonous paint on children's toys. Tomorrow it will be something else. Some of the scares are legitimate.

Corruption is endemic. Everyone can be bribed and expects to be. It is how things happen here and how they have pretty well always happened. It is a legacy of the centralized government of empire, which had always depended on officials to exercise its will, officials who lived many thousands of miles away from accountability and therefore had the scope to become local tyrants. Communist Party cadres are the most recent embodiment of these officials, but they are merely the heirs to an imperial tradition.

In consequence, TWL 'strongly discourages any proposals to staff, including meals, entertainment and personal gifts of any sort'. And every link in the supply chain has to be checked and rechecked. TWL even employs an outfit called Verité to shadow-audit its auditors. 'The closer a product is to being shipped,' says Tony, 'the greater the likelihood of corruption.'

But, and it's a colossal but, China remains the place to get anything made, anything at all. 'The universal habit here,' says Tony, 'is to say yes. Then they find a way of doing it.'

The trade fairs are unimaginably huge. Shanghai is about to stage an expo for fishing tackle and sporting goods only. It will be roughly the size of Hyde Park. In Yiwu, a couple of hundred miles from Shanghai, the permanent Small Commodities Market is apparently the size of several Hyde Parks. 'And on Alibaba.com,' says Tony, 'you can find, quite simply, everything', and he brings up the website on a computer. Under 'briefs, panties, thongs, and boxers', Alibaba.com gives us a choice of 1264 manufacturers.

At which point Jenny the Merchandise Manager arrives with the specifications for my underpants. I find myself studying those specifications with an interest I never thought I'd feel. 'Legs and waist must have elastic tunnelled and twin needle flat locked down on the raw edges. Elastic must overlap by three cm at the start/finish of waist and each leg. The front has a dart at the gusset seam. Front panel is double ply bagged out and fully enclosed into the centre front panel seams.'

Nothing, it seems, is left to chance. The fabric must be 'carded A grade cotton single jersey at 135 GSM', and it must undergo lab tests for 'dimensional stability, spirality, colour fastness, stretch and recovery'. And on my medium-size pants the dart on the gusset must be 6 centimetres long. I borrow a ruler. The dart on my gusset is 6 centimetres long. Precisely.

Having been drawn up in New Zealand, the specifications for my pants were put out for tender with accredited Chinese businesses. The company that won the tender had to make up a sample batch that was checked in this office, then sent to New Zealand to be rechecked. Then a pre-production sample, accompanied by authorized lab test results, underwent the same double inspection. Then a final post-production sample, in other words a specimen drawn from the completed order, was checked. Only then came permission to ship.

TWL negotiated a price FOB, in other words all costs involved in getting my underpants made and loaded on to a ship were borne by the manufacturer. After that TWL paid all costs.

Jenny's research has also unearthed the bill of lading. My underpants left the factory of Kingstar Light Industrial Products in Quanzhou on 17 October 2006, grouped into packs of five, labelled and ready to go on sale. There were 15,000 packs: 1500 small, 3300 medium, 3450 large, 3450 XL, 1800 2XL and 1500 of the comically gargantuan 3XL. In other words medium is no longer the median size. Since sizes were standardized, New Zealanders, like the rest of the West, have got fat.

The 75,000 pairs of underpants, weighing 4837.5 kilos and occupying 24.796 cubic metres, were packed into a container by the manufacturers, who declared to the quarantine authorities that the container was free of live organisms, material of plant or animal origin, soil and water. The container was driven to the port of Xiamen, shipped on the Cosco *Longbeach*, and transferred to the ocean-going *Maersk Niigata* which sailed south-east for twenty days and docked in Auckland on 9 November. From there the underpants were distributed to stores and offered for sale to the variously proportioned men of New Zealand, whose backsides they now embrace, drips absorb and erections restrain.

The shipping was handled by Kuehne and Nagel, a logistics company. Logistics means the business of shifting stuff. Kuehne and Nagel own almost nothing. The ships are not theirs, the stuff is not theirs. They merely handle the complex organizational work that I shrink at the thought of. They are a vast concern, originally German but with offices in practically every major port in the world, including Shanghai.

I ask Tony whether he could wangle me an invitation to visit Kuehne and Nagel, and he promises to try. And he tells me that he has already contacted Kingstar Light Industrial Products in Quanzhou and they'll be happy to show me round the factory. Meanwhile he shows me round his office.

The place is industriously quiet. Young Chinese employees are sitting at computers, surrounded by piles of samples. Here are bras and toys and Christmas decorations. Here are socket sets, fishing rods and saucepans. Clothing samples are being checked on a white table under bright lights. And against one wall stands a row of what look like shop-window mannequins that have suffered quadruple amputations.

They turn out to be fit-test dummies, made in Canada and frightfully expensive because of the finicky precision with which they were built. To a tolerance measured in tenths of a millimetre these figures represent the official standardized proportions of the human beast. Here is the small male human being, there the medium female human being. And there, at the end of the row, that pair with the bulging arses and the slumping guts, are Mr and Mrs 3XL.

All the apparel that comes through this office is slid over

these dummies to test for fit. I run a finger over the stomach of Mr Large, stopping politely above his genital bulge. His Canadian skin is slightly furry, like a mouse's skin.

Staff turnover, says Tony, is high, not only in this office but throughout Shanghai. There are just so many jobs available for anyone who can speak English. *51job Weekly* is a paper that consists only of employment ads. 'It's fat,' says Tony, 'seriously fat.' Only this week one of his staff quit at lunchtime, telling no one. He just went away and never came back. 'But he did leave a nice polite message on his computer.'

When Tony asks if I have any further questions I have only one. 'I realize,' I say, 'that this may be a sensitive matter, but can you tell me roughly what price TWL paid the manufacturer for my underpants?'

'I knew you'd ask that,' says Tony, sighing. 'And it's not that simple. Things have to be put into context. The difference between the wholesale and the retail price, what the punter sees as profit, has to pay for a host of things: customs, freight, shipping, distribution, QC, CSR, my wages, this office, the lot.'

'Of course,' I say. 'But all the same, if you could give me a rough idea.'

'Hang on,' says Tony, 'I'll ring my boss in NZ.'

He scrolls through a list on his mobile phone, then presses a button or two. 'Hello,' he says, 'is Nick Tuck there? . . . Oh OK, I'll ring back later.'

Tony looks surprised when I stifle a laugh.

I never do discover the unit price of my underpants but I don't really need to. If TWL can sell five pairs in New Zealand for NZ$8.59, the price per pair at the factory gate is approximately, allowing for shipping costs, overheads and all the rest of it, bugger all.

I spend much of the day in the TWL office on the eighteenth air-conditioned floor above humming Shanghai. Over the course of that time what seems to be extraordinary becomes ordinary. This is a place of procurement. It procures essentials, like underpants, and inessentials, like toy dumper trucks the colour of butter. That it should exist twelve hours by air and twenty days by sea from the place where these items will be sold is an absurdity, but an unquestioned one. And in one way there is nothing new about it. China has been trading with the West for a couple of thousand years. The Romans prized Chinese silk before Christ was born. And on the *Antiques Roadshow* much of the porcelain that the experts say learned things about came from China.

But silk and porcelain were uniquely Chinese. The West didn't know how to make either. The West does, however, know how to make underpants and plastic dumper trucks. It's just that China does it cheaper.

When I was a child, the words 'Made in Japan' meant cheap and nasty. Now 'Made in Japan' means top-quality stuff. And the same process is already happening in China. There are still plenty of enterprises turning out trash, but the quality and complexity of Chinese-made goods is improving almost by the day. Increasingly they are making hi-tech stuff – televisions, phones, computers – that is as good as anything anywhere.

A lot of this has been achieved by reverse engineering. In other words the Chinese have taken Western products to pieces, found out how they work, and started making them themselves. There has been huge theft of intellectual property, including the theft of brand names. Over recent years Chinese factories have made fake Heineken beer, Polo shirts, Head and Shoulders shampoo, Gucci sunglasses, Toyota cars, Yamaha motorbikes, Viagra, Calvin Klein briefs and every brand of Swiss watch under the sun.

You can buy a complete Windows operating system or Adobe Acrobat for a New Zealand dollar. They have also, and I'm impressed by this in particular, written new Harry Potter stories published with Rowling's name on the jacket. I would not be surprised to learn they were better written than the original.

The Chinese government has implicitly connived in the process. Especially in the early days of the boom, the Chinese government set out to ensure that the influx of Western ideas and money would profit China more than it profited the West. The West was so desperate to gain access to this unthinkably huge new market that the Chinese government, who retain unbrookable central power, held the whip hand in all negotiations. They used the whip with subtle effectiveness.

So China is growing richer. Eventually it will price itself out of the market and the manufacture of plastic dumper trucks will shift to wherever labour is cheaper. But that day will be a while coming. For out in the provinces behind Shanghai, in the however many million square miles of China that appear on the map as a dauntingly vast chunk of Asia, there are a billion peasants. They work the soil pretty much as they have worked the soil for ever, as dynasties have risen and fallen. They have been dragooned into wars, forced to build walls and palaces, subjected to taxation and natural disasters – a particular speciality of China – but they have gone on going on. And now, for the first time and irrevocably, things are changing in a single generation. The bright lights of the cities and the sexy roar of capitalism are seducing their children. Those children are flocking to town to earn money. Not much money but more than their parents or grandparents or any of their ancestors have ever made, and with the possibility, most importantly, of more still.

No one knows for sure how many people are shifting in search of the new wealth. I have read estimates of 300 million. It is the biggest human migration in history. After almost half a century of being forced by law to stay where they were on their tiny plots of land, the Chinese peasantry is coming to town, and particularly to the east coast. Thousands arrive in Shanghai every day.

China is changing, fast. And China is one fifth of the human race. The effects will be felt, are being felt, everywhere.

O'Malley's on the Tao Jiang Road is a pub in the international manner. Set behind tall walls and apparently guarded by a single elderly man on a campstool, it consists of a little garden, a covered courtyard and a warren of low-slung bars and rooms, in a remote parody of an eighteenth-century coaching inn. There is Guinness on tap, of course, that global signifier of synthetic Irishness, plus the usual international brands like Foster's, Heineken and Carlsberg, all of which target the ever-growing itinerant class of global capitalism. The bar staff are local, impeccably deferential in waistcoats and white shirts. The price of beer is reasonable in Western terms, in Chinese terms outrageous.

The Kiwi night, as Compton Tothill predicted, has hauled perhaps fifty people out of this vast metropolis, drawn by a shared familiarity with some islands in the South Pacific. Comfort food has been laid on – chicken nuggets, fish and chips, with real knives and forks. And everyone talks business. Business is why they're in China. And it seems that business is why they're at this bash. Business cards are being exchanged everywhere I look. I find myself drinking with a moon-faced local who went to university in New Zealand. He represents a new plastic debit card that employers can give their employees. As far as I can tell it's the electronic equivalent of luncheon vouchers. It is going to be big, he tells me, business is already beginning to boom. When I ask about numbers he sidesteps the question. When I ask again, more directly, he sidesteps more thoroughly, feigning acquaintance with a man at the far end of the bar. I watch surreptitiously as he hovers at the man's shoulder a while, waiting to pierce a little conversational knot, then darts in with his self-introduction and his water-melon smile. A few seconds later he is exchanging business cards, and doing most of the talking. It's going to be big, he is saying, business is already starting to boom.

Compton Tothill, the old China hand, isn't hard to spot. He has an air of quiet certainty and comfort, like seasoned oak. His patrician vowels, formed in the Anglophile suburbs of Christchurch, have developed a hint of Asiatic intonation. Perhaps sixty years old, he worked for twenty or more years in Taiwan, retired, returned to Christchurch and found that he was, in his own words, no longer a Kiwi. The threads had snapped. His old friends thought differently from him. So back out he came and has now been in Shanghai for six years.

But it's clear that he feels that it's a little indecent to talk about himself, and he deftly swings the conversational searchlight on to me. What has brought me to Shanghai.

'Underpants,' I say. 'I'm trying to trace a pair of underpants back to source.'

'That must be terribly interesting,' he says, 'but please excuse me, I'd better circulate.'

Another bar is dominated by a tall young man whose eyes sparkle with zest. He's from Te Puke in the North Island. He grins and laughs and talks too loud, fired by beer and youth. People instinctively excuse his manner because of his infectious energy, his radiant delight in the here and now. He struts like a rooster, fiercely thrilled by his own independence.

'I won't be modest. It's pretty good,' he says, when I ask about his command of Chinese. Modesty was the last thing I expected but I don't say so. 'I've set up a trading company.'

'Trading in what?'

'Anything. You want something made, you come to me. I'll find it for you. Simple. I've built up connections. I love it. See that bloke over there. He wants ironwork for going round the verandas of old villas. I'll get it for him. I know several forgeries. Easy.'

'Forgeries?'

'Yeah, forgeries, metal places. They'll make anything here, anything you want.'

He talks of his upbringing, his frustration at the slow pace of New Zealand, and his imperial business ambitions. But it transpires that his empire is not quite as expansive as his manner. He spends four days a week drudging for an English language school.

The man who wants the veranda ironwork is a shearer from Oamaru. When not shearing, he builds boats and renovates houses. Frank and cheerful, he's been bewitched by Shanghai. 'I didn't know what to expect but Christ, I fucking love it. Have you had a massarjee?'

'A what?'

'Massarjee. It's everywhere. You go in for a haircut and one thing leads to another. Cheap as chips too.' He giggles. 'There's this street in Pudong where the sheilas just come up and grab you by the balls. Beautiful girls they are too.'

The man's wife, who was not privy to the preceding conversation, is equally taken with Shanghai. 'You know back home I used to say, "Look, there's another bloody Asian." But they're lovely people, aren't they? So kind and always smiling.'

There's a fervour in this gathering that I quite enjoy, a sense of mateyness in a strange place, a shared sense of novelty. I meet a former pupil of Shirley Boys' High who is trying to convince the newly rich Chinese to drink wine, and a farmer from Hawke's Bay who has come here to get a gadget manufactured, a gadget that he's invented and patented. It has something to do with stock control. But his main interest seems to be the use to which the locals can put a bicycle. 'What's the best load you've seen on a bike?' he asks.

'Five dead pigs,' I say, because yesterday I saw a bike carrying three.

'What about a fridge?' says the farmer. 'Full size. I saw this guy buy a second-hand fridge at a market, strap it to the side of his bike and head off with the bike leaning at forty-five degrees. Bloody amazing.'

'How did he pedal?'

'He pedalled all right, don't you worry,' says the farmer, then moves away to talk to someone else.

When I leave around 11 p.m. the main streets still thrum with people, surprisingly various in age. And I seem to be the only one who's a bit pissed.

But I wouldn't be surprised if the booze came soon. With capitalist success and capitalist stress and capitalist self-indulgence and capitalist loneliness and ferocious capitalist advertising, I suspect that in ten years the late night streets of Shanghai will be different. Fat with money the singleton children of an urban middle class will monopolize these streets, shouting, happy, and rendered clumsily inaccurate by Guinness, Foster's, Heineken and ready-mixed, sweet as peaches, bourbon and Coke. Though by then, of course, all of those drinks, or indistinguishably similar ones, will be made in China. Perhaps, indeed, they already are.

5

Walk Upright and Speak English

Tony Pendleton keeps his word. He rings me first thing in the morning to tell me that Ben Schlatzl from Kuehne and Nagel, the logistics company, will pick me up from my hotel at eleven. They're going to show me the port my underpants went through.

Before Ben arrives I go to the bank to change money. There seems to be only one teller, and she does not appear to be telling. A miniature security guard spots me looking baffled and steers me through the crowd to the woman's desk where she checks and rechecks my traveller's cheques and passport, completes a form in triplicate, stamps all three copies with what looks like an Ming dynasty seal on a stick, then hands everything back, whereupon the security guard, chattering cheerfully, leads me to a stool. In front of the stool a wall. On the wall a screen. Set into the wall a drawer. Following gestured instructions from the guard, I put my documents in the drawer and it sucks itself shut. My documents then appear on the screen under the hands of a bank teller whom I imagine to be just the other side of the wall but who, for all I know, could be half a building away. The hands check and recheck the cheques and the passport, summon a supervising pair of hands to check the checking, then the original hands gather up my things and disappear for rather too long. When the hands return they are holding a wad of banknotes that they count in a whirring machine before laying them alongside my passport in a drawer. The same notes and passport then appear in the drawer on my side of the world. Their sudden arrival jolts me. I feel as though I've been watching a movie that vaguely relates to me and then suddenly it has become flesh.

I changed US$2000. There are about seven yuan to the US dollar. The largest denomination bill, which bears a picture of Mao looking airbrushed and plumply benign, is worth 100 yuan. The sheer bulk of the notes I get is embarrassing. It's a wad to stop a bullet. It's too fat for my wallet. It would exceed a peasant's lifetime earnings. I cram my pockets with my Westerner's wealth, feeling cosseted, insulated by sheer money. Notes are intoxicating. I am reminded of the best pay packet I ever received. I earned it as a student for spending a month up a ladder painting gutters and it came in a sealed brown envelope. I took it to the toilet to open. It held 120 pounds in twenty-pound notes. Between finger and thumb I riffled their fibrous lineny texture. Then I kissed them.

Ben Schlatzl is young, German and handsome. Dressed for business in suit, tie and overcoat, he sees me in the lobby of the hotel, nods, assesses my clothes, walks past and sits on a couch to await someone more businesslike.

'Are you Ben?' I say.

He stands to shake my hand, dissembling his surprise at my scruffy trousers, my open-necked shirt. His manner is genial and his English admirable, apart from the ritual German transposition of v and w.

The Kuehne and Nagel car is a seven-seater people mover with a front end like the bevelled tip of a chisel and upholstery of deep and creamy leather. But Ben apologizes for it. He assures me we would be in something altogether more sumptuous if we did not have to pick up three more people, the head honcho of Kuehne and Nagel's Shanghai branch, and a brace of financial analysts from Switzerland. We are to meet them at the Jin Mao building in Pudong, the tallest of Shanghai's buildings, where the Hyatt hotel begins at the fifty-third floor.

The company driver maintains the standard for company drivers. Faced with a wall of pedestrians he drives hard at the feeblest of them. Where the road is clogged, not once does he permit anything to nudge past him. And I note with interest that he has graduated beyond sounding his horn. He flashes his lights instead. It feels classier than sounding a horn but is no more effective.

In the lift up to the Hyatt, Ben and I are accompanied by three jewellery-draped Australian women with upper arms like turkey wattles. The women are heading for, and energetically discussing, breakfast in the Crystal Ballroom. One of them is obsessed with the prospect of crêpes, which she pronounces to rhyme exactly with pipes.

The view from the fifty-third-floor lobby is majestically unsurprising. It is merely Shanghai and more Shanghai and an awful lot of cloud. 'Twenty-one million people,' says Ben, 'and growing every day.'

Nearby they're erecting the world's tallest building. But it won't hold the title for long. A Malaysian building will be taller, and the Malaysians started first. But the Chinese will finish first because they build faster. They've had plenty of practice. Since the late eighties Shanghai has put up more than 5000 buildings of fifteen storeys or more.

The two Swiss analysts seem absurdly young. They are doing Asia in a fortnight, visiting businesses with a view to advising their investors where to bung their surplus francs. Wednesday was Bangkok. Yesterday Hong Kong. Today and tomorrow Shanghai. 'If I am organizing my trip better,' says one, 'I would go to U2 concert in Singapore, but I am getting the dates wrong.'

Providentially for me Kuehne and Nagel has laid on a tour for them of Shanghai's new port. When the boss turns up I am moved to the front seat so that the four German speakers can talk business together. They do so in English. I presume that it is a courtesy to me, but when one of the analysts hands over gifts of Swiss chocolate, they all lapse into German. It seems that because of the United States, Microsoft, and perhaps a remote vestigial effect of the British Empire, English is the language of commerce.

'How wulnerable,' asks one of the baby analysts, 'is K&N to economic cycles?' The boss explains that K&N is not wulnerable at all. It owns next to nothing and staff are easy to shed.

'What about recruitment?'

'No problem. We just trawl the universities once a year. If they can walk upright and speak English, we hire them.'

The present port of Shanghai is tidal and it requires constant dredging. It also occupies land that has become real estate almost beyond price. Worst of all, it is only the third biggest port in the world, after Singapore and Hong Kong. The situation is entirely unsatisfactory. So Shanghai is building a new port. It will be the biggest in the world, of course. They are building it on an island.

After an hour of driving the urban landscape at last gives way to a wide flat delta and my first glimpse of Chinese agriculture. Concrete-block farmhouses squat amid rows of vegetables, grizzled fruit trees, ponds for fish, ponds for ducks and stands of bamboo. Men and women till the soil with spines hunched by their work. A few tunnel houses, like Anderson shelters fashioned from plastic, have been blackened by their proximity to Shanghai. The sky here is no less grey than in the city centre. It is impossible to tell whether the horizon is the meeting of air and land or of air and water.

It is water. The land falls only a foot or two and becomes a featureless sloppy sea. We pass a sign the size of a house announcing 'Tangshan Free Trade Port Area' and we are suddenly on a bridge with no apparent end. It streams away from us in a series of identical shallow humps, walking on stilts across the open sea, shrinking with perspective to a pencil's width, a hair's width and then melding into the cod-grey sky. This bridge is twenty miles long and six lanes wide. It joins the mainland to the new port. The Chinese built it in a couple of years.

The Chinese have always had a penchant for doing work on a large scale. You have only to think of the Great Wall, or of the numerous imperial palaces that were put up by one dynasty only to be razed by the next. The power to achieve these things stemmed from the emperor. Defy that power and you died. Obey it and you still stood a fair chance of dying.

The Great Wall is famously visible from space. Less famous and quite invisible from space are the bones of the dead builders. Their numbers ran into the millions. It was effectively slave labour, the sort of labour that built so many of the things over which we tourists like to clamber and coo, moaning as we do so that these days we lack the grand vision.

Today the force behind the great construction projects is government money. Billions of yuan have gone into the construction of roads and railways and power generation. For all its ferocious rate of change, China is still run from the centre, as it was under Mao, as it was under the emperors.

The bridge snakes on, its sections mesmerically repeating themselves. Before long I can see neither the land behind us nor the island ahead. We are simply on a bridge over the open sea beneath a low and dreary sky. In the plush air-conditioned van, Germanic voices talk of stock price volatility and P/E ratios and freight volumes going forward. Tyres whirr on the mint-fresh tarmac. Below the bridge a rusted fishing boat lurches and flops, hauling a net through oxtail water.

A final giant curve of the bridge and we approach the island. Until recently it was home to a fishing village. Unfortunately for the fishermen, the surrounding water that provided their livelihood proved deep enough to accommodate the largest of container ships. There isn't a fishing village there any more.

A portal has been blasted through pinkish rock, beyond which a road winds off to a public viewing platform. But we are privileged guests. Kuehne and Nagel has clout. We present our credentials to what seems like military security and are waved through and round a bend to where the new port opens out. To say it is colossal is to say that the Spice Girls were a little vapid.

The island has been dynamited and bulldozed flat. Behemothic machines are shovelling gravel and grading the land and laying bitumen. The area already prepared would house, at a guess, perhaps 2000 football pitches. But only at a guess. The scale exceeds the capacity of my mind to assess it.

I live in Lyttelton, the largest port in the South Island of New Zealand. It has half a dozen wharves for ordinary ships, and a single deepwater berth that can accommodate a single large container ship. Shanghai's new port deals only in giant container ships. Ten berths are already operational. Forty more are under construction. A giant container ship can be unloaded and reloaded here in eight hours. At full capacity this port will turn round 150 of these ships a day.

And what ships. Their steel sides rise like cliffs. The windows of the bridge are comically small, like eyes on a brontosaurus. The superstructure that houses the crew is like a matchbox on a house.

Each ship is attended by crimson straddle cranes, monstrous motorized beasts on stilts, that pluck a container from the hold, slide it in between their giant legs as if suckling it and then lower it on to a waiting truck.

In the holding area stand thousands of forty-foot containers, huge stacks of refrigerated containers and an acre or two of open 'flat racks' supporting machine parts too big for any containers. And the place is still only 20 per cent operational.

We crawl along the wharf's edge, dwarfed by everything. Even the baby financial analysts have fallen silent to gawp at the reality of global trade, the sheer quantity of stuff being shifted in big metal boxes. China makes the stuff and pumps it out through here. If you think of China as a giant sow in farrow, this port is one of the teats at which the world comes to suck.

Barely anyone goes on foot. There is no equipment here that a man could lift on his own. The human beings are operators of tame mechanical monsters. Every movement of a human arm, every press of a finger, every turn of a wrist is magnified by hydraulic power to shift tons. There is little to see except flanks of steel on a scale that dizzies. Far out I watch the rectangular stern of a ship lose definition as it fades into the grey. Some weeks from now it will tie up at a less impressive port than this one to disgorge its load. The containers will disperse to various destinations, their great iron gates will swing open, and the stuff will scatter to warehouses, to distribution centres, to shops. And at the far end of the chain stand you and I, the Western consumers, in our cheap Chinese underpants.

'It's wery big,' says an analyst. Hard to improve on that. It is wery big.

The place is run from a control tower like the bridge on the USS *Enterprise*. Windows grant a complete view of the port, but no one looks through them. When supervisors need to see what's going on they go to any one of a dozen screens from which any of a thousand surveillance cameras can be manipulated with a three-inch toggle. I am allowed to have a go. I zoom in on the only human figure I can find, idling at the base of a straddle crane like an ant in a forest. But as he takes shape on the screen in his hard hat and orange boiler suit it becomes clear that he is not idling. He is striding along the wharf, clipboard in hand, but his purposeful progress makes no dent on this territory of giants. I am half a mile away from him. I can see that he hasn't shaved. He will never know I watched him. I can sense how dictators become excited by power.

Most of the employees in the control tower are loading ships on screens. They transfer colour-coded containers into holds with a couple of movements on the keyboard. The only noise is the clicking of mice. Those clicks are changing the shape of the world's economy.

In the car park outside the control tower the Kuehne and Nagel boss is unimpressed. 'If this had been Hong Kong,' he says, 'we would have had a tour guide in a short skirt with perfect English.'

The boss has spent most of his working life in the East. I ask him how well he speaks Chinese.

'I have a wife to do that,' he says and laughs.

For my benefit, I suspect, we stop at the lookout where the less privileged tourists gather. It's midday on a weekday. There are no vendors of ice creams here, no souvenir shops, no children's entertainment, nothing to do here except overlook a port, and you have to drive twenty monotonous miles of bridge to get here. Yet this unfinished industrial landscape, constructed without thought to anything except utility, has pulled a substantial crowd of excited Chinese people. I am captured inadvertently on the memory disks of a hundred digital cameras, their automatic zooms getting little whirring hard-ons as they seek a point of focus.

'You help me please,' says a grinning old man with a belly like a ripe gourd. He is wearing a fleece vest with a picture of a canoeist on the left tit. The legend 'Mild Seven Outdoor Quest' is embroidered beneath it. He hands me his camera and poses chuckling in front of a chunk of rock on which the name of the port is spelt out in characters a couple of yards tall. Beside the title stands a vast anchor. 'You get the an-cher,' he says pronouncing the ch as in chop, 'you get the an-cher.' I get the an-cher. The man is inordinately pleased.

No doubt the tourists have come to gawp as I have gawped, but I also sense that they have come to revel. And what they are revelling in is a sense of national pride. Here, in front of them, is a physical embodiment of China's resurgence, of China reasserting its rightful position in the world.

The financial analysts, who have been terribly grown up and serious and who have spoken like a transcript from the business pages, become infected by the holiday happiness of the crowd. They extract cameras the size of Nice biscuits. They photograph the tourists, the port, Ben, the K&N boss, me, Ben, the K&N boss and me together.

Back in Shanghai a couple of hours later Ben shows me round the two floors halfway up a skyscraper where Kuehne and Nagel does business. Business consists of 700 or so Chinese employees seated at computer screens. All that any of them are doing is organizing the shipment of goods from China to the world. They never see the goods or the ships. They merely provide the service, organizing the packing of LCLs (less than container loads) into FCLs (full container loads), putting the FCLs on to ships and sending them away.

'What about importing?' I say. 'China must import something.'

'Follow me,' says Ben. At the end of the room a dozen employees sit slightly apart from the 680 or so others. 'Our import section,' says Ben.

China does import stuff. It imports colossal quantities of raw materials such as iron ore. It imports huge amounts of scrap metal by bulk carrier. It imports plastic waste such as old DVDs and bleach bottles, which it recycles into, among other things, baby bottles. And it imports unimaginable numbers of empty containers.

Ben gives me a Kuehne and Nagel map of China, a brace of Kuehne and Nagel pens and a little Kuehne and Nagel pouch with a zip on it. All are made in China. I unzip the pouch and out springs a Kuehne and Nagel frisbee, instantaneously expanding to four times the size of the pouch.

'Thank you,' I say, 'my young dog will love it.' He will, too. I'll throw the frisbee, he'll sprint after it, leap and grab it, shake it fiercely to break its neck, then pin it with a paw and shred it. One Chinese knick-knack down, a billion billion to go.

Ben hands me on to Jiamen who is cheerful, fluent in English and charged with taking me to the CFS, the Container Freight Station, near the soon-to-be-replaced port of Shanghai. The CFS is where LCLs are made up into FCLs.

The afternoon traffic is as dense as a Cup Final crowd but more aggressive. Stalled in long jams the drivers fizz like flies in a bottle. The CFS lies only a few miles from the office but the stop–start battle of the drive gives me plenty of time to extract the story of Jiamen's life. He has lived China's recent history. He could hardly have avoided it. And yet he tells the story with a gentle matter-of-factness.

He was born at the height of the Cultural Revolution when Mao's paranoia sent millions of bourgeois intellectuals to remote villages to learn to be peasants. Bourgeois intellectuals meant educated urbanites, which simply meant people who might see through Mao.

Jiamen had no toys. He played in mud. He got one new set of blue serge clothes a year at the Spring Festival. Being a bright child he was recruited to the elite Junior Communist Party, which was like Scouts but with political rhetoric in place of dib dib dob. His first school textbook was a reader that had to be learned by heart. The catchy first page ran 'Long live Chairman Mao. Long live the Communist Party. Long live the People's Republic of China.' Thereafter the story line improved a little. 'My father is a worker. My mother is a worker. My uncle is a soldier.'

It was the banal brutality of every dictatorship, and none of it worked. Bourgeois intellectuals didn't become peasants. Peasants didn't become communists. In fact, probably no one became a communist, not even Mao. Mao was a great man. He began with good intentions. But as is the inevitable way of things, power screwed him up. He became as mad and murderous as Stalin. Or as numerous Chinese emperors.

In the West for the last half century, history has touched few of us. It has been by and large a spectator sport, something to be ignored or deplored or argued over. Some people are always affected by political decisions, but few are grossly damaged by them and fewer still killed. Mao's whims killed millions. We can know the facts but it remains hard to imagine the reality of it, and that it was so very recent. What I find especially hard to conceive is the absence of choice. People did as they were told, like children. The authorities were omnipotent. Fear reigned.

As people did what they needed to do to survive, the truth went into hiding. Everyone wore the official party line because the alternative was death. But when the foot eventually came off the throat, everyone reverted to what they'd been before the foot came down on the throat, unless they were dead.

Jiamen remembers the day Mao died: 9 September 1976. Aged ten, Jiamen was required to patrol the streets of Shanghai to ensure that no child played games or laughed. Solemn music played on the radio.

I can't help reflecting that in that same month, at the end of the hot summer of 1976, I was about to head for university. Half a dozen of us who had been at school together said goodbye to that period of our lives by renting a boat on the Thames and spending six days drunk. The difference between my life and Jiamen's was luck.

Thirteen years later I was in New Zealand and Jiamen was in Tiananmen Square.

'Were you afraid?'

'No.'

He should have been. Still no one knows exactly how many protestors were shot. It may have been thousands.

'The authorities panicked,' says Jiamen. 'In Shanghai they handled it much better.'

According to Jiamen the mayor of Shanghai, Jiang Zemin, defused a similar demonstration by ordering the parents of the protestors to round up their children. And apparently that same mayor stood before another crowd of protestors and recited the Gettysburg Address to them in English. Whatever the truth of his actions, Jiang Zemin emerged with great credit. He became the next General Secretary of the Communist Party and in due course the President of the People's Republic of China.

In 1998 he came to Christchurch. I was attending a book launch next door to the hotel where the president was due to dine with New Zealand's prime minister. A few hundred protestors had gathered to bang drums and chant Free Tibet, though I remember doubting at the time whether any of them could have found Tibet on a map.

Chinese officials refused to allow Jiang Zemin to witness the demonstration. But the protestors were not breaking New Zealand law and the police refused to shift them. The result was a stand-off. The problem was solved by parking half a dozen buses between the protestors and the entrance to the hotel. Jiang Zemin arrived by limo, was hurried through the door and saw nothing. He was no doubt aware of the demonstration, but he couldn't be seen to be aware of it. At the time it seemed absurd, an infantile game of let's pretend. On mature reflection, it still does.

'What,' I ask Jiamen, 'does the average Shanghai youngster know about Mao, the Cultural Revolution and so on?'

'Not much,' he says, 'and why should they? They want to make money and spend money. They're getting smug.'

'And the party, what will happen with the party? Can they retain power?'

'The party's wising up. They've got more and more non-party experts advising them. They're learning from overseas. It's easiest for everyone else just to say to hell with it and get on with making money. Everything's going well. People are proud of what's happening here. They're getting rich.

'Lots of stupid people in the West get China wrong. They've always got China wrong. There's a lot of anti-foreigner feeling here, against Japan, against the States.'

'And yet there are thousands of foreigners here.'

'Yes, but most of them don't really live here.' And he tells me about Jinqiao, an enclave for expats with its own stores and social clubs. It sounds like a modernized Somerset Maugham world. 'They play cricket,' says Jiamen, as the driver swings terrifyingly across a stream of traffic, through a set of gates and pulls up in front of the Container Freight Station. Its doors are flanked by a pair of lucky lions.

Just inside the doors we meet a pile of artificial kidneys. The pile is the size of a bungalow. These 'hollow fibre dialysers' are stored in white cardboard boxes stamped Asahi Kasei Medical Co. Ltd. The company is Japanese, but the manufacturers Chinese. This pile is 'buffer stock', Jiamen tells me, for the world.

Beyond the 10,000 or so kidneys the warehouse stretches away, brightly lit and scrupulously clean, and built on the sort of scale that I am becoming used to. The far end is invisible. Forklifts pick up pallets of this, stacks of that and whirr them to the open side of the building where containers wait.

Most containers, such as the one that held my underpants, bypass such places as this. They are filled and sealed at the point of manufacture and taken straight to the port. Here are only the small orders, the part loads. But they seem to comprise, well, everything: boxes of vermicelli, moisturizing lotion, batteries and paper cups. Over there are piled boxes of chopping boards, cling film, ballpoint pens, whiteboard pens, permanent marker pens, toothpaste and Colgate branded toothbrushes. Here's an island of women's underwear, alongside another of boxed 3M overhead projectors to be dispatched to classrooms for the use of teachers frightened to turn their backs on their pupils. Sandpaper, mitre saws, steering racks, 7-gallon air compressors, jacks. A mountain of 40-inch 6-wheel plastic creepers, whatever they may be. Their brand name is DuraLast.

There is stuff here destined for Turkey, for Brazil, for Nigeria, for the States, for Belgium, for everywhere I've heard of and plenty of places I haven't. Here are running shoes bound for Limoges and pallets of strawberry 'jelly shoes', whatever they may be, addressed to Rushton Ablett of Northampton. Northampton was once the heart of the British shoe industry.

The sheer variety and vastness and absurdity of the place makes me giggle. I wander from aisle to aisle reading the information on boxes. Here is ordinariness by the ton. It's the whole mundane world of fixtures and fittings. It's the stuff your house is crammed with, the cutlery, the garden furniture, the synthetic Christmas tree, the baubles on the synthetic Christmas tree, the fairy lights on the synthetic Christmas tree, the toys you'll wrap for your children and place under the synthetic Christmas tree. Here's even a mound of cardboard boxes containing rolls of the paper that you'll wrap the presents in. And all of it made by people who have no concept of Christmas.

Clothes are everywhere: a caravan-sized heap of boxed T-shirts, and wheeled rack after wheeled rack of identical skirt and blouse combinations, the skirts black, the blouses a fetching pattern of black and vomit yellow. Each matching outfit is wrapped in cellophane. 'GOH' is their acronym, Garments on Hangers. And they've been ironed, because it is cheaper to iron them in China and transport them in such a way that they do not crease, than it is to compress them and have them ironed on arrival. The label should, but doesn't, say 'Ironed in China'.

According to Tony Pendleton the Chinese are the best in the

world at packing containers. Whenever New Zealand customs have to unpack a container to check its contents, they can never, without exception, fit all the stuff back in. I watch the champion packers at it. They work with cheerful commitment, disappearing into a container with stuff, emerging without it and going to fetch more, under the supervision of an old hand with a three-dimensional mental image of what goes where inside this soon-to-be-sealed metal cavern.

The only time I have ever stepped inside a shipping container was on a fishing trip in New Zealand. A friend of a friend had planted an old container in a paddock and converted it into a holiday home. It had a kitchen in one end, a bathroom at the other and in between it slept three large fishermen with ease.

'There are hundreds of warehouses like this,' says Jiamen.

'Hundreds?'

'Maybe thousands,' he says.

I return in the evening to the restaurant where my incompetence with chopsticks was such a success. How quickly we establish routine. It's born of timidity, a need for security in a random world. And yet how limiting it is. I am almost fifty. I have travelled a fair bit but I have risked almost nothing. What has prevented me tasting the world to the full is simply the tyranny of habit.

But there are compensations to habit, such as finding oneself recognized on one's second visit to a Shanghai restaurant. Indeed, I seem to have become a minor celebrity. On my arrival at the door, the acidic features of the maîtresse d' light up to the extent that they are capable of lighting up. I smile and say 'ee' which I think means one, though I hold up a single finger as back-up.

It is early evening and the place is quiet. Ms Acid leads me past a parade of smiling waitresses, seats me at a table and speaks peremptorily over her shoulder. A girl with a face that would not look out of place in a yurt brings me a large bottle of beer, unordered. 'Goodeveninghowareyou,' says the waitress who looks about fourteen, and then she giggles. Within thirty seconds I've received the novel-length menu and half a dozen paper towels in anticipation of scattered food and excess perspiration. And my jacket, which I've placed on the back of my chair, has been sheathed in plastic, presumably in case my ungovernable chopsticks, in addition to scattering food about the table, start biffing it over my shoulder.

The towels come in handy. An apparently innocuous plate of chicken in peanuts has been coated in the same stuff that ruined yesterday's cabbage. But the crab meat and the distressed looking vegetables and the Tsingtao beer are a joy. When I leave I get a farewell that wouldn't disgruntle royalty.

It's drizzling. Above the street hangs a truck-size picture of Rafael Nadal, the grunting Spanish tennis star with the anthropological face. The photo is dominated by the tumulus of his left bicep, whose existence he highlights with sleeveless shirts. My mother in Sussex has remarked on this bicep. Now the Chinese have the chance to remark on it.

Nadal is in town along with Federer and all the other millionaire racquet-men, all nestled no doubt at this very moment in air-conditioned rooms on some astronomically numbered floor of some multiply starred hotel indistinguishable from the one they nestled in last week in Atlanta or Rome. China is joining the world.

I wander awhile, lit by just the right amount of beer, relishing the anonymity and strangeness. On a street bench sits a virulently coloured plastic clown. It's Ronald McDonald, crosslegged in hooped leggings and perpetually grinning at nobody, at everybody, at Shanghai. Next to him sits a shrivelled ancient with a face like a basset hound, looking the other way. For one of the very few times in my life, I wish I had a camera.

6

Dining with Dirk

*C*hina Daily tells me that Milton Friedman, champion of the free market, has died. I hope that before he keeled over he got to see Shanghai traffic.

I wouldn't have recognized Mr Friedman if he'd come up and shaken me by the hand, but in the 1980s I kept bumping into his ideas. In 1982 I left Thatcher's Britain where everything was changing in the name of free-market reform, and went to live in Canada where everything was changing in the name of free-market reform. Five years later I pitched up in New Zealand where I found an ostensibly Labour government selling state assets to American corporations in the name of free-market reform.

China contracted Milton too, for it was during this same period that Deng Xiaoping began the process that resulted in China's industrial boom, the boom that made my underpants. Deng called it 'socialism with Chinese characteristics'. What he meant was capitalism under central control. This is not a history book, but in China, as everywhere, the past is written in the present.

Until comparatively recently, China lived alone. The Romans had bought its silk, but they never did more than brush the fringes of China's western frontiers. When Marco Polo's account of his travels in China was published in the fourteenth century, the West became fascinated with the place, but still very few people actually went there. It was only a little over 200 years ago that the West became seriously interested in trading with it. And the Chinese found this difficult. China had always traded and was keen to continue to do so, but on its own terms. And those terms were dictated by China's justifiable sense of superiority. China coveted no European goods, and at the same time it saw itself as it had always seen itself, as the Middle Kingdom, the undisputed centre of the civilized world. All peoples beyond its borders were barbarians. If they came to China they had to come as vassals, paying homage to the emperor. All of which would have been fine had not Europe developed a taste for tea and porcelain. It imported vast quantities of these, but sold China nothing in return.

In 1792 Earl Macartney set out to put things right. He led an expedition to China, taking with him a hundred people, a letter of flattery from the king, and sixty-six crates of things that he hoped might interest the Chinese: telescopes, a horse-drawn carriage, Wedgwood vases, a planetarium, portraits of the British nobility, a hot air balloon and other indispensables. He also brought gunpowder and guns. The Chinese sniffed a big fat rat.

They obliged Macartney to leave his weaponry on the coast before letting him proceed to what was then Peking. Meanwhile they adorned the British baggage train with banners proclaiming 'Ambassador bearing tribute from the country of England', which wasn't quite how Earl Macartney saw things.

As the British party approached Peking they travelled on

roads paved with granite and they crossed bridges made of marble. Within Peking lay the fourteen square miles of the walled Tartar City, and within that city the Imperial Palace. Here were parks and pleasure gardens, artificial lakes and hills and an abundance of eunuchs. Their faces were painted, their voices treble, their appearance in every way hideous. And, having been deprived by surgery of other pastimes, how they schemed.

The presence of the unseen emperor hung over the place. He had the mandate of heaven. That mandate meant that certain streets were for his use only, and only he could wear pearls or yellow cloth, and only his robes could be decorated with a five-toed dragon. Anyone granted a formal audience with the emperor had to kowtow. And that, for Earl Macartney, was a bit of a tickler. Macartney saw the audience as a meeting of equals. The Chinese emphatically didn't.

The kowtow required the supplicant to prostrate himself at the foot of the emperor's dais and bang his head on the floor three times. Then he stood to bow. Then it was back to his knees for more head-banging, up for another bow, and so on. The full kowtow required an aggregate of nine bangs of the head. For the earl this was nine too many. He was the king's representative and the king banged his head for nobody.

Over months of wrangling, several solutions were proposed, including the idea that Macartney should kowtow to the emperor at the same time as a mandarin of comparable rank kowtowed to a portrait of George III. In the end, and probably just to get rid of him, the emperor granted Macartney an informal audience at which he conceded precisely nothing. And thus he bought China a host of problems.

What Macartney wanted was trade concessions. What Macartney got was a letter advising the King of England to be obedient to China. The letter also stated that China had no need of British goods. Nor did it. But the rest of the world had need of Chinese goods. The result was an imbalance. Money flowed into China but none flowed out. It was exactly the same situation that is worrying the United States right now.

Two hundred years ago it took the British thirty years to find the solution to their problem. It proved wondrously simple. It was opium.

The British owned India. Ships by the thousand sailed from Britain to India full of goods to sell. They then sailed on to China to collect Chinese goods to bring back. But from India to China they sailed with unprofitably empty holds. What could be better then than filling those holds with Indian opium to sell to the Chinese and thus to pay for the goods purchased. So the British became drug-pushers. Within a few years they had turned millions of Chinese into junkies and the profits were wonderful. So wonderful that the French and the Americans joined in with enthusiasm.

Understandably the Chinese were upset. But by then the Royal Navy had developed greater firepower than anyone else in the world. Any hint of resistance from the Chinese, and in went the gunboats. When they came out again it was with better terms of trade in the captain's cabin. And thus the glorious British Empire both sapped the human capacity of its trading partner and balanced the books.

It's a complex story that took a century to work itself out, but the eventual and inevitable conclusion was that by shameful means predicated on superior weaponry, Great Britain and other Western powers gained footholds on Chinese territory, including Hong Kong and the port of Shanghai. To the Chinese it was nothing less than a slow invasion by barbarians. They have a point.

When the Qing dynasty collapsed in 1911, largely because of Western activities, China lay open to the world and the world poured in. Shanghai became a hub of international trade and it boomed. Or at least it boomed for the foreigner. The average Chinese citizen gained nothing.

The remnants of that foreign occupation still stand on the south bank of the Huangpu river, the area known as the Bund. Here are the boastful buildings erected by British banks, American oil companies, German engineering firms. They are the art deco equivalent of today's skyscrapers, their stone facades now blackened by the leprous air.

What is now the showpiece of the Shanghai Pudong Development Bank was the 1920s headquarters of the Hongkong and Shanghai Bank. When built it was an assertion of British imperial smugness, designed expressly to be the big boy on the Bund, the building you noticed from the river, the building that sang of solidity. Construction took two years.

You enter through a revolving door that looks to weigh several tons and pass between two bronze lions that appear to weigh several more. The domed ceiling is set with a mosaic of Apollo. More mosaic panels depict the eight banking capitals of the day: London, New York, Paris, Calcutta, Bangkok, Tokyo, Hong Kong and Shanghai. London is represented by a pre-Raphaelite Britannia looking plucky in front of St Paul's. The bits of the lobby that aren't mosaic are marble.

The mosaics are in remarkably good shape, largely because the building became City Hall and the mosaics were plastered over so that they didn't corrupt the people. The mosaics stayed plastered over until 1998 when the people, presumably, were beyond corruption.

Beyond the lobby, lies the main banking hall. Its roof is supported by four of the largest single-piece marble columns in the world.

Step out of the bank, cross the road, climb the steps on to the riverside promenade, battle through the tourists, elbow your way into a space against the railing, look across the Huangpu river, behold Pudong and see what the new money has done.

Pudong is the flat north bank of the Huangpu. In 1990 it was vegetable gardens and pig farms. Today it's Manhattan, but without the old bits. It's futuristic, all mirror glass and domes on stilts and monstrous cupolas set a thousand feet into the sky. It bellows ostentatious competition, a simple masculine game of mine is bigger than yours.

I buy a postcard of Pudong to send to my mother. The card looks recent enough but when I compare it with the cityscape in front of me I find that most of the gaps in the skyline have been filled since it was taken. Curiously, the photo appears to have been taken in sunshine. I have yet to see sunshine. The tops of the tallest buildings right now are wreathed in the standard Shanghai grey-brown swirl of what is possibly cloud and definitely dirty. The river has the colour and the consistency, and for all I know the chemical composition, of sewage.

The tourists are doing the standard things, taking photographs, unwrapping snacks, and following tour guides like little flocks of ducklings. A lot of the guides have battery-powered microphones, the better to compete with their rivals ten yards away. One man standing on a chair bellows through an old-fashioned megaphone. But what is immediately noticeable is that almost all of the tourists are Chinese. They mill cheerfully in cheap polyester suits and point complex miniature cameras across the river. The faces of many tell a story of a hard life. Their skin is weathered leather, except over their cheekbones where it is polished vellum. Their teeth are, to say the least, idiosyncratic. And the tourists are small, small even for Chinese people. These people have had a life of little rice and fewer vegetables. But they haven't yet got the hang of tourism. They are far too happy. Unlike bumbagged Westerners, dutifully pecking round Athenian ruins or the pretty bits of Prague, these people are having a holiday, not performing a rite. They grin and touch each other. They seem delighted to be exactly where they are. They point and coo across the water at the Pearl TV tower, the huge Hyatt building, the new China. I can't help interpreting their mood as being related, at least in part, to pride. Just as at the port, they seem proud to be witnessing what China has built and is becoming. Do they feel perhaps an old ancestral surge announcing that China is the Middle Kingdom once again? And is there in their glee a hint of revenge?

As Jiamen mentioned, and as others have told me, there is xenophobia in China. It is understandable. Over the last two centuries foreigners have brought nothing but problems. Mao's peasant revolution was not primarily a communist takeover. It was the establishment of a new dynasty, and it was a reassertion of Chinese sovereignty over China. Mao effectively resealed the Chinese borders so as to keep foreigners out.

Mao's rule led to crippling poverty. As it did so, the Chinese peered across the China Sea and watched Japan enjoying leaping prosperity. Historically the Chinese had always seen their neighbours as a backward race who had cribbed such culture as they had from China. For a couple of thousand years that had been a fair assessment.

But when the West came knocking in the nineteenth century, things began to change. China's attempt to reject the West had disastrous consequences. In contrast, the Japanese, by and large, welcomed the newcomers and learned. Japan prospered. China faltered and fell. The nadir was reached in 1937 when Japan occupied first Manchuria then large tracts of China, including Shanghai. The Japanese occupation was as grisly as all Japanese occupations. The story of Nanking, where hundreds of thousands of people were raped, mutilated, slaughtered, is a match for pretty well anything in the history of human brutality.

Then, despite its defeat in World War Two, Japan rose from the ruins to unchallenged industrial supremacy in Asia in less than thirty years. For the Chinese it was galling. But it was also instructive.

So when Deng Xiaoping made the first steps towards the new way he showed that he had learned from Japan's example. He made absolutely sure that, this time round, any boom in China would be a boom from which China would profit. And it has been. Foreign capital has been welcomed but it has been allowed in on strictly Chinese terms and has been exploited to China's benefit. The direct tangible consequence is that right now I, the big-nose Westerner, am wearing Chinese-made shoes, socks, trousers, shirt and underpants. And it's a statistical near-certainty that you are, too.

China has also followed Japan's example in investing its profits in the United States, to such an extent that Chinese investment is now propping up the US dollar and the drunk-on-debt American shopper. If every yuan was pulled out of US Treasury bonds, those shoppers would suddenly find themselves unable to buy on credit. But those yuan are not going to be pulled out because what the American shoppers are buying is made in China. Walmart alone buys around 1 per cent of what China makes. No wonder the crowds on the Bund are grinning.

'Are you English?'

The speaker is wearing the standard unobtrusive suit and is accompanied by his wife. He asks where I am heading and I say that I'm just walking down the Bund.

'We will walk with you,' he says. It's a statement rather than a suggestion, but I don't mind. His English seems excellent and I want to ask questions. He falls into step beside me. His wife drops a few paces back.

'My wife does not speak English,' he says, and smiles in a manner that I'm afraid I can only describe as charming. If Dirk Bogarde had had a Chinese mother this is how he would have looked. Even to the quiff above his forehead.

Dirk is an academic, specializing in ancient cultural artefacts. He tells me a bit more than that, but, perhaps unnecessarily, I am wary of identifying him.

Now that I have a captive local to quiz in my own language I find it hard to start. What I want to say is, 'Tell me about China.'

'What a lot of tourists,' I say. 'And they are all Chinese.'

'Yes,' he says. Again that suave smile.

'You're from Shanghai?'

'I have lived all my life in Shanghai.'

'You've seen a few changes then?'

'I have seen a lot of changes.'

'Do you approve?'

'Some of the changes have been good. Some have not.'

'What changes have not been good?'

'A lot of poor people have come to the city.'

'But surely poor people always come to cities.'

'Yes.'

I feel that I am being deflected by a smooth curved surface. I have an eerie sense that Dirk knows what I am going to ask before I ask it, as if we were rehearsing dialogue from a not-very-interesting play. At the same time, it is clear that Dirk is enjoying himself.

'Is Shanghai becoming Westernized?'

'Yes. But it is still Chinese.'

'Can you define what you mean by Chinese?'

For once Dirk does not reply immediately. I look at him. He smiles and stops to light a cigarette. His wife catches up with us. He ignores her. We have reached the end of the raised promenade. He isn't going to answer the question. Unless not answering is meant to be the answer to the question. But I don't think he's that subtle.

'Tell me,' I say, 'if you were a tourist in Shanghai where would you go?'

'The Yuyuan gardens and temple.'

'Is it far?'

'My wife and I will go with you.'

I feel a twist of unease, as if I had just seen a chess opponent make a pawn move that was insignificant of itself but that opened a whole new avenue of possible threat.

Dirk steps into the traffic. His wife doesn't. Dirk crosses the jammed road somehow without running. I follow. We leave behind remarkable Pudong, the sewage river, the palatial Bund and Dirk's wife. We battle through roadworks, and reach a remnant of old-style Shanghai that can't have long to live. Here are two-storey ramshackle buildings with alcoves and courtyards and murderous loops of electrical wiring and men in low stalls staring up at small televisions, and women squatting on the pavement beside polystyrene trays of dying soft-shell crabs. I glance back and Mrs Dirk is thirty yards behind us.

As we near the temple the buildings smarten. Here are shops as the West sees shops, with window displays and lighting and a cash register. The roofs are traditional Chinese in style but modern in execution.

'For the tourists,' says Dirk.

At the Yuyuan temple entrance I am struck on the ankle by a remote-controlled toy.

'Hello mister,' says a grinning salesman. 'You want car?'

Dirk speaks abruptly in Chinese. The man ignores him.

'You want car?' he says. 'Very good quality.'

It's early evening and the temple is closing but the old man at the gate is happy to take an entrance fee from me.

'I shall wait here for you,' says Dirk.

The place is deserted. I cross a courtyard set with incense burners. There's a stall selling jewellery, and what appears to be a cafeteria. The structures are wooden, seemingly modern, but built to look old. Balconies are set beneath low, sweeping, upturned eaves in a style that could only be Chinese. It's the sort of roof one would see in blue illustrations on ancient porcelain. The ends of the roof joists are carved with figures. The place feels a bit like an airline ad. And here in bang central Shanghai I suspect that its principal purpose is to titillate us tourists.

Beyond the last courtyard is a roofed shrine, all dark gold and crimson. Against the far wall stands a row of vast figures, presumably divine but noticeably human. Elaborately dressed in ceremonial war robes, most of these gods carry swords and wear moustaches. I would find it hard to worship a moustached god.

In a corner sits a robed monk, immobile, his hands joined on a plain wooden desk, his head bent over his hands. He is intent, unaware of my presence. I go closer. He is paying devout attention to his mobile phone.

I rejoin Dirk at the gate. His wife has found him and is looking peeved. As I approach they are having a pointed conversation. When Dirk sees me he turns on his most urbane smile.

'Did you have a good time?'

'I saw a monk with a mobile phone,' I say.

'Yes,' says Dirk. As he speaks the monk runs past us out of the temple, his robe flaring to expose bright yellow socks. He has his mobile phone in one hand and in the other a can of Diet Coke. And we set off again, through the new-built, fake-old Yuyuan shopping precinct, with zigzag bridges over fishponds and knick-knacks on sale and abnormally hygienic eateries. Most of the tourists are once again Chinese.

I have ranted before about the synthetic nature of tourism. But it still astonishes me the way an agreed notion of a place is arrived at and promoted and sold to people so that they visit with a certain expectation which the place then does everything it can to gratify. New Zealand is as good an example as any. It puffs itself as, and the phrase is not only tautologous but also, obviously, dishonest, '100% Pure'. And the standard route that tourists follow round the country is designed to reinforce that dishonesty. The tourist route is effectively a parallel world to the one inhabited by New Zealanders. Though I suppose that in the end tourism is no different from selling pink and black underpants. You advertise to create the perception of a need, then you gratify it.

Dirk's wife lags behind again. I am not sure why I am still in

Dirk's company. I decide that I may as well broach a subject that I know I understand too little.

'Tell me about the party,' I say.

'The party?'

'Yes. How do you become a member?'

'We will discuss it over dinner,' says Dirk.

He's shifted another pawn, brilliantly. But this time I try to parry. I don't know what Dirk wants and I feel ill at ease. I tell him I have to go back to my hotel to make some phone calls. It's trueish. I need to get Ruth to organize a flight to Quanzhou, but tomorrow would be soon enough for that.

'What time will you be free?' says Dirk. It's the first question he's asked since his opening line.

'Not till about 7.30, I expect.'

'I will meet you at your hotel at 7.30. See you later.'

I don't believe I've told Dirk the name of my hotel. I don't wait for him to ask.

There was something disconcerting about Dirk's calmness, his basilisk geniality, his disregard for his wife. Half an hour later, lying on my hotel bed drinking a cup of black tea, suddenly and sickeningly it occurs to me that Dirk may be a government agent sent to check me out. Equally suddenly I swat the idea away as melodramatic absurdity, and ring Ruth. She promises to find me a cheap flight to Quanzhou, and suggests that I also visit Wenzhou and Yiwu, both of them industrial boom towns.

'I wouldn't mind seeing somewhere that isn't booming,' I say. 'Somewhere even pretty, perhaps.'

Ruth promises to try to think of somewhere, but she doesn't sound too confident.

At 7.40 I go downstairs. Dirk is sitting on a sofa in the lobby. He's reading a newspaper. I feel an urge to return to my room before he sees me, but it's too late.

'Hello Joe,' he says in that same unruffled tone, 'have you eaten snake? You must eat real Shanghai food tonight.'

I feel impotent, outmanoeuvred.

'I know a good restaurant near here,' I say, partly because I am tired from a day of walking the streets, but also because I have studied the whole of the menu at that restaurant and there is no mention of snake.

'We go to where there is a street of famous restaurants. They are real Shanghai restaurants.'

'Is it far?' I say, like a child.

'It is not far.' He smiles handsomely.

I follow Dirk out into the street. Outside Watson's Your Personal Store we pause.

'My wife is shopping,' says Dirk.

She emerges from the shop without purchases. As soon as Dirk catches sight of her he sets off. I go with Dirk.

Not knowing your destination lengthens any journey, and Dirk seems less inclined towards conversation than this afternoon. We embark on the long march. In streets still crammed with cars and people, I rapidly lose any sense of where I am. I feel discomfited by Dirk's wife's lagging presence, Dirk's seeming disdain for her, my tired legs and my sense that this evening will prove fruitless and dreary. I am going along with this man's will only because I lack the strength of character simply to leave. I consider ducking off down a side street, running into the crowd like a fugitive, but am prevented partly by a residual courtesy imprinted in childhood and partly because somehow Dirk knows where I am staying. I must have told him, I suppose, but I don't recall doing so. Unless, of course . . . I swat the idea away again.

We walk at pace for perhaps an hour, most of it in silence. From time to time Mrs Dirk catches up with us while we wait to cross a road. She says nothing.

Of all the streets we walk, the street of famous restaurants turns out to have the fewest pedestrians. Dirk silently studies external menus, makes a decision and leads me upstairs past tanks of fish in urine. The fish don't swim. Some float at a soon-to-die angle; the rest just hang and gulp. I expect I shall soon be eating one of them. But there don't seem to be any snakes.

Half a dozen pretty young waitresses with the facial characteristics of Inuits are watching a television set high on the wall. The only patrons are a doll-like Chinese girl and a prematurely balding Western man in his twenties. Such hair as he retains resembles a lank shower curtain.

'An Introduction to Shanghai' supplied by my hotel said, and I quote, 'A favourite Chinese sport is fighting over the bill in restaurants. It is considered polite in China to offer to pay the bill once or even twice, even when you are clearly the guest.'

I tell Dirk that this meal is on me.

'Good,' he says.

He consults the menu but not his wife or me. Having ordered the meal in a tone of voice far sharper than he has used to address me, he swivels his chair to face the television. So does his wife.

The show they watch is like a third-form talent contest. In front of an adolescent studio audience, a girl aged perhaps four-teen cavorts in too much make-up and a skirt that is more or less a belt. On a stage lit green and purple, the girl either sings or mimes 'Don't Cry for Me Argentina' in Chinese. When she finishes, the adolescent audience cheers, claps, stamps and whistles and then, at a gesture from an invisible floor manager, instantaneously stops cheering, clapping, stamping and whistling. And Dirk, the distinguished academic of ancient artefacts, is transfixed. So's his wife.

I find myself eavesdropping the only other diners. The balding young man is from Yorkshire. I note with pleasure that his side of the tablecloth is littered with failed chopstick work.

He teaches English, and he talks exclusively about teaching English. His dining partner says nothing.

'I 'old up flashcards. You know flashcards?'

She looks blank.

He dives below the table, rootles in a sports bag and pulls out a card a foot square with a picture of a bottle on it and the word 'bottle' written underneath it.

'I 'old up the card and they say bottle.'

The girl's expression doesn't flicker.

'My students always understand me,' says the Yorkshireman, his dreams of sexual congresss crumbling before the girl's impassive mask, 'I just doan't know why you doan't.'

A dish of slithery bits arrives at our table. I capture one at the first attempt. It is chewy and bland.

'Is it good?' asks Dirk. It is the first time he has spoken since ordering, the first time he has looked away from the television.

I make a gesture of ambivalence.

'It is pig's stomach,' says Dirk.

I immediately suspect that this meal will be a series of dishes chosen with the sole intention of disconcerting the Westerner. But Dirk's wife works her way steadily through the pig's stomach with every appearance of pleasure.

China doesn't need fast food. It already has it. Within minutes of ordering we've got a dish of what appear to be cockles in what appears to be custard, some small spherical purple vegetables, noodles, pork that is mainly fat, blackened boiled eggs in sauce, a whole fish which I presume I have already met, and no snake.

As Dirk turns his attention to the food, I strive to open a conversational vein.

'You said you would tell me about the party.'

'Yes.'

I wait.

'I was a party member for five years. I did everything good.'

'And then?'

'Tiananmen Square. I was at Tiananmen Square.'

I am immediately suspicious. I suspect that middle-aged

Chinese now claim to have been at Tiananmen Square in the same way as rather more than middle-aged hippies claim to have been at Woodstock. But Dirk's face has acquired a sort of thoughtful intensity that I haven't seen before.

'I was a leader of a student faction. Three friends from my class died. The army picked up the bodies in the early morning and took them away. They burned them. Families were looking for their sons. They were gone.'

The truth of his tone is unmistakable. My suspicions evaporate.

'I was in prison for three months. Every day I had to write down what I did. I wrote the same thing. One day the police chief said to me, "I don't want to keep you here, but the authorities, you know."'

'And then you were released?'

'For ten years I could not get a visa to travel. It was stamped on my passport. No visa. But now it is forgotten. I can travel for my work. Things are better. Soon the young will take power in the party. It will happen. They will need help from outside China, but it will come. The time will come.'

'Inside ten years?'

'Inside ten years.'

And that is pretty well that. Dirk pays appalling attention to the fish. He chopsticks the front third of the fish behind the gills, holding his plate off the table and his head over the plate and he sucks at the cheeks and neck and flanks, sifting the flesh from the bones and spewing a constant stream of detritus back to the plate.

But I think at last that I have got a handle on Dirk. He is no government man. He just wants to practise his English. He also sees me, I believe, as a sort of trophy. By being a Westerner, I somehow vindicate his youthful protest against authority. In addition I suspect that I am a pawn in the obscure game of chess he is playing with his wife.

The Yorkshireman pays his bill and his impassive doll immediately leaves. He picks up his bag and follows a couple of yards behind her, drooping. The waitresses are still watching television. When Dirk has finished with the fish and I am able to look at him again I gesture towards the waitresses.

'What do they know of Tiananmen Square?' I ask.

'Nothing,' says Dirk.

He orders a bottle of rice wine and pours me a glass. His wife, in her sole non-alimentary action of the evening, reaches across the table and chinks her beer against my wine. 'Chus,' she says.

'Chus,' I say.

It is only later as I am walking back through the night, seeking landmarks to guide me and hugely grateful to be alone again, that I realize she was trying to say 'Cheers.'

7

We Made Your Pants

Quanzhou, where my pants were made, is in Fujian province, two hours flight south of Shanghai. As I wait at the airport, eight young waitresses are undergoing morning inspection. Dressed impeccably in frocks and pinafores they are lined up like the household guard. The role of queen is played by the female manager who would be a shoo-in for a film part as one of the more doctrinally pure guards in a concentration camp. She picks at imaginary defects in the girls' uniforms. When I approach she details one of the girls to attend to me. The girl smiles enchantingly and chains my rucksack to the table leg. It's six in the morning.

I have developed a penchant for dumplings. In English the word conjures baked balls of suet, half submerged in a casserole like mines in the Channel during the war. But here dumplings are little wads of savoury minced meat wrapped in a skin of I don't know what, steamed, readily chopstickable and served with a bowl of vinegar for dunking. They come in half dozens.

I order a dozen. They are superb, the coffee dire. The coffee costs more than the dumplings.

My fellow passengers on the Air China plane are seemingly all businessmen. Every one of them wears a white shirt, no tie and a dark-blue suit that catches the light.

At Quanzhou airport I am met by a driver sent by the underpant company and a couple of amputees. The amputees are keen to touch me with their stumps. The driver spits abuse at them and flails at them with a clipboard on which my name is written in careful capital letters. The amputees are hard to dissuade. They have undergone a lot worse than flailing with a clipboard. As we emerge into sharp, surprising sunlight they shamble after us, whining, wheedling and striving to give me the full visual benefit of their deformities.

The driver loads me into a van, fires the engine and reverses without looking. I am reasonably confident that he isn't trying to further disable the beggars, but he is clearly unconcerned that he may. As we pull out of the car park one of them smears his stump against my window. I momentarily expect the sewn and puckered skin to ooze a snail trail on the glass.

We drive through a ruined industrial landscape. In the West the words 'ruined industrial landscape' suggest roofless warehouses, crumbling chimneys, a scene of former thriving. Here it means a scene of future thriving. Quanzhou is in the process of seemingly planless growth, of chaotic development.

The driver speaks no English so I am left to stare through tinted Toyota glass at spectacular areas of rubble, detritus-strewn yards in which people squat to work, tottery edifices of bamboo scaffolding and crude brown brickwork, with mortar oozing from between the bricks like cake filling. Scooters and mopeds throw up squirrel tails of dust. Lorries bounce through potholes, lumbering fat-nosed lorries that I think of as Bedfords and associate with the fifties and smog-smothered London.

Quanzhou feels different from Shanghai, as if I've shifted

back down a rung or two on the ladder of industrial evolution. Here the air is bright with dust and sun, and there remains evidence of how things have been for millennia. Interstices of land are still parcelled into neat terraces of vegetables surrounding an unlit one-room hovel. I catch glimpses of a wide and foetid river, and on the ruined roadside a man leads a water buffalo by a nose ring. We swing through a gate and suddenly I am in the forecourt of the factory that sewed my pants. I feel a smug little swell of achievement. And I realize that when I began this quest I didn't dare to expect I would get even this far.

Kingstar Light Industrial Products Ltd looks like a cheapish, newish polytechnic. A central admin block is fronted by a courtyard and flanked by twin four-storey buildings that could be labs or lecture rooms. It's impeccably clean and apparently deserted, but when I open the door of the van I hear the hum of work.

Terrence the factory manager greets me at the entrance to the office. Prompted no doubt by his contract with The Warehouse, Terrence has set aside the whole day to show me whatever I want to see. He sits me down in the samples room and has a girl make coffee in a little plastic percolator. I have learned already that coffee is the modern drink, the drink of the new industrial urban China. Coffee looks forwards, tea back.

The room is crammed with displays of underwear. There's more women's stuff than men's stuff, but still an entire wall is devoted to men's underpants. While a phone call summons Terrence from the room, I study them. They resemble what you would see on the shelves in any Western department store, largely because they are what you would see on the shelves in any Western department store: Diadora underwear, Classic Collection America's Brand underwear, Pringle underwear, plastic-wrapped underwear stamped 'Offre Speciale', 'Love Is . . .' boxer shorts for Britain and a three pack of George brand Stretch Hipster Trunks already marked with a price of six pounds.

When Terrence returns I am appraising a pair of hipsters between finger and thumb. I drop them hurriedly.

Terrence is pumpkin-faced and water-melon grinning, reminding me for no reason that I can justify of Mr Youkoumian in one of Waugh's African novels. But beneath the affability I sense a hard-nosed quality, a ruthlessness even, that is going to be kept hidden today.

From my pocket I pull The Warehouse briefs, the briefs that I bought in a store several thousand miles away, and hold them up like evidence in court.

'You made these?'

Terrence takes them, studies the stitching, stretches the waistband and hands them back.

'Yes,' he says.

'How significant is The Warehouse to your business?'

'The Warehouse?' asks Terrence.

'TWL. The New Zealand company. How big are they for you?'

'Oh,' says Terrence, 'we don't think of clients as big or small.' But it soon becomes clear that The Warehouse is small. Kingstar deals in serious quantities. One order from a German retailer was worth over 4 million US dollars.

'How many garments is that?'

'Over 4 million,' says Terrence with a twinkle. 'TWL does not do volumes like that. But is a wery good customer. They give wery exact specifications.'

That Terrence sells knickers to Germany 4 million at a time may explain his pronunciation of very.

The factory makes 60,000 dozen pieces of men's underwear a month, 100,000 dozen pieces of ladies' underwear and 200,000 dozen pieces of lingerie (the distinction between the last two being, I presume, that ladies don't wear lingerie). That's over 4 million garments a month. Most of them go to Europe. None goes to China. Not a single bra. While the corporate West salivates over the Chinese market with its billion potential consumers, the corporate Chinese salivate over the Western market with its billion actual consumers.

Terrence was born in Manchuria, and he, too, remembers the day Mao died. He was five years old.

'The radio played wery sad music. Everyone had to wear a white flower made of paper. There was no amusement for the whole month.'

He is an emphatic advocate of the new capitalist China. 'There were only two ways, change or death. And there are still only two ways, change or death. There will be political change some time, change at the top. You will see.'

'You mean a revolution, democracy?'

'You will see. There will be change.'

But he's not especially bothered about it. I sense that he knows where the power lies and that is with the new money. The old order simply has to snuggle up to it to survive. He does not find government intrusive or meddlesome or restrictive. He doesn't know the rate of income tax, but believes it is under 20 per cent. His business is business.

'Where does your cloth come from?'

'We make it here.'

'You weave it yourselves?'

'We do not weave. We knit. Knitting is different. Weaving is many threads, knitting is one. I show you.'

Kingstar Light Industrial Products Ltd was founded by a local couple in 1994. It now employs 600 workers, most of whom live on site in dormitories behind the admin block. Manufacturing happens in the twin buildings that face each other across the courtyard. One makes knickers for both sexes. The other makes bras.

Terrence leads me across the deserted courtyard and into the ground floor of the underpants building. A line of knitting machines is chuntering, fed by an aerial web of cotton yarn and tended by a couple of flitting silent youths. The cloth is knitted in the form of a tube. I stand and watch a tube grow perhaps a foot in a minute, the mechanism that creates it moving far too fast for me to see how it does it. The machines were made just across the water from here, in modern industrial Taiwan. Each machine is surrounded by fans to blow the dross away from its delicate innards.

'Single jersey knit,' says Terrence, handing me a wad of cloth to feel. It is slightly elastic and it feels like underpants. 'We knit all our own cloth. Most of it is single jersey. Your briefs are single jersey.'

'And the yarn, where does that come from?'

'We get it from agents and brokers. They get it from the west, I think, but I don't know.'

'The West? You mean the States or somewhere?'

Terrence laughs. 'No no, the west of China. Xinjiang province I think.' And he makes a gesture implying that all this happens a very long way away from here and is no concern of his.

'Can you find out?' I say. 'I need to go there.'

Terrence's forehead bunches. He thinks it unlikely that his suppliers will tell him their sources, for fear that he'll cut out the middleman. But he promises to ask.

Apart from cotton yarn, they also use spandex, which is apparently the generic term for Lycra. It's an elastic thread, made by some petrochemical process. But there is none in my pants.

The cotton unwinding from a row of conical bobbins is all white. It is possible to buy naturally coloured cotton, but it is a grim beige, the colour worn by women who don't expect their knickers to be seen by anyone but doctors. According to Terrence, all other naturally coloured cottons are fake.

The factory dyes most of its own material. In the dyeing room bolts of cloth are lowered into murderous baths of dye. The smell scours my nostrils, like a cold remedy.

After dyeing, drying and relaxing, the cloth is laid out 120 layers at a time on a massive white table, the length of half a cricket pitch. Templates are laid on the top layer, fitted like a puzzle to minimize wastage. Then a youth cuts vertically around the outlines of the templates with a gleaming fine-toothed saw. It goes through the cloth like an electric carving knife through a pile of sandwiches. The result of each deft cut is 120 raw bits of underpant.

'How many pieces of cloth in my pants?'

'Eight,' says Terrence without hesitation, and he seizes specimen pieces from assorted piles and assembles a pair of underpants around his own crotch, explaining the process of double-bagging and other technicalities, until the pieces become too numerous for him to hold in place and they fall to the floor. He laughs and leaves them there.

The sewing room on the floor above is pure factory. Perhaps 150 girls and a dozen or so boys are sitting at machines under bright fluorescent lighting. Most have their ears plugged with little Walkman radios. Each has a single job to do, a seam to sew or an edge to hem. Having sewn it they drop the result into a cloth bag and do it again and again and again. They pay little attention to me. And almost without exception they are beautiful – high-cheeked, fresh-skinned, black-eyed, lithe and impassive, like a roomful of Tutankhamen masks.

'Labour is a big problem,' says Terrence. 'We have to go further to find it every year.'

Most of the workers in this room have been lured from the back blocks of Sichuan province, which is a long way away from here and then some. At the Spring Festival, when the whole of China gets on a train and goes home to family, many of these kids stay in Quanzhou. If they took the train to Sichuan, then the battered bus to their provincial city, then hiked over the misty watercolour ranges to the villages of their birth, by the time they arrived it would be time to start coming back.

Sichuan is emptying. Seven out of ten families there have

'lost' someone to the east coast. They come here because here is where the wealth is. The population of cities like Quanzhou is simply unknown. If you took a census here, by the time you'd done your counting the result would be out of date. By thousands. The current best estimate of the Quanzhou population is 7½ million, the size of Greater London, and pushing on for twice the population of New Zealand. And until a week ago I'd never heard of the place.

China has always done big cities. Even in Marco Polo's day there were several cities with more than a million citizens. The population of London at that time was about 80,000.

Quanzhou has swollen before. In the thirteenth century it was the extreme eastern end of the silk route that stretched to the Mediterranean, and it was one of the great ports of China. But then Quanzhou chose to resist the Mongols. The Mongols took badly to being resisted.

Six hundred years later, during the European expansion into China, Quanzhou did not become one of the 'treaty ports'. Nearby Xiamen, known to the Brits as Amoy, took that role and it grew in consequence. But now the whole east coast is flourishing. And the scale of that growth is unprecedented.

Terrence is attuned to underwear fashions in the West. He confirms my prediction that boxer shorts will die. My prediction was based simply on experience. As much a victim of trends as everybody else, I bought a pair of boxer shorts a few years back. I found that they bunched at my thighs like a furled skirt.

Boxer shorts can be worn comfortably only by skinny youths in jeans ten sizes too large, jeans whose waistband drops to mid-buttock. That look is on the wane, presumably because it's hard to skateboard with the crotch of your trousers between your knees. Moreover, the West is running low on skinny youths. Today's rich kids are fattening like eunuchs. To compare the children of Christchurch with the workers in this factory is to observe the consequences of wealth. Western youth is plumping up. Computers keep the kids indoors and sedentary. And if they do go out, their parents drive them wherever they want to go because the hills are alive with paedophiles.

And then there's marketing. Kids are advertised to with unprecedented sophistication, if sophistication is the right word to describe a process of ruthless psychological manipulation in pursuit of profit. One of the easiest advertising targets is the natural childish appetite for fat and sugar, especially when accompanied by a childish inability to know when you're being manipulated.

Over the course of a couple of decades, a PE teacher I used to work with did an informal annual survey of the school's intake of 13-year-old boys. He simply asked them to climb a rope to the ceiling of the gym. Every year the number who made it shrank. And every year the number of kids built like wobble-titted Buddhas grew, kids who would grasp the rope and heave hard but whose feet just wouldn't leave the gym floor.

Shanghai's many KFCs and McDonald's are already thronged, but it will be a while yet before China has to widen the seats on its aeroplanes and before its streets are clogged with shambling pallid monsters whose waists are wider than their shoulders. For purely aesthetic reasons, I hope it never happens.

Boxer shorts are being supplanted by hugging hipster trunks. I watch a girl sew on a waistband. The waistband is yellow, the trunks black. Her fingers whizz like the flashing components of the knitting machine downstairs. The action she performs takes longer for me to describe than it does for her to perform. What was two items becomes one and tumbles into her production bag and she starts again. The waspish end result is destined for Turkey.

The waistbands are embroidered with the legend 'Exceed your limits', about which I propose to make no comment for fear of becoming shrill. Picking up an incomplete garment, Terrence illustrates the difference between the cover stitch and the overlock stitch. One is for beauty, the other for strength but by the time he's finished explaining I've forgotten which does which.

The waistbands are made in a factory elsewhere in Quanzhou. I ask if I can visit it, and Terrence looks momentarily disconcerted. He tells me they are 'wery busy'. I plead. He promises to see what he can do, then leads me to the quality control room where a couple of girls check underpants endlessly for faults. And then we're back in the courtyard.

'Would you like to see bras?' asks Terrence.

'Not really,' I say. 'My mission is underpants. But I would like to see where the workers live.'

They live in two purpose-built blocks behind the factory, one for the boys and one for the girls. The blocks resemble the offspring of a school boarding house and an army barracks, with communal ablutions, dorms of four to six beds each, thin mattresses, a refectory on the ground floor with formica tables and fixed stools, an unlovely recreation room, a small shop for staples and balconies running the length of each floor overlooking an outdoor basketball court.

'The boys play basketball every night,' says Terrence. 'They play wery good.'

In the centre of the court these lads from remote and mountainous Sichuan have painted the NBA logo and a vast Nike tick.

'And the girls?'

'The girls go into town on dates,' says Terrence, grinning. 'But it is dangerous in town at night. They have to be home by 11 p.m.'

Employees must be sixteen years old and may work no more than sixty hours a week. They are paid piecework rates and they don't earn much, except by the standards of subsistence peasant China. Most manage to send money home. They last a year or two at the factory then either marry or move to other work in the region. Few return to their province.

And that is more or less that. Like most places long imagined, this factory, this place where my underpants come from, has turned out to be spectacular only in its ordinariness.

I am aware that I was ripe for being deceived. Terrence knew I was coming. He had time to prepare a Potemkin tour of his factory, a common habit of Chinese businesses that want to please the Westerner. But I saw no evidence of sham, and I am reassured by the thought that The Warehouse accreditation system vets its suppliers far more rigorously than I can.

I have a hotel booking but Terrence insists on cancelling it and drives me to what he says is the only habitable hotel in Quanzhou. In the back of his Honda Accord are several badminton racquets. 'How's your badminton?' I ask.

'Not good,' he says and he runs his hand over his plump little gut. 'Too fat.'

The hotel is tiered like a low-slung wedding cake. My room on the fourth tier costs 300 yuan a night. Though not palatial it would accommodate a dozen workers with ease, and two dozen at a pinch. It's mid-afternoon. I draw the curtains and stretch out on the bed. Only a mile away from where I lie drowsing, several hundred sewing machines are humming away under deft Chinese fingers – overlock stitch, cover stitch, another pair of underpants for the lumbering West. And I realize that here in China I am beginning to feel embarrassed by my size and by my wealth and by the unearned ease of my life. But not embarrassed enough to keep me awake.

When I open the curtains on the late afternoon I meet an elderly man. He is the other side of the window, cleaning it. We are face to face. I step back in surprise. If he stepped back in surprise he'd fall thirty feet to a car park. The ledge he's crouching on is a foot wide. He has a bucket and a rag and he is attached to the building by nothing whatsoever. I smile at him but he does not smile back. He just shuffles along the ledge to the next window.

In the hotel's business centre, where I go for a map of

Quanzhou, I am accosted by Jack. Jack's from Malaysia. Jack is voluble, Jack has a handshake like an industrial clamp, Jack repeatedly refers to Jack in the third person as Jack, and Jack is keen to know where I'm from.

When I say New Zealand, Jack is keen to tell me more about Jack. Jack's a big businessman. Jack had a rubber plantation but Jack burnt it down because there's no money in rubber. Jack is planning to erect factories on his land. Jack is going to make a lot of money from his factories. Jack is looking for ground-floor investors.

'Give Jack your business card,' says Jack in the manner that does not entertain the possibility of refusal. I give him my card. Jack whips off his glasses and scrutinizes the card as if it were a potentially enriching lottery ticket.

'It don't tell Jack your company name.'

'I haven't got a company name.'

Jack replaces his glasses and stares at me with intense theatrical puzzlement. His mouth is set like a goldfish's mouth.

'What you do?'

'I'm a writer.'

'Pah,' exclaims Jack with a disgust that rocks him on his feet. 'Pah.' He mimes a fat spit. 'Writer no good. Jack think you investor. Invest in Jack's factory. Writer no bloody good.'

At which point my Sussex upbringing wells stoutly within me. 'Sorry,' I say.

'But,' says Jack, suddenly brightening and tucking my card into his wallet, 'Jack give you a call later, OK?'

'It's a deal,' I say.

The business centre doesn't stock maps of Quanzhou, but the girl at the desk does tell me where to eat. There is a street called Delicacy Street. In what appears to be the city's sole concession to tourists, Delicacy Street is signposted in English.

The street is lined with eateries that spill on to the pavement. One restaurant does only donkey. Another specializes in dog. I don't mind people eating dog – although I am aware that the diners wouldn't mind whether I mind or not. What happens to a dog's carcase is as immaterial to me as it is to the dog. But I do mind how the dogs are kept and killed. At least I mind hypothetically. I am not going to try to find out.

I don't know why, but I cannot bear animal suffering, even on a screen. As a child I found Lassie films unwatchable. As an adult I still do. And yet I can watch news footage of mothers wailing in bereavement or of flyblown children about to die of hunger, and be unmoved.

The restaurant I select at random does a bowl of bones in dishwater set into every table. The waitress lights a burner underneath my bowl, which brings the broth to the boil. She then brings me assorted foodstuffs to cook in it. I get two bowls of something similar to lettuce, one of unidentifiable sliced vegetables, another of unidentifiable sliced vegetables that may be unidentifiable sliced fruit, some dumplings, and two bowls with saucers over them. I lift one saucer and a shrimp jumps out. I recapture it then peep under the other saucer and see what look like four-inch millipedes.

On the whole I consider I manage the meal well. The lettuce wilts on contact with the boiling broth so I just dunk it and eat. It tastes like hot wet lettuce. After some chopstick incompetence with the fruit and vegetable pieces, I tip the lot in. Over the course of the meal I manage to retrieve perhaps a third of them. The two-thirds is no great loss. The dumplings, in contrast, are easy to chopstick, easy to cook, easy to extract, and impossible to eat without squirts of meat juice drenching your shirt. Then I hesitate over the live stuff.

I wouldn't boil a dog to death, obviously, nor a cat. Nor a chicken, nor a mouse, nor, I think, a lizard. But I'm not bothered by shrimps. In other words I draw a line somewhere between boilable animals and unboilable ones, but I'm not sure why that line lies where it does. Perhaps the only moral difference between boiling a cat and boiling a shrimp is the degree of difficulty – and maybe the cat's capacity to scream. But anyway I chopstick a shrimp, dunk it and release it. Horribly it surfaces with what appears to be a momentary bid for life. A nanosecond later it is dead. Thirty seconds later I am peeling and eating it. It's a fine shrimp. And I feel distinctly Chinese. But I do hold all subsequent shrimps under water for a second or two before letting them float to the surface dead. What you don't see didn't happen.

I murder my first millipede with a sense of expectation. I've seen them often in markets and noted that they're priced above shrimp. I let the beast cook for a minute, then haul it out, blow on it and set about peeling it. In a very short time I am left with lots of bits of exoskeleton and no meat. I don't know if I've overcooked it or undercooked it or just happened on a skinny millipede. I haul the next one out after fifteen seconds. It's no better.

There are millipede eaters two tables away. I spy on them as they extract a beast after a seemingly arbitrary cooking period, pull off the front claws and suck them. I try the same with my third millipede to no discernible effect. My neighbours then bite off the head and spit it to one side, shove all that remains into their mouths, chew vigorously and spit a stream of legs and exoskeleton back to the plate. I manage the head-spitting fine. What I don't manage is to find anything resembling flesh. In the end my millipedes deliver a net energy loss.

By further spying I learn that with all one's bowls emptied it is customary to haul the bones from the broth and gnaw them. I don't. Instead I order three Tsingtao beers in a row and enjoy watching Quanzhou pass by. The bill when it comes is hard to decipher but for the remarkably low cost of the meal and six words of English printed across the bottom. 'It's an honour to pay tax,' it says.

8

At Beautiful Success

The Buddhist temple of Kaiyuan in Quanzhou was established in 686. It covers a substantial acreage. Two ancient stone towers stand at the east and west ends, each shaped like a stack of inverted umbrellas and elaborately carved with Buddhas and warlords. Between them lie courtyards, flower beds, piles of builders' rubble and a series of shrines and halls. And at seven o'clock on a warm morning it's as much a place of recreation as a temple.

People exercise alone or in groups wherever they wish. Here are smiling, don't-care dancers such as I saw in public parks in Shanghai, a troupe of elderly women doing a sort of choreography with bamboo staves, elderly men writhing in the slow absorbed elegance of what may be t'ai chi, numerous middle-aged women cheerfully failing to hit shuttlecocks, and a man in a suit. He is marching slowly on the spot. He raises both hands above his head. Then he raises one leg straight out in front of him like a shelf bracket. A hand comes down to touch the toe.

The other hand comes down to touch the toe. His balance never wavers. Each hand rests a moment like a butterfly on a leaf, then up it goes again, down comes the leg and he's back to marching. I watch him for fully five minutes from smack in front. I make no effort to pretend I am not watching him. He doesn't notice.

I like all this. I like it because it seems unreflexive. It does not seem driven by vanity. No one is doing it because they've been told that they should. No sweaty solitary women are pedalling bicycles to nowhere, no balding men are grunting through sit-ups, and no one is covertly admiring his own biceps in a mirror. And the bodies seem better, suppler, lighter here, as though gravity were less compelling. And the people smile.

Dropped by a bird, a fruit the size of a plump cherry lands on my leg and lodges between my thighs. I've seen this fruit on sale in markets. I think it's a longan. Peeling apart the pitted yellow skin, I nibble at the glassy flesh, and am pleased by the unfamiliar tartness.

The forecourt of the main shrine to Buddha is studded with ancient trees. One fig tree is 800 years old, a mulberry 1400, older than the temple itself. When this tree was a sapling, Viking longboats were sweeping on to British beaches. The roots of other trees rise above ground like buttresses, clumsily patched in place with cement. A man walks past me backwards. He lopes at a standard walking pace. I watch him turn left and climb a set of steps without looking over his shoulder.

The main shrine is enclosed on three sides and is built entirely of timber and bamboo. The only metal is an ancient bell rung by a log on a rope. Even this early in the morning the air is dense with smoking joss sticks. A few beggars with stumps, apparently resident, haul themselves across the courtyard to wheedle at the wealthy foreigner.

Kneeling to a golden Buddha, an old woman offers banknotes, holding the cash in both hands above her head. She prostrates herself a few moments, mutters a bit, then stands, drops the cash through a slot in a vast donations box and toddles off about her business.

Another woman, stout and trousered, performs an elaborate ritual with little painted sticks. She kneels on a cushion and intones some sort of imprecation, then stands and flings the sticks to the floor at Buddha's feet with a little urging shout, as if throwing dice on a craps table. She studies the sticks. Divination of a sort, I guess. Then she does it again.

The woman looks about my age so she was born into Mao's China. Throughout her impressionable years she was subject to its ideological bombardment, its doctrinal, millennialist tyranny, its pragmatic lies. Officially Mao abolished God. In fact, he sought to supplant God. Images of Mao were more widely disseminated than any image of any human being in history. The intention was simply to transfer the human instinct for belief on to another figure. It was crude myth-making, effectively indistinguishable from any other cult.

In one way it succeeded. People did revere Mao, though their reverence was closely allied to fear. But from a longer perspective, it failed. All the legal, tyrannical, propagandist and military efforts to scrub this woman's brain clean of all beliefs bar one failed. And in essence I suppose they failed because Mao died. It's as simple as that. Which is why every enduring faith on the planet insists that its object of devotion, Muhammad, Jesus, or L. Ron Hubbard, lives for ever.

And so, when Mao fell, the temple still stood, surviving yet another of the crashing waves of Chinese history.

I cannot pretend to understand the intricacies of Chinese religious belief. What I have gathered is that it is dominated by three main threads: Buddhism, Taoism and Confucianism. They intertwine like snakes, and any effort to disentwine them is to destroy the complex living knot.

The most puzzling of the three religions is Confucianism,

because it was never a religion. Confucius was roughly contemporary with Plato. Essentially he was a social philosopher. He concerned himself with how best to organize society, and many of his ideas persist. Indeed, they have become engrained in Chinese thinking.

He argued that the family was the foundation of society. In China it still is, as evidenced by the vast migration of the Spring Festival. He argued that the young owe a duty of respect to their elders. In China, the young still pay that duty. There is nothing much in the way of social security for the elderly here, because nothing much is needed. In the home of my interpreter Ruth, for example, four generations cohabit. That's the norm. Confucius would approve. He would also approve of the decorous public behaviour of the young.

It was Confucius who proposed the practice of recruiting the best and brightest into government by competitive national exams. Such exams have a 2000 year history in China, an intellectual meritocracy established when power in every other society in the world was based on inherited privilege or religious hokum.

Like Plato, Confucius scoffed at democracy. No one believed more strongly than he did that a government's sole concern should be for the people governed. But allowing the unwashed to elect their leaders on the basis of their appearance, bribery and rhetoric was, he maintained, no way to appoint the best people to the job. And if you look around the democratically elected parliaments of the West, you can't help thinking that he may have had a point.

A country was best governed, according to Confucius, by a dictatorship of selfless and morally superior people who were trained for the job. Sadly for him, and indeed for the human race, the selfless and morally superior have a habit, once promoted to power, of becoming the selfish and morally appalling.

In short then, Confucius was a conservative patriarch, a

decent man and a pragmatist. But he never concerned himself with metaphysics nor did he ever lay any claim to divinity. Why there should now be temples devoted to him, I don't know. Myth-making once more, I suppose.

Buddha, too, was more or less contemporary with Plato. He was Indian, but his teaching caught on in foreign lands more than it ever has in India. In China its popularity with the authorities has waxed and waned over the dynasties, for purely political reasons, but in the public mind it has just gone on going on.

As far as I understand it, Buddhism as conceived by Buddha, isn't a religion either. It is rather a system of psychological self-help that aims to achieve mental peace. Being as screwed up as everyone else, I've often resolved to learn more about it, but being as feckless as everyone else, I've never got round to it. Perhaps I'll learn more on this trip. But what I can say with some confidence is that the woman throwing sticks at his feet and the woman offering him cash would have puzzled Buddha greatly.

Laozi or Lao Tse may or may not have existed, though if he did, it seems that he, too, flourished around 500 BC. There must have been something in the water. Lao Tse may or may not have founded Taoism, and Taoism may or may not be a coherent system of religious and philosophical beliefs. Essentially Taoism stands in antipathy to Confucianism. Where Confucians propose organizing human society in order to make it better, Taoists propose doing nothing. Which presumably is why Taoism was embraced in the seventies by the dope-soaked sons and daughters of Californian dentists. But Taoism seems to accommodate such a multitude of metaphysical strands, from traditional Chinese ancestor worship to traditional Chinese medicine, via polytheism and a belief in 'the way', whatever that may mean, that I hesitate to call it anything other than a welter of superstitions.

In short, the Chinese don't have an official state religion, and as far as I can tell they barely have any religion as we in the West understand it. They seem just to pick the rituals that please them, cross their fingers and get on with stuff. It means they have to make do without popes, and vicars in cable-knit sweaters, and televangelists with wigs and a fondness for secret whoring, and Mormon youths with haircuts and one-piece underwear, and lunatic ayatollahs, and doomsayers with placards in public squares, and anti-abortionist murderers, and guilt, but somehow they seem to get by.

Nevertheless they do have one overriding belief and that is in luck. The Chinese don't so much worship as hedge bets. I have been told I don't know how many times that the number 4 is unlucky because the word for it sounds like the word for death, and that other numbers, at certain times, but not always, are lucky. The notion of luck, in China, is ubiquitous. And it is barely distinguishable from prosperity. The two ideas appear to overlap completely in the Chinese mind, exactly as they do in the English word fortune.

My earlier image of throwing dice on a craps table was deliberately chosen. The Chinese are inveterate gamblers. Without the Chinese every casino in New Zealand would struggle to make a profit. And though there is officially no gambling in China, you can judge its popularity by the number of notices forbidding it. And also by the massive growth of casinos in Macau since that region returned to Chinese control. Even when playing innocent whist in the park, the Chinese slam down their cards as if they were playing for millions. China worships luck. And China worships prosperity. And it's getting an overdue dose of both right now.

Outside the Kaiyuan temple you can buy paper money to burn for the benefit of your ancestors. You can also buy almost anything you might want to eat. In a medieval alleyway, with its bikes and its ruts and its ramshackle hovels and its scary wiring, there's a covered market, dark as sin and stinking, its drains clogged with vegetable scraps and blood. I'm a sucker for markets, markets like this, with food making no effort to disguise its origin. All of it was growing yesterday. Much of it still is.

Turtles in buckets, fish in polystyrene trays, eels, lizards, snakes and toads in nets, all bar the lucky ones still breathing. A bunch of duck innards hangs from a hook dripping fluids on to the mudguard of a bike. The chopping boards on which ducks are dispatched and fish scaled and turtles shelled are concave with years of murder. Pigeons cower in a cage. A toothless woman rolls a square of dough and a dob of spiced giblets into a crimped dumpling like an orange segment. Then she makes another. And another and another. Her movements are deft and thoughtless. She rattles out conversation with a woman who carries her shopping on a bamboo shoulder pole with a hook at each end. Plucked black-skinned chickens sit on display with combs and beaks intact, their wings and necks and rumps raised, the whole bird trussed like a crown of beef.

Vegetables and fruit I've never seen are piled and peeled and sliced and cored and sold. Cleavers flash. A three-foot hammerhead shark lies dead on a slab, a freak. A man in a vest sits behind it, smoking. It's all he has to sell. It's his day's work. Women wash intestines, stuff them with what seem to be other intestines and knot the ends. The noise is constant, social, sharp-edged, flaring into rows like sudden squalls, as quickly calming. A woman behind a pile of dogfish watches me open-mouthed as I pass through, but few others give me more than a glance. That glance instantly assesses me as a tourist, a gawper, and dismisses me as an irrelevance to trade.

On the way back to my hotel, battling through bicycles, buying churros fresh fried in a smoking vat, I think of the Lyttelton supermarket where I buy my groceries at home. The apples there have little stickers on them, the healthy stuff has a paternalist tick on it, and the meat comes in trays with cushioned bases to absorb the distress of blood.

Terrence has managed to arrange for me to visit the elastic factory where he sources his waistbands. On the way there I tell him all about my morning at the market and the temple. He is politely uninterested. He speaks only to point out a substantial factory devoted entirely to the manufacture of zips. Then he turns on to the premises of the Meida Elastic Fabric Company.

The company vice-president is gruff, monoglot and a champion smoker. I consider myself no slouch in the tobacco department but I don't even try to compete. From the moment we sit down in his office to the moment he steps into the factory proper, a matter of something over an hour, he is never once without a lit fag. Quite often he has two. When he crosses the office from desk to cupboard, a distance of perhaps twelve feet, he leaves a lit cigarette in the ashtray at each end of the journey.

He insists on making us tea. It's an elaborate process involving a perforated brass tray with a waste-water pipe leading from it, a spirit lamp, a small kettle, a smaller tea pot, cups the size of thimbles, endless tipping of hot water into and out of every one of these vessels and constant smoking. The tea leaves are coarse and black. The tea when it arrives is the colour of reasonably-late-in-the-evening urine.

'This tea,' Terrence tells me in a reverent whisper, 'costs 4000 kwai a kilo.' That's about NZ$800. My appreciative sips imply that it's worth every kwai and then some. It isn't. It tastes pretty much as it looks. But the vice-president seems gratified by my performance.

With Terrence as linguistic intermediary, and one whom I suspect takes more liberties than I'd wish in translating my questions, I learn that Meida, which means more or less 'Beautiful Success', was founded in 1990. It has prospered in much the same way as Kingstar has, and now, like Kingstar, employs several hundred young workers from remote provinces. It houses them in an accommodation block that was clearly built by the same unimaginative architect.

The factory makes elastic straps. It makes straps for bras and knickers, waistbands for underpants, straps for anything that has to cling to human flesh. Its principal raw material is, I'm not astonished to learn, rubber. A little of that rubber comes from Malaysia, but most of it from Thailand.

I ask Terrence to ask the vice-president precisely where in Thailand, because I'll have to go there.

'Thailand is wery dangerous,' says Terrence and he does not forward the question. When I press the point, saying that I shall be going there regardless, Terrence simply switches his attention to the vice-president who, now that he no longer has to concentrate on tea-making, is able to devote his full attention to smoking.

Meida also uses spandex, which it imports via agents from Taiwan and elsewhere. Though there is no spandex in my pants, the vice-president fetches a spool of it for me to admire. With grunts and grins and a couple of hundred cubic metres of smoke he urges me to finger the stuff and test its stretchiness. I use my tea-appreciating noises again, and again they are well received. I think the vice-president likes me.

As far as I can gather the waistband of my pants is made from elastic thread. That elastic thread consists of a strand of rubber wound around with polyester thread. It is then knitted, and the resulting stretchy strap is sewn into a turning at the waist like an enclosed belt. It's elasticating at its most rudimentary.

To see less rudimentary elasticating I am taken to the factory floor. At the door the vice-president takes a drag on his fag that would fill six pairs of lungs, drops the butt into an ashtray the size of a rain barrel, and plunges through a wall of rubber strips like the hatch your luggage takes too long to emerge through at the airport.

117

The noise is thunderous. The workers have earplugs. We don't. In order to ask a question I have to place my lips so close to Terrence's ear that it looks like love. I soon give up and just look. When either Terrence or the vice-president addresses me I smile, nod and understand nothing.

All the machine workers are young men. Their function is simply to ensure that the machines keep doing their job. Overhead runs a vast web of threads, but not far enough overhead for comfort. The threads are almost invisible, like gossamer, and I am terrified of blundering into them, bringing a clattering machine, or all the clattering machines, to a halt, and everyone turning to stare at me, my skull wrapped in broken threads like the ropes of Lilliput, and on my face an idiot appeasing grin. After five minutes my neck aches from precautionary hunching.

The threads feed machines that knit whatever has been programmed into them. My companions hold the products up for my inspection: a plain white rubber band as in my underpants, a delicate frilly pattern for bra-edging, narrow fancy shoulder straps, and branded waistbands with a furry finish achieved by a process that I can't ask about and anyway probably wouldn't understand the description of. A bin contains a mile or more of continuous waistband, an inch or so wide and embroidered with the words 'Pierre Cardin'. And there are similar writhing masses called Fila and Uomo and, so elegantly, Bum Equipment.

On the stairs between floors it is possible to be heard and again I ask where the raw rubber comes from. 'Thailand,' I am told once more. I press as insistently as I dare but get nothing more specific.

On a lower floor a machine is sucking an endless strip of rubber from a cardboard box. The strip, perhaps half an inch wide, runs between guides and on to blades that split it into several narrower strips and then on to further blades and more blades after that. They keep splitting the rubber until it has become thread. I stop by the machine and feign an intense interest in its workings. At the same time I nudge the cardboard box surreptitiously with my foot until I can read what's printed on the side. 'Thai Filatex Public Co. Ltd, Bangkok,' it says, and there's a complex street address but I am being urged towards the dyeing room and I don't have time to note down the address without making it obvious what I am doing.

The dyeing room holds vats of dye that look as though they would dissolve flesh. The air is corrosive.

In the packing room great bundles of elastic strap of every conceivable hue and design, from pastel featheriness to lurid chunkiness, are bound and wrapped and sent away to be sewn into garments that are then sent further away.

Back outside, my friend the vice-president lights a cigarette or two and addresses me at length with gruff good humour, coughing in appreciation of his own no doubt excellent jokes, and apparently convinced that within the last hour I have become fluent in Mandarin. Then this strong decisive man offers me a hand like a wilting petal. As Terrence drives me away through the gates of the Beautiful Success Elastic Fabric Company we just avoid colliding with a team of water buffalo.

9

The Picturesque Poor

China doesn't have motorbike gangs. China is a motorbike gang. Crossing Quanzhou in the morning rush hour I several times find myself acting as an island in a river of low-powered motorbikes. If I stand still the bikes flow around me. If I move forward they flow around me just as deftly. It takes an act of will to keep moving forward. Face, I believe, is what the colonial European felt that he needed 'out East', by which he meant the appearance of decisiveness. It works. Look confident and people defer to you. Show weakness and they overrun you. But confidence is hard to fake.

I'm heading back north towards Shanghai, taking in a couple of boom towns en route, and I hope a bit of boom-free rural China. My first stop is Wenzhou where I'll meet Ruth. I'd like to go by train but there doesn't seem to be one, so I have the prospect of spending most of today on a bus. I hate buses. Few things depress me more than the sight of captive passengers looking out of the windows of long-distance buses. And one of those few things is being among those passengers. The smell, the serriedness, the sense of being herded, the associations with school trips and old people's outings make me shrivel.

'Our Smiles Greet Guests From All The World,' announces a running light display in the Quanzhou bus station. 'Our Enthusiasm Warms All Passengers On A Trip.'

The tone and nature of the bus station resemble the tone and nature of any bus station anywhere, which tells you precisely how smiled at and warmed by enthusiasm I feel. Poor people battle with too many pieces of luggage held together by too few pieces of string. Every announcement of a bus evokes a sudden free-for-all surge to the entry gate, like the crowd being released into a Harrods sale.

The bus driver is a bus driver. By which I mean that he is curt, surly, unhelpful, the arrogant paramount chief of a tiny mobile kingdom. He resents passengers. But his bus is a wonder. Instead of fifty dispiriting seats and a smell of puke, there are perhaps fifteen pairs of bunks, each with a sheet and a pillow and a bag to put your shoes in. I nab a top bunk. The bunk may be only half an inch wider than my backside and several inches too short for my Western frame to stretch out fully, and the pillow may be seriously undernourished, but it's an immeasurable improvement on what I'd expected. I can lie near the roof in effective isolation and when not drowsing, watch rural China drifting by in silence on the far side of the glass.

The last sight I have of Quanzhou is a vast billboard showing an idealized panorama of the city on which has been superimposed the grinning mug of Hu Jintao, the present General Secretary of the Communist Party of China and the Paramount Leader of the People's Republic of China. He looks like the punchable class swat.

Beyond Quanzhou we head north on a flash new highway. It spears through a landscape of reddish soil, little plantations of what I think are banana palms, and innumerable villages. The older buildings have an upturned roofline like the profile of a Red Indian canoe. In the fields stand tethered goats, cattle and water buffalo, and there are ponds of captive ducks like netted snow.

As the coastal plain rises to gentle hills the landscape becomes inimitably Chinese. The agriculture is on a tiny scale endlessly repeated. Every valley holds a village and every village has no plan. It has just grown to the little that it is and stayed that way, a few unpaved tracks and a scatter of houses. Some houses are old and dark and low, others new and dark and low. The old ones are crudely built of stone or timber; the new are crudely built of brick or block. The sloping land around and about them is terraced into tiny plots. A maze of irrigation channels runs off the hills and round the rim of each plot, plots shaped like kidneys or lozenges or bean pods. On most there isn't room to turn a tractor, which is fine because there are none. Motive power is the water buffalo, relieved by the human frame and the occasional ox.

The peasants look as though they have been placed there by the Campaign for Picturesque Poverty. They wield primitive tools, they hunch under shoulder yokes, they wear conical coolie hats and their clothes blend drably into the land.

Though I am lying down, travelling at fifty miles an hour and separated by glass from this world, I recoil from the hardship. These people's parents and grandparents and great-grandparents worked this land the same way and ended as they started which was poor. It's a vista of going on for the sake of going on. And to me, a child of the modern West for whom progress was a given, for whom it was always implicit that I should follow my own way and not my parents' way and make of my life what I would, this subsistence life I am staring at looks as bleak as misery. And I guess that it looked this way to the peasants' offspring, because they all seem to have gone. I see no one in the fields under thirty years of age.

Beyond the villages the hills recede behind one another in ever fainter shades of green, the view so often depicted in Chinese watercolours whether painted a thousand years ago or last week.

I stretch out on my bunk to the extent that it is possible and I drowse. In waking interludes I reflect on the state of my quest. I've pretty much done the easy bit. I've now seen where my underpants were made, and who made them and how. I've seen who ordered and bought them and how they were shifted from the Middle Kingdom to the land of the long white cloud. But henceforth I shall have to go further afield, to trace the rubber and the cotton back to their sources as raw materials, and I shall be acting on less definite information. It seems daunting. For now, however, it can wait. I am keen to see a few bits of non-pant China. I curl foetally on my side and watch this alien country pass by.

When we arrive at Wenzhou bus station in the early evening, there is no sense of Confucian restraint. The place is cacophanous, frantic, aggressive. My hotel is only a few hundred yards away but in walking that distance I am accosted by perhaps thirty women trying to sell me bags or belts, and twice that number of men trying to sell me bags or belts or women. The sales pitch is fierce and unremitting.

The hotel lobby is moderately plush, but my room sings of sales reps and cynicism. The joinery is don't-care shoddy and the carpet is nylon. The plug sockets spark, and the sheets on the bed are gritty, with only an inch of overlap at the sides of the mattress, and none at the head or toe. Free-standing plastic cards advertise prostitutes. The photographs of sexual ecstasy are unconvincing. The minibar contains Scotch, beer, noodles and condoms.

Wenzhou has boomed like the rest of the east coast, but that boom is a self-made boom and an almost anarchic one. When Deng Xiaoping established zones for special economic development, in other words for capitalist industrialization, he did

124

not include Wenzhou. Wenzhou was left to struggle on under the old system where every enterprise was state run and controlled by party cadres.

But Wenzhou watched the special economic zones forge ahead and decided that it wanted some of that. So Wenzhou sprouted a mass of private businesses. They were all illegal. The only way they could survive was to attach themselves to state-controlled enterprises. To achieve this they needed party officials to connive. The party officials were only too happy to connive. Soon every state-run business, most of which were commercially beyond hope, had a mass of thriving little businesses attached to it like barnacles on a ship. The whole system depended on rorts, backhanders and corruption. The party ostensibly retained control in Wenzhou, but only by changing its supposedly communist spots. A miniature version, in other words, of China as a whole.

Most of the new enterprises were single-household concerns making mundane domestic items such as socks or buttons. Some went under but others prospered. The city resembled an industrial petri dish. Those businesses that prospered were immediately replicated. And because the whole shebang officially didn't exist, there was no system of commercial law to govern it.

As the ideological grip of the state loosened in the nineties the illegal enterprises became quasi legal, and Wenzhou became one of the great manufacturing towns of the nation. Many of the new businesses worked with leather. Today, only twenty-five years on, the Wenzhou region is the second largest maker of shoes in China, which also happens to make it the second largest in the world.

This city, in other words, embodies the Chinese instinct to do business. Fifty years of totalitarian repression had starved that instinct of oxygen but did not come close to extinguishing the coals. One gust of air and they flared like a beacon.

As I go in search of dinner before bed, the streets feel as the American west must once have felt, crowded with newcomers sniffing at opportunity. There's an immigrant rapacity here, nothing tender, nothing settled. The place is choked with people and cars and noise and vendors of everything. Wedding fireworks of clamp-your-ears ferocity go off at unpredictable intervals. I seem to be the only person who jumps.

The proprietor is standing at the entrance to his four-table dumpling restaurant. Beside him there's a stack of bamboo steaming-baskets, like jungle cake tins. I ask if he serves beer. Or rather I say 'Have, have not beer?' and mime the question mark. He beams at me and launches into an oration that I cannot understand but which clearly indicates that his is probably the most impressive range of local and imported beers in the whole of Zhejiang province, all of them chilled to the brewer's specifications and awaiting only a connoisseur like myself to appreciate their subtleties, and furthermore he is offering them this evening at an unparalleled discount simply because he is feeling good about the way the world is spinning. I take a seat. He tells me to wait just a moment, then he trots across the road to a little shop. When he comes back he is carrying three bottles of Tsingtao.

He pours the beer into a beaker made of plastic so thin that it yields between my finger and thumb and crackles as I drink. The beer is warm and the dumplings scalding. But the proprietor is genial, and so convinced that I am fluent in Mandarin that he addresses me throughout the meal. A girl I presume to be his daughter drops in. She shows dad a filling she's just had at the dentist. Then she shows it to me. It looks a fine filling and I say so. '*Hao*,' I say, 'Good.' The girl couldn't be more pleased, and she too has a nice long chat to me in Mandarin.

At midnight, full of beer and dumplings, I'm in bed listening to the night sounds of Wenzhou. They are like day sounds. This city crackles like a plastic cup. The phone rings. 'Hello good night you want massarjee?'

I decline politely, replace the receiver and snuggle to the extent that it is possible to snuggle into gritty sheets. The phone rings.

'Hello good night you want massarjee?'

I lay the receiver on the bedside table, where it squeaks for a while, then bleeps, then falls silent.

I breakfast with Ruth and an Italian. The Italian works for a liqueur company that he refuses to name, so I presume it's posh. He's here to source merchandising for his brand: key-rings, sew-on patches, ashtrays, the disposable paraphernalia that bombards us with subliminal plugs. I've never given a thought to where such stuff comes from. It comes from here.

'China eees most cheap place,' he says.

At my request Ruth has hired a car and driver for the day. So far my underpants have taken me only to the urban world. Today I hope to taste a smidgin of rural China. I'd like to crumble some Chinese soil in my fingers. I'd like to slap the rump of a water buffalo.

Wenzhou is built on an estuary. The water looks as inviting as the Victorian Thames. As the driver fights our car on to a ferry, I am assailed by a memory of the cross-Channel ferries of my childhood. On those ferries loading was rigorously marshalled. Polite English families in polite English cars waited politely in queues. One by one they were beckoned aboard by a man in a boiler suit who would urge them to within worrying inches of the car in front. Here in Wenzhou, boarding is a free-for-all. What gets us and everyone else on board is attitude. And because everyone's got it, the result is fair.

It takes a while to get into water buffalo territory. Battling out through the industrial fringe of the city we get stuck behind an ancient truck laden with what appear to be rolled-up quilts. They are pink and padded and held in place by a mesh of rope. They bulge off the flatbed like a vast pink cabbage, stretching high above the cab and far out beyond the wheelbase. At every pothole they bounce like belly flesh. Gradually a gap widens in the mesh of rope and at a particularly severe jolt half a dozen quilts spew through it. I expect the lot to go but they don't. The truck carries on oblivious.

I ask Ruth to tell the driver to stop, and then to tell him to help me collect the quilts. This requires us to dart into the three-lane highway, seize a quilt and dash back to safety. The driver is half-hearted about the whole business and none of the traffic cedes an inch to us. Presumably they don't see our act as charity. They see it as opportunism. We cram three quilts into the boot and the rest in the back seat where they gradually expand to smother Ruth.

I ask Ruth to tell the driver to catch the lorry. He looks surprised and then he laughs. So he, too, saw it as opportunism. But he slips very happily into the role of driver in a pursuit. During his overtaking manoeuvres I find it simplest just to close my eyes. And I envy Ruth her airbag of quilts.

A mile up the road we flag down the truck. It pulls over, stops, and a small man climbs out of the two-man cab. Then six more small men climb out of the two-man cab. All seven of them look aghast. When we offer them the quilts they look astonished. Without losing their look of astonishment or, as far as I can tell, saying thank you, they stuff the quilts back under the mesh and climb back into the truck.

We follow a river valley up into the mountains. Sun slowly thins the mist. Wherever the valley widens enough to permit habitation and cultivation, there is habitation and cultivation. An hour out of Wenzhou we stop at my request and I wander back down the valley a little to a bridge. Beside the river a withered couple tend their skerrick of land. Both wear coolie hats. Their movements are the movements of the old. Their heads are like the shrunken skulls of Maori warfare. She chops a furrow with a mattock. He scatters dung from a bucket. I can't tell whether the dung is animal or human. They don't speak.

Beside the empty road a woman sits on a campstool with a bucket of sugar cane sticks, chopped ready for sucking. On the other side of the road three workmen wait for a lift to town. They stare at me in unison, like curious cattle. I offer them a wave and a breezy '*Ni hao*.' No response, nothing, just the same unabashed stare.

An old woman is crossing the bridge towards me. I lean on the parapet and look down river. I sense her stop at my side. I turn and say hello. The woman is carrying a plastic bag of empty plastic bottles. She says nothing but reaches out and strokes the hairs on my forearm, studies them in frank amazement. Few Chinamen have hair on their forearms. No Chinaman has fair hair on his forearms. Indeed, no Chinaman has fair hair.

She starts to murmur, to wheedle. She pats her sparse scalp then her chest, and delivers a weak but theatrical cough. One of her front teeth is crowned with gold. She coughs again and starts to whimper, stroking my arm again, pleading. I give her a few yuan from the back pocket of my jeans. The gift intensifies her whimpering, her pleading. She strokes my arm with greater urgency, as if it were the stroking that did the trick, and she tries to return my hand to the pocket from which charity came. She weeps and coughs. I stride away across the bridge, too fast for her to pursue.

Away down river on a beach of pebbles, they're staging wedding photos. Marriage here is a bureaucratic formality. You fill in forms and send off for a certificate stamped by a drudge in an office. But the new urban middle class has to find ways to spend its wealth, and in the main streets of the larger towns, shops have opened up to sell wedding photos. Their windows show the same fake and sugary snaps that have become fashionable in the West, the same posed shots in picturesque places that the happy couple have never previously visited and never will again.

Inside the shops the salesgirls sit with clients and go through album after album. From watching through windows I've noted that the grooms seem just as interested as the brides, but then I suppose love does that. And one happy couple has chosen this valley to immortalize their union.

Photographers' umbrellas have sprouted on the beach and duckboards have been laid across it to save the rented dress from soiling. The bride is helped into a rowing boat, the groom joins her and a flunkey pushes them out into the shallows. The bride squeals and clutches the gunwales.

The photographer calms her. He has removed his shoes and socks and is wading in water that reaches halfway up his calves. He persuades the bride to trail a languid finger in the flow, and the groom to curl a loving arm around her. The bride's dress is the purest white, which is standard in the West, of course, but startling in China. For two thousand years or more the custom in China has been to wear white only at funerals.

A few miles further up the valley two places of worship stand side by side. One is a typical village temple, crudely built of concrete. A painted plaster dragon runs along the length of the roof ridge, a fierce claw raised as if to strike. A padlock the size of a pineapple prevents me opening the gates, but through the grille I can see the standard mannequins of devotion with their beards and bellies, looking about as divine as bus drivers. Outside the gate a concrete shrine like a drinking trough is littered with the dog-ends of joss sticks.

Alongside it stands a modern Christian church. It looks the genuine article but for two details: the clock on the tower tells the right time and the windows are of golden mirror glass. Between the two buildings there's a plot of cabbages the colour of battleships, and almost directly overhead runs a half-built highway on stilts, a dwarfing thing, carving through the red earth, disdaining the harsh geography.

Some of the scattered hovels and houses look derelict, but outside the house closest to the church a bright-eyed woman is assembling little coloured baubles. She's the caretaker of the church and keen to chat. Through Ruth she tells me that the government did not pay enough compensation for the land that they took to build the road, and that there is no secondary school in the valley so the young have to board in the city. Many of them don't come back. She doesn't blame them. There's nothing for them here, she says. The village is ageing and shrinking.

And all the while she deftly makes what turn out to be decorative curtain hooks, an example of one of the literally hundreds of thousands of tiny household enterprises that have arisen in and around Wenzhou in the last two decades. As this cheerful, sparkling woman natters, her husband sits on a stool with a bowl of noodles and a plate of pancakes, a sallow skinny man with the eyes of a fish on a slab. He slurps the noodles noisily into his mouth, and stares at me in frank amazement. Absent-mindedly he tosses scraps of pancake to a tiny yellow cat. The village is midday silent.

We stop to eat in a town wedged high in the mountains. Tumbledown shops sell second-hand plumbing, old men in vests watch the world pass by and stray dogs strut the streets and bristle at each other. The dogs it seems are interbred, all reverting to a single ginger type of medium height and a strange plumed tail that arches upwards to expose an arse like a pencil sharpener.

The restaurant is dingy, smoky, dirty, busy and lovely, with plastic tablecloths, a littered floor and constant hubbub. Lunch begins with a fierce argument between my driver and the proprietor over I've no idea what. Thirty seconds later all is smiles. We consume beans with pork, pork with bamboo, prawns with ginger, wilted green stuff, a paddyful of rice, lots of beer and salted tail-fish with red peppers. Tail-fish consist of a head followed immediately by a long tapering tail. The tail is meat-free bone. So is the head. The driver demonstrates that I am supposed to suck it, but the pleasure to be gained from doing so eludes me. The entire extravagant meal for three costs 110 yuan. And I may have been ripped off.

I wander after lunch, leaving Ruth and the driver to snooze. A couple of alleyways back from the unprepossessing main street I find a village built of wood. It dates back a thousand years or more. Lunchtime beer may have softened me, but I find the place enchanting. It's still inhabited, genuinely it seems. A primary school squealing with kids stands beside a pond that's refreshingly fenceless. Stone-lined irrigation channels run everywhere, crossed by arching bridges of timber. A terrace of single-storey wooden dwellings flanks the main channel. On the communal shaded veranda a few old men sit round playing cards and a lot of old men stand round them watching.

For sure the place has been tarted up to emphasize its ancient prettiness, but that does not erase its ancient prettiness. Apart from some of the temples, and the skyscrapers of Pudong, these are the first pretty buildings I've seen and the only old ones. They were built with an eye to something beyond mere utility. How many such buildings have been flattened in the last century by an ideological bulldozer or an economic one? I don't know.

The old village merges seamlessly into the new. One minute I'm on the ancient timber veranda failing to understand the rules of Chinese whist; the next I'm in a ramshackle contemporary street of concrete and corrugated iron where women sit threading necklaces beside displays of brooms and plastic bowls and woven coolie hats that no one is buying. Puppies nose through rubbish. Washing hangs like bunting and chickens wander with a slash of pink aerosol paint across their backs. A puppy scatters the chickens in an explosion of squawks and flappings.

A few hundred yards further on the village ends in neat sloping terraces planted with maize and turnips and 200 varieties of cabbage. Beyond them are the steepling limitless mountains.

10

To Yibloodywu

Ruth and I take the train to Jinyun. Speakers in the ceiling relay music at a volume just below a level that demands attention. We get 'Jingle Bells' and 'Nessun Dorma', followed by 'Auld Lang Syne', whistled. A Buddhist monk rises from the seat diagonally opposite mine and toddles up the aisle with a saucepan. The saucepan is enamelled and battered and shows the remains of a floral pattern that I recognize from my mother's kitchen in Sussex. Five minutes later the monk returns. His saucepan steams.

Just as Chinese bus drivers resemble bus drivers anywhere, so Chinese railway employees would slide seamlessly into what I remember, without affection, as British Rail. Their ties are loosened to precisely the required number of inches. Their surly lack of interest in their passengers is bang on. The only difference is that there are a lot of them. One woman carries a stool. Her sole job is to step on to it at intervals, reach up to expose the yellowing armpits of her blouse, and rearrange the luggage on the racks.

Most passengers eat. They nibble sunflower seeds, spitting husks into bags or on to the floor. They delve into parcels and extract cakes, leftovers, sweets, fruit.

Jinyun played no role in the manufacture of my underpants. We're going there merely to break the long journey to Yiwu with a dose of Randomville, China. According to Ruth the place is mountainous, scenic and popular with film-makers. But it's small.

'How small?'

'I think about a million persons,' says Ruth.

Few of the million are in evidence near the railway station. I see only grand but empty boulevards and grand but empty coffee bars, plus a shop called Wankelong Motors. Wankelong Motors sells exactly the sort of little motorbikes that deserve to be called Wankelong. But who it sells them to is a puzzle. There's nobody about except a posse of workers fashioning a median strip in the grand but empty boulevard.

It comes as little surprise that our hotel is grand but empty. It's got an empty marble lobby and an empty cocktail bar where the seats are cubes covered in primary-coloured cloth. 'Lobby Bear,' is how the hotel directory describes the place. 'Located in the lobby it praides all kind of brand bear cocktail fresh juice and delicious.'

The brand bears available are on display in a glass cabinet like medical specimens: two bottles each of Heineken, Budweiser and Tsingtao. When I order a Tsingtao, the waitress extracts one of the two in the cabinet. In the middle of the room under an arch of plastic foliage, a baby grand piano plays itself electronically. 'Smoke Gets In Your Eyes', jazzed up. I carry my beer to a cloth cube. The waitress follows me all the way, then presents me with my tab. When I've signed it with my room number she takes it straight to reception for processing.

I am a reasonable linguist. I readily grasp linguistic structure and I pick up vocabulary quickly. But my Chinese has progressed little, partly because many of its sounds are alien and partly because the grammatical structure is unlike anything I've met. But it's the characters that foil me most. I cannot fix them in my head, so I have no mental image of the sounds I am trying to reproduce. In consequence, though I may learn a phrase in the morning and think I've mastered it, when I reach for it later in the day I find it has dissolved.

But one phrase has taken very firm root: '*Yo may yo ming sing pyen?*' is how I see it in my head. It means 'Do you or don't you have postcards?' My mother likes to get postcards and I like to please her. But postcards, I have discovered, are not a Chinese habit. I have trotted out my request in fifty post offices, shops and hotels. Sometimes it has elicited a shake of the head, proving that at least it's been understood. More often it has elicited bewilderment.

The three smart girls at reception, whom I have all to myself, understand my request, I think. They consult in a rapid-fire verbal huddle, then one scurries to a back room and reappears with a more senior woman. '*Yo may yo ming sing pyen?*' I repeat. The girls nod as if to say, 'That's what we said he said.' The senior woman says 'One moment', withdraws to her office and returns in a little more than one moment with three furling postcards. All show the hotel and nothing else. It is called Sunny Hotel. It is not a lovely building.

'Lovely,' I say, 'thank you', and there is much rejoicing.

I ask for stamps and I am told I will have to go to the post office. I ask where the post office is and I am told where to find a taxi.

I say I don't want a taxi. I want to walk. I ask for a map and I am told that there isn't one. Clearly, a town with only a million inhabitants is too small to merit one. Why, it's only three times the size of New Zealand's capital city.

Can they perhaps draw me a map showing where the post office is? I am told which number bus to catch.

'No, no,' I say, 'I want to walk.'

135

I am told it is far too far.

I explain that I am a champion walker, and I mime a vigorous walking style, swinging my arms like a guardsman. When the girls have stopped giggling they tell me that the post office is in the old town. I feel I am homing in on hard information.

And the old town, I ask, now where might that be, and I indicate the points of the compass with chopping motions of my hands followed by a hunch of my shoulders and an upturning of the palms. When the girls have once again recovered, one of them leads me out of the main door and points me towards the old town as if she were aiming a robot at a distant target. I set off walking like a stiff-armed automaton then turn to see the effect of my clowning on the girl. She's gone.

Round the corner from the hotel a line of unwanted taxis sits waiting, their drivers idling, smoking, flattening newspapers across the steering wheel as taxi drivers do the world over. The buildings are all new. Shiny apartment blocks stand amid rubble with no paths leading to them, as though they had sprouted overnight like mushrooms. A hummock is crowned with a kiddipark. Its swings and climbing frames, all fresh as paint, are barren of children. It seems that I'm walking through a new-built ghost town.

I follow the river downstream. The valley is carved on a grand scale, but the river flow is paltry. On a wide slow bend the stream occupies only a third of its bed. A foetid litter-strewn lagoon has formed on the outer edge. A weir in the river would serve as a dam had not a hole been knocked through it. Downstream from the hole women rub hard soap into old clothes, rinse them, wring them and slap them against rocks as if trying to kill snakes with them.

Further on a man smokes and fishes the afternoon away. I smoke and watch him. I watch for a quarter of an hour. Throughout that time he squats without moving, in a posture that no Englishman over the age of six could hold comfortably for thirty seconds. He trots his float time and again down the same five yards of turdish water, twitching it upstream at the end of each run. His bait is too tiny to be visible. He doesn't notice me. He catches nothing.

Gradually the grand new buildings give way to dingy older ones. Then I round a bend and up ahead where the valley narrows to a gorge I can see the old town. The buildings cling to the steepness like a fungus. It's clear what has happened.

Like every city in this province, Jinyun is expanding. The town planners must have simply decided that the gorge was too costly a challenge. So they just let the old place be and are building a new town next door, a town for cars and plumbed apartments and tomorrow's China. No doubt the new town will soon be humming, but as a visitor one could hardly fail to prefer the old version. The streets wind like coiled string. Within their narrowness, cars and pedestrians do battle for dominion and by and large the pedestrians win by force of numbers.

I ask a chunky woman the way to the post office. She is standing beside, and clearly the proprietor of, a bicycle taxi. The bike is ancient, like a village policeman's bike in a Bertie Wooster story, gearless and made of iron. If it hit a wall it wouldn't buckle. It tows what looks like a pair of old-fashioned pram wheels with a plank between them.

'OK OK,' says the woman, when she finally grasps what I want. She pats the plank and urges me to climb aboard. I climb aboard. She shouts something joyous, straddles the bike, stout in her trousers, stands all her weight on the left pedal, breaks the inertia, transfers the weight to the right and pedals me up a slight slope. I should be looking at the passing scene but my gaze is transfixed by her taut backside, the worn seat of her thick cloth trousers, the mighty exertion of those legs.

'OK OK?' she shouts back at me, still standing her full weight on the pedals for every strained half-revolution.

'OK,' I say.

'OK OK OK!' she exclaims, delighted by the conversation. Our route levels out and she begins to sing, her legs still working like pistons. Pedestrians stare at me. They must see few big-noses, up here in the mountains where the mists roll. A vendor with bits of pig on a tray gazes at me open-mouthed, following me with his whole head. We swing into a cobbled alleyway, the bell on the handlebars warning pedestrians with exactly the same tinny noise as on my first bike, forty-five years and half a world away.

'OK OK OK.'

I look up to see the familiar green logo of China Post. My driver throws an exuberant gesture at the place, like a local who has just led a doubting archaeologist to the lost city.

'*Hao*,' I say as I dismount.

She looks puzzled.

'OK OK,' I say.

She beams like a torch and asks for three yuan. I give her ten, a couple of dollars, and refuse the change.

Her face ignites. 'OK OK OK.' As she cycles away she turns to wave with a smile as wide as Christmas. And I feel a little shabby. I earn the mantle of Mr Generous by spending only insignificant sums. It feels fraudulent, patronizing. Perhaps I should pay only the prices asked of me. They're probably inflated anyway.

Old Jinyun is a fine town to wander in. It crackles with brio. The little streets are dense with small-scale commerce, sellers of knick-knacks, brushes, candied fruit, dried fruit, fresh fruit and fruit impaled on wooden kebab sticks. I cross an old bridge to an unlit covered market where there is barely room to walk between the high-heaped goods. I finger a cigarette lighter, ask how much, and am pleased to note that I understand the answer. Out of the volley of language, the unbroken stream, a couple of recognizable sounds have emerged like islands. Sometimes it is better not to try to listen. It is better just to relax and hear. Thirty years ago after I had been living in Spain for a few months, I realized that when I was drunkish, my comprehension of the language was close to total. Sober I paid too much attention. My conscious mind overrode a less conscious one, and I translated in my head as I went. Beer is good for you.

And so's a haircut. In other people's eyes my hair has become the reverse of itself. No one sees the hair; they see only where it isn't. I am defined by my baldness. To the young that baldness is an instant signifier, like a flag run up a mast reading 'of no interest'.

But I still notice my hair. When it reaches a certain length it becomes ticklish on my neck and curls at the edge of my ear and the need for a haircut becomes a constant niggle like low-level background noise.

A youth is watching a television mounted high on the wall in what strives to be a salon. Cheap plastic bowls have been spray-painted silver and there are fancy bottles of European shampoo. But the walls are scuffed and fat flies tour the ceiling. I suspect this place is for women, but I don't care. I announce that I don't speak Chinese, a phrase I now deliver with such fluency that it appears self-contradictory, and I mime the snipping of scissors. The youth blushes and smiles. The smile crumples the whole lower half of his face.

The chair he relinquishes and urges me to occupy is identical to the one in E9, my last classroom, the room I spent a decade teaching in. The black vinyl seat has even split at the front edge in the same way and is exuding the same mustard-coloured foam. I sit and submit. There is a pampering pleasure to such submission.

The youth does a pointless tour of inspection of my scalp then sets to work: shampoo, scalp massage, towel rub, then tiny scissors and utter absorption. He's little more than half my size but as he razors the back of my neck I note in the mirror that his fingers are half as long again as mine, like a gibbon's fingers.

'How much?' I say when he's done.

'Five kwai,' he says. A dollar.

I give him ten because I don't have five. He tells me to stay where I am and scampers to the vegetable shop next door and then to the shop beyond, where a man is squatting to saw at an aluminium window frame.

'Forget it,' I say with gesture and he smiles that crumpling smile and blushes and we are both happy.

On my way back to the new town I hear 'OK OK OK.' Mrs Chunkylegs is pedalling a fare seriously uphill but still has the energy to call out to me and wave. I like this place. I like the energy of it, the cheerfulness, the livingness.

I dine with Ruth in the sort of cheap little restaurant I have become fond of. Occasional cockroaches scuttle over the walls. Our main dish is duck in sauce. I delve with chopsticks and extract, to my surprise, a mussel still in its shell. I suck it clean of sauce. The sauce is excellent. The mussel is the duck's beak.

The train to Yiwu in the morning is full of young soldiers, and more are packing the platform, saying farewell to their soldier mates.

Confucius, that champion of deference and decorum, would not have been impressed by them. They smoke in the non-smoking carriage. They block the aisle to form a card school. They shout down the carriage and throw things to each other over the heads of other passengers. And they have occupied our reserved seats. Ruth is tiny, but she takes on these young men with magnificent vigour. When they don't take her seriously she doubles that vigour. I stand mute behind her, striving to look tough. No one pays me any attention. Ruth has right entirely on her side but the youths in our seats don't budge. They indicate two empty seats in the next compartment. Ruth argues. The boy-soldiers shrug.

'Where is your commander?' asks Ruth.

They indicate the seats opposite the two empty ones. We peer round the seat back and there is the commander, stretched out across three seats, snoring. The soldiers laugh. We take the two empty seats.

The train is full and still filling. A soldier lifts the commander's sleeping head, slides into the seat beneath it, and lays the head on his lap. The cradled sleeper half wakes. The soldier lights a cigarette and places it between his commander's lips.

As we pull out of the station, a line of half a dozen soldiers on the platform salutes quite smartly. The last soldier in the line is gulping with distress, his Adam's apple bobbing, the skin bunched around his eyes, his mouth like the arch of a bridge. But he keeps his body stiffly erect. None of the soldiers on the train looks out of the window.

They wear a coarse green uniform of jacket and trousers, with gold buttons and red and gold epaulettes. But no two wear the same style of shoe, and from beneath their jackets peep the collars of dissimilar shirts.

I ask Ruth whether they are recent recruits on military service. She relays the question to a withdrawn and friendless youth beside her. Apparently, most of this rabble have been in the army for at least two years.

They rule the train. No civilians upbraid them. No ticket inspector seeks to quash their boisterous disregard of the rules.

Is there some hangover here from Red Army days, some residual fear of their power? I put the idea to Ruth but she was born at the start of Deng Xiaoping's reforms and is a child of the new commercial China. She says only, 'The soldiers are very dirty. They are using rude words.'

And besides, she is engrossed in a film. The train is equipped with screens, and a dubbed American movie is showing. 'This director,' says Ruth, 'make a movie called *Backward Mountain*. When we see it we laugh. It is about two cowboys falls in love. Very funny.'

Beyond the window every scrap of less-than-vertical land is planted with mandarins, or perhaps tangerines, the fruit like baubles on a Christmas tree. An hour further on and all is tea bushes.

Yiwu is flat. It squats inland on a coastal plain that stretches to Shanghai. Its new railway station lies in wasteland several miles out of town. The town is coming to meet it. The roads are there, plots are marked out for development, and some factories are already built, standing alone now, awaiting a tribe of cousins who won't be long.

Yiwu is another of the success stories of the modern China. It was a rural town of no account, but it had plans, and being situated as it is, it had opportunity. If you look up any of the Yiwu civic websites, you can get a sense of the energy and purpose that is driving this nation.

Like any city council website in the West the text is crammed with jargon and ambition. The difference is that Yiwu means it.

Since the reform and opening policy, Yiwu has resolved to execute the development strategy of Building the City by Prospering Commerce unswervingly, using the commodity industry as a leader to drive regional economy, and become a large market city and strong economy city from a traditional agricultural small county . . . Yiwu have successively gained such honors as being the National Technical Project Advanced City, National Sports Work Advanced City, National Culture Work Advanced City, Zhejiang Civilized City, Zhejiang Educational Strong City, etc.. Furthermore, it has been awarded the National Double Support Model Cities Award four consecutive times.

Today, Yiwu appears a prosperous scene with a flourishing market, developing economy and steady society. The commodity industry has been leading industry in the regional economy. Currently the Yiwu commodity market possesses an area of 1.5 million sq.m. and has 40,000 stores, collects 28 categories and about 200,000 varieties of daily goods. Throughput is nearly 10,000 tons, market business volume is on top of the nationwide large special markets for 12 successive years, and has been granted the unique market title of being one that 'pays attention to quality', and 'keeps promises' by the State Quality Supervisory Inspection and Quarantine General Bureau. Furthermore, the Yiwu market has been an international commodity distribution center and the important base for foreign merchants to purchase commodity . . . It has also cultivated a group of predominant industries, scale enterprises and famous products of socks, ornaments, zippers, cosmetics, shirts, cultural articles, pen-making, toys.

But this is all modest stuff. A paragraph or two later, as he outlines Yiwu's future, the author gets properly energized. You can feel his hope in the crumbling syntax.

In the new century, Yiwu develops with the times, exploits and innovates, puts forward the aim of walking in giant steps, and strives to become in the top 10 of world commodity fairs in the next 20 years and construct a truly international commodity city . . . with the lowest cost, best credit and best service . . . let informatization d[r]ive industrialization, industrialization boost informatization, walk new industrialization road, make the brand of commodity, made in Yiwu famous in the whole world."

The town fringe is a mass of businesses. Where Wenzhou flourished through cottage industry and loopholes in the law, Yiwu followed a more officially approved path. The factories are newish and purpose built to make the world's small commodities. And they make underpants too, which is why we came.

When Ruth began her research, it was companies in Yiwu that she rang first. When they heard that I was a prospective buyer from New Zealand they were all over her. Now that they know the truth, they've disappeared. I don't blame them. They have businesses to run and no time to waste if they are to make 'made in Yiwu' 'famous in the whole world'.

I leave Ruth in the hotel getting nowhere with underpantists on the phone and I head out on foot. I'd like to see the one and half million square metres of Yiwu Commodity Market. I've read a little about it. It sells everything, not to the public but to agents who come from round the world. There are, for example, several hundred stalls selling Christmas decorations. Somewhere near here right now is a machine operator knocking out a million plastic angels a day before toddling home to too little rice.

Yiwu is also at the heart of the counterfeit business, the production of fake brand-name sunglasses and the like. Now that China has joined the World Trade Organization, it is under increasing pressure to clamp down on commercial rip-offs. It responds by periodic blitzes, all of them heavily publicized. Television news and the obedient press show pictures of government bulldozers running back and forth over mountains of pirated DVDs. But it's mainly window-dressing. The business still thrives and costs Western companies billions. At the same time it highlights an absurdity.

When people buy Ray-Ban sunglasses, for example, or Rolex watches, they don't buy them because they are the best. They buy them for the brand. The brand confers status and a sense of merit. The brand is a sort of juju.

That fake Ray-Bans and Rolexes sell by the million is not so much a commercial truth as a religious one. Boil it right down, and what you're left with is a superstitious half-belief in certain charms or tokens. Which also, by a curious coincidence, happens to be the religious stance of most of China.

Yiwu is plug-ugly. Its centre is dirty, clogged, frenetic, grace-less. Everyone drives like a paramedic. You can taste the air. I ask at a couple of places for postcards but am less than aston-ished to find none available. For one thing, by the time they were printed they would be out of date. For another, it would be hard to take a pretty picture of Yiwu.

The grass in a civic park has been bleached by more feet than it can take. Buried beneath the park is a low-ceilinged shopping mall holding a crowded KFC, a hundred clothes stalls and a roller-skating rink. If you're a male teenager in Yiwu it is fash-ionable to take your shirt off and roller-skate extremely fast backwards, performing dance steps as you go, striving to look bored, while avoiding infants, incompetents, beginners and fre-quent two-foot-wide rough-cast unpadded concrete pillars. If you're a female teenager in Yiwu it is fashionable to look unim-pressed.

In the streets there are traces of a former Yiwu. The window of a traditional Chinese medicine shop holds a stuffed fawn looking understandably startled, a lacquered turtle, preserving jars full of sea horses and garfish, contorted roots, several dried lizards that look as though they died in agony, a six-foot snake and a statue of an ancient sage scrutinizing a plant. A customer goes first to a white-coated doctor who listens, questions, then issues a prescription. This is then dispensed by white-coated assistants. They extract dried ingredients from shelves and drawers and beautiful porcelain vases, weigh them with preci-sion and hand them over in a paper-wrapped bundle that looks exactly like a portion of fish and chips. You take the bundle home and make soup out of it.

Traditional Chinese medicine is giving way to its Western counterpart. The rate of change is directly proportional, I sus-pect, to the rate of growth of Yiwu's Commodity Market. But traditional Chinese medicine can't be all bad. The Chinese have always lived a long time. During the Ming dynasty, several hundred years ago, civil servants received a pension only when they reached the age of seventy.

I wander the industrial suburbs expecting to find signs in English to the Commodity Market. I find the 'Yiwu Wonderful Factory' making I don't know what but with a guardhouse at its entrance complete with guard. I find places making towels, decorative ceramics, glassware, necklaces, calendars, all the stuff that comes to find you as soon as you buy your first house, and that never goes away. Yiwu is a source of the stuff that you have to make an active decision to get rid of.

The exuberance of the promotional material I quoted above seems at odds with the city I see. The place feels joyless. It infects me with gloom. And under a granular sky the thought comes to me, as it has several times on this trip, of where this is all heading.

China is booming. It is booming by making. It can undercut the world by having almost unlimited cheap labour. China also has a penchant for commerce, a penchant that was caged for forty years. The result is this eruption of industry.

China also succeeds because it has lax laws – lax labour laws, lax pollution laws, lax intellectual property laws, and lax enforcement of even these lax laws. The country competes but plays to different rules. It will cut any corner. An article in *China Daily* this week announced that fatal workplace accidents had fallen 10 per cent in comparison with the same month the year before. This month only 7321 people died at work. That's a mere 250 people a day who said goodbye to their families in the morning, went to work and never came home.

China is no longer in the grip of any sort of political or social ideology. Those in power have only two objectives. The first, as always and everywhere, is to stay in power. The second is to make China rich. In that aim they are entirely at one with the people they govern. The aim of the second objective is to help them achieve the first objective.

The headlong rush towards prosperity is unsustainable. No amount of window-dressing for the Olympics, no string of international agreements, no battery of environmentally friendly projects opened by Hu Jintao and other toadies, can disguise the obvious truth that China is soiling itself and using itself up.

It burns thousands of tons of low-grade coal a day. It increases its power generation capacity each year by the equivalent of the British national grid, and almost all of that power is generated by coal. Every city I have been in has created its own particular pall of grey and brown. Seven of the ten most polluted cities in the world are in China. Here in Yiwu it is hard to imagine the sun shining. And there is no doubt that local officials all over China connive in masking pollution problems and in evading such laws as exist.

To be sure, away to the west of Yiwu there are millions of acres of empty rurality just going on going on, but the effects of what's happening in industrial China are reaching back into rural China. Water in particular is a worry. China has never abounded in water. Now the stuff is becoming scarce and dirty, especially in the north. Recently the third largest lake in China turned toxic. Only half of China's sewage is treated before entering rivers and lakes. In places, the mighty Yangtse can now be waded. According to government figures, and the Chinese government is not known for inflating a problem, over 90 per cent of urban water is contaminated by industrial or organic waste. The city of Shanghai is now looking to the sea for its drinking water. It plans to build the world's largest desalination plant.

In short, the charge up Industrial Wealth Street is entirely understandable, but what's further up the street does not look pretty.

I never do find the Yiwu Commodities Market. I don't much care. I know what I'd find there. I'd find commodities on a scale that would be unimaginable if I hadn't already imagined it. It would be a banal surprise that I can't be bothered to go on seeking.

Ruth is waiting for me in the lobby of the hotel.

'Any luck with the pant makers?'

She shakes her head.

'Let's go to Shanghai.'

She nods her head.

11

They Play Cricket

It's a poor people's bus, with seats of bone and shock absorbers that don't. The poor fit these seats better than I do. One man has brought his knees to his chin and curled his arms over his head and is sleeping as I imagine a small ape might sleep when it's raining. Ruth eyes our fellow passengers with evident distaste.

'Many bad people coming to Shanghai,' she whispers, 'many bad people from far away.'

I rest my head against the streaked and juddering glass. The land is flat as a tablecloth, all muted greys and browns, little settlements of no distinction, nothing to hold the eye. At Hangzhou half a dozen people battle off the bus with parcels, at the same time as a dozen battle on. If one person went down he would be trampled.

In the hundred or so miles from Hangzhou to Shanghai some stretches of farmland remain, but the future is written beside the road in the form of sudden isolated factories and bulldozed

149

spaces and gleaming warehouses the size of aircraft hangars. These are the forerunners, the scouts. Ten years, at a guess, and this gap between cities will be no gap, merely a vast and birdless corridor, a conurbation built by the new wealth. Shanghai will be a city of 50 million, ancient Hangzhou will be a suburb, and everyone will drink the sea.

But I am pleased to be returning to Shanghai. The constant novelty of moving is an assault on the head, a demand on perceptions. It is a comfort to slip back into somewhere even slightly familiar. I glimpse the crab-claw summit of a downtown skyscraper and a mental map of the inner city drops over the place like a thrown sheet. I know where I am again.

The poor are restless, anticipatory. They stand before the bus halts, regathering parcels from the racks, from under seats, re-encumbering themselves with their battered ragtag stuff. The bus slows, then swings unexpectedly through 180 degrees. Those standing are too tightly packed to fall. They sway in the aisle like seaweed. A hiss of doors and the people battle their way off. In China, no one alights.

Through the window I watch them divide and fan out like a river delta, and then they are gone. Shanghai, that earns one dollar in every twenty that China earns, that receives one dollar of overseas investment out of every ten that China receives, has swallowed forty more Dick Whittingtons.

Ruth is checking under the seat, then checking again along the rack.

'They steal my laptop,' she says. Her face is tight with anger.

We scour the empty bus but she's right. One of the Dick Whittingtons has filched her computer from the rack and melted into the city with it. I feel guilty by proxy and offer her money which she refuses. But she lays into a bus-station supervisor with impressive lack of restraint. The supervisor responds with an impressive lack of interest. He offers her no sympathy, no forms to fill in, no number to ring. What he says, quite clearly, though I don't understand a word, is 'tough'. The free market demands losers as well as winners.

Before my flight home I have two days to fritter in Shanghai. Aware that I have barely scraped at the surface of this huge city I buy a guidebook, though not without misgivings. With it comes with a free phrase book. I study them both in a back-street eatery over wonderful fried rice that is so cheap it is effectively free. My misgivings about both books are confirmed.

The phrase book has a chapter on shagging, though it chooses to call it 'romance'. Halfway down the list of phrases designed to steer you through the minefield of interracial intimacy are the words 'push harder'.

Now, I have never used the phrase 'push harder' in a sexual context, nor have I heard it used, but I suppose that, at a stretch, I can just about imagine someone wanting to use it. What I find improbable is someone committing the Chinese phrase to memory just in case. And what I find even more improbable is someone fumbling for the light switch, the phrase book and the reading glasses in mid-shag, turning to the relevant page and, well, let's consider the guidebook.

It misses reality by a similar distance, but in a dissimilar way. In common with all guidebooks I've seen, it reads like the bastard child of a Sunday supplement and a travel brochure.

'Half the fun of being in Shanghai,' says page 139, 'is ordering a brand-new wardrobe of tailor-made clothes.'

Oh really. Half the fun?

'The city is justly famed for its skilled tailors, and you'll spot them tucked away down the side streets, beavering away at their antique sewing machines. The best place to kick-start the creative process is the city's fabric market, one of the most colourful places in . . .' No, I can't go on. It's not just the stress on 'fun', that mantra of our age, but also on shopping and the picturesque, those staples of holiday-making. And look at the language – 'justly famed' . . . 'tucked away' . . . 'beavering' . . .

'the creative process' . . . 'colourful'. If that lot doesn't make your guts writhe, or make you doubt the writer's honesty, we are very different creatures.

But I have to admit that without the guidebook I would never have known that Shanghai had a Museum of Public Security, and with an afternoon to kill and no underpant research I can profitably engage in, I visit it. It's a hundred years old and housed in a concrete tower impressively shorn of anything resembling an aesthetic touch. Several security guards lounge in the foyer without apparent function. I pay eight yuan to a girl sitting in front of a glass cabinet that holds a fetching display of helmets. Having sold me the ticket the girl disappears. I cannot find the entrance to the museum. The security guards watch my puzzlement without making any effort to relieve it. I push through a door, turn a bend in the corridor and discover a bank of monitors showing live surveillance-camera pictures of the outside of the building. I am unsure whether this is an exhibit. A highly animated security guard arrives and lets me know, with some vigour, that it isn't.

Back in the foyer I show my ticket to another of the guards. He gestures towards the corner. I shrug and remain in front of him. He sighs, gets up, and leads me to the lift.

The fire-fighting hall on the third floor has not drawn a crowd. Remarkably I am the only person admiring the hoses of various diameters, and the expressions of solidarity and good-will from the Kuala Lumpur Fire-fighters' Association.

But the police hall on the floor below has a smattering of visitors admiring the photographs of corpses: corpses hanged, corpses shot, corpses stabbed, corpses drowned and corpses dismembered. And here's the actual cleaver that did the dismembering.

A glass cabinet holds a badly stuffed police dog. Opposite are pictures of him when he was alive, alongside some splendidly graphic snaps of the wounds he managed to inflict.

A collection of confiscated porn looks disappointingly tame – Feng meets Li for some kissing and rubbing, all done in hand-drawn pastel – but the guns are enjoyable. There are perhaps fifty cabinets of guns. Some are police guns but most are bad people's guns. Here are guns disguised as walking sticks or fountain pens, pocket-sized machine guns, and one especially natty weapon that fires its bullet not horizontally but upwards at an angle of forty-five degrees.

The lift opens and its chrome doors release twenty-five primary school kids. They look as educationally stimulated as all kids in museums do, until one of them finds the photos of corpses. His delight draws the others. Good to see the young learning the virtues of public security. It's useful knowledge. They still have public executions in China.

The condemned are paraded into a stadium, made to kneel and shot in the base of the skull. A doctor is usually in attendance because organs have to be removed quickly and skilfully if they are to command decent prices on the international market.

Apparently, if you are charged with a capital crime in China you stand a 99 per cent chance of being convicted of that crime. Most people end up confessing, thereby obviating the need for a tedious trial. I read recently, though not in the Chinese press, of a man who initially denied a charge of murdering his wife. But after a few days and nights of polite questioning he changed his mind and admitted the deed. Yet he wasn't executed. His wife, you see, turned up to save him.

Feeling that I may as well do a little more tourism before dinner I head for Mao's house. It is well signposted until I reach where it should be and find a towering Four Seasons Hotel, with marble round the flower beds, sprinklers in the flower beds, doormen dressed like Regency dandies and a foyer done in the sofa-and-pot-plant look that is the reassuring international code for bland security with room service. Mao, who apparently used to search his crotch for lice whilst interviewing Western dignitaries, might not have been impressed.

In these last two days in Shanghai I have only the one appointment. It is with the secretary of the Shanghai Cricket Club. We've arranged to meet in an Irish pub called the Blarney Stone.

I arrive early. The pub is Irish in the traditional international sense. You can get a Guinness, a Kilkenny or a Scandinavian lager and it comes in a pint glass. On a big screen there's a British football match. The bar staff are Chinese; the prices aren't. The roof beams are low, the furniture wooden and deliberately crude. I doubt there's a city in the world now without such a bar, except for perhaps Dublin.

It caters for expats, of course. As it did in the 1930s Shanghai crawls with expats. And as in the 1930s many of them live a life effectively segregated from China. While I wait for David to arrive I flick through *That's Shanghai* magazine. It is crammed with ads for gated foreign estates. 'Spacious luxury villas with private gardens, beautifully landscaped natural surroundings and a professionally managed clubhouse,' runs an ad for Lakefront Villas. 'Your family deserves the best.' The photo shows a scattering of suburban palaces in best American neo-classical. They are set in the middle of what looks like Augusta.

The Emerald is a 'Fortune 500 living community'. The ad shows an apple-pie mom with exactly the sort of teeth you'd expect. She is kneeling before her winsome seven-year-old and adjusting the straps on his winsome satchel. 'Jerry,' runs the riveting dialogue, 'is it all right for you to go to school alone?'

'Of course mom,' says little Jerry, 'it is only a short distance walk inside The Emerald. In other words there's absolutely no danger of my being abducted by any of those unhygienic slant-eyes who work for a dollar a day in daddy's factory.'

The second sentence was edited out during production, but its ghost lurks as subtext.

Cricketer David doesn't live in a gated community. He's married a Shanghainese, fathered children here and now thinks of Shanghai as home. In short he's gone troppo. He's even acquired a car and learned to drive in the local manner.

A former first-class cricketer in New Zealand, he now runs a manufacturing business, and his conversation twinkles with awareness. He sees all the ironies of belonging to a cricket club in Shanghai. But half the playing members, he informs me, are now Chinese.

With him is a grinning young Scouse journalist, a sub-editor for *China Daily*.

'But the paper's censored, isn't it?' I say.

He laughs like a bath emptying. 'Of course,' he says. 'It's a crap paper. There's some subjects you know you just can't touch.'

'Doesn't that sort of, well, cramp you a bit?'

'Do I look like I care?' he says. 'It's not as though I'm going to be here for the rest of my life.'

He hopes to write novels.

More friends arrive. We stand in a loose circle at the bar, drinking in rounds, no glass ever empty, elbows sucking up slops, laughing with increasing volume. The conversation is sharp, honest, relishable. I could be in any of the pubs where I have spent uncounted evenings over more than thirty years. Late in the evening we move to a faux-rustic table to eat. Too numbed by lager to care, I order whatever the bloke next to me is having. It turns out to be a mixed grill, chops, eggs, sausages, bacon, just protein and grease, the West on a plate.

Bursting out of the pub around midnight, I am momentarily surprised to find China still there, smelling, tasting, looking, feeling, being different, and I am very pleased to see it. I like it here. I wallop back along Huaihai Road singing.

12

May I See Your Trees?

It's more than a month before I can get away again. The second leg of my research is harder to organize. I need to find the source of the rubber that went into the waistband on my underpants, the source of the thread that went into the cloth, and the source of the cotton that went into the thread.

I find Thai Filatex, the rubber company, on the internet. It's based in Bangkok. I send them an email. I also email Terrence at Kingstar asking him once again whether he can find out where his thread comes from.

After a week I have heard back from neither. I put Ruth on to Terrence, asking her to ring him, email him, pester him in a way that I find uncomfortable but that she seems to quite enjoy. I also ask her to dig up some wholesalers of cotton thread and to find out where they get it from.

Meanwhile I keep on at Thai Filatex. I send them the same email again, then more emails, offering references testifying to my blameless character and my innocence of purpose. No response. Nothing.

Ruth is soon back to me. She says that Terrence has spoken to his agents but they just won't tell him the name of their suppliers. They are afraid he'll cut out the middleman, and he doesn't want to upset them.

'Is he telling the truth?' I ask.

'I think,' says Ruth. 'That is typical Chinese business.'

I believe her, and at one remove I believe him.

Nevertheless from other suppliers of thread, Ruth has managed to confirm that Xinjiang province, way out in the west of China, is almost certainly the source of the thread in my underpants, because only there does China grow the sort of cotton known as long staple. Long staple means long fibre, and long fibres mean softness. The harsher cottons that go into denim, say, or tablecloths, are short staple. But for next-to-the-skin comfort, the sort of comfort that advertisers can write lush and sensuous prose about, long-staple cotton is the only option. I shall go to Xinjiang.

Thai Filatex has still not replied so I ring the number on their website. A voice answers in Thai. I say my name and speak slowly in English. The phone goes dead. I ring again and get no answer. But now that I know they exist I book flights. I'll spend a few days in Thailand, enough time I hope to see rubber trees being tapped, then head for the distant province of Xinjiang where the cotton grows. I am delighted to discover that my travel agent has never heard of Xinjiang, nor of Urumqi, its capital city. Nor had I, of course, until recently, but I don't tell her that.

And then my dog Jessie starts to die. She's thirteen. Until now she's come on every walk with my younger dog, padding five miles or more a day, staying close to my side but still managing the distance. Then suddenly she can't. Her range shrinks and her appetite with it. She sleeps more and more. In the days leading up to my departure she becomes a husk of the dog she was, tottering only a few yards before sinking to the ground.

The vet suspects cancer but there is no point in opening her up. She doesn't seem to be suffering, though the vet gives me a vial of morphine just in case. The day before I leave I dig Jessie's grave, high on the hill behind my house in the shade of a walnut tree. And I give a friend sealed instructions on how to bury her.

On my last evening she's as weak as water. I hope she'll die. She doesn't. When I have to leave for the airport in the morning she is lying on the deck. I kneel beside her and stroke her and kiss the top of her head. Her muzzle is grey but the fur of her ears is as silky as when I first stroked it thirteen years ago. In those years she and I have walked thousands of miles. I once worked out that we've walked right round the world together, and then some.

I say goodbye, kiss her again, walk away, look back and she has turned her head to watch me go. I go. I go to Bangkok. To find the source of the rubber in a pair of cheap underpants.

Six-thirty the next morning and I'm on the seventeenth floor of a hotel in Bangkok, wearing the complimentary dressing gown that guests steal. My feet are on the windowsill, the soles against the glass, and I am watching the sun rise like a cocktail cherry through the city fumes. I can feel its heat already through the double glazing. And down below me lies smutty-sweet Bangkok. Once they called it the Venice of the East. They wouldn't now. From the hotel window it looks like a milder Shanghai. The tower blocks and construction cranes and freeways, the cityness, extend all the way to a horizon of haze and dirt. But this place isn't quite so far gone as Shanghai. Pollution gathers round the city's rim like the noseband on a horse, but high above the city centre is an expanding patch of Cambridge blue.

Directly facing my window stands a house-sized picture of a BMW grille. The Thai script that accompanies it looks half Arabic, half Roman. A similar sized poster on the flank of a tower block depicts the King of Thailand. His Majesty looks like a bank clerk on holiday. He wears I'm-serious spectacles, an open-necked shirt and a camera slung around his neck.

The bank-clerk king overlooks a web of elevated roads, already thick with traffic this early in the morning. The traffic is not the tuk-tuk quaintness of a brochure. It is the same Japanese and Korean vehicles that line the roads at home in Lyttelton or the suburban cul-de-sac where I was brought up in England and where my mother still lives. Immediately below me I can see the neglected remains of what was once a canal. Beside it is a Buddhist monastery. In its courtyard I can make out the orange dots of monks.

After breakfast, the foyer of the hotel is a milling mass of Western tourists. At the door of the hotel the commissionaire is all teeth. 'Good morning sir. I get you taxi. What you want? You want shopping? You want sightseeing? What you want? Where you go?'

I know exactly what I want and where I'm going. From the internet I have learned that Thai Filatex occupies Mahatun Plaza Building on Ploenchit Road, and I have found Ploenchit Road on a street map. It seems to be a principal thoroughfare, which I find encouraging. Less encouraging is the heat. Immediately beyond the plate-glass doors, one pace from the air conditioning, there's a wall, a barrier of hot air, fat with moisture.

It was warm enough when I arrived last night at midnight but now the air is like an assault. A hundred slow yards down the road and I can feel the warmth a quarter of an inch beneath my skin. My wrists have swollen and my watch strap itches. This isn't the dry heat that I learned to cope with and almost enjoy in central Spain. It's the sapping humidity of the equator, where it helps to be dark of skin and small. Perhaps this heat explains the Westerners in the foyer, all of them dawdling in the comfort of air conditioning, delaying their emergence into this airborne cruelty.

A coffin shop displays huge wooden caskets carved like ceremonial canoes. Stalls on the street sell mangoes peeled and sliced and served in plastic sachets, pineapple slices on sticks, melons, guavas and the famous stinking durian like a spiked puffer fish. Here it seems is a place without seasons, where tropical fruit is always fat.

Other stalls cook. They offer fried bananas, entrails on rice, and dubious soup from a cauldron. You take it away in a small plastic bag, like a goldfish from a fair. How you drink it, I've no idea.

An old woman threads marigolds on a string, votive offerings to be bought and given to Buddha. Shrines abound, private ones in shops and alleys, public ones in squares. Most carry the standard statue of the cross-legged fatso, but others show a slimmer younger Buddha standing upright and looking markedly Indian.

Beneath a bridge over one of the extant canals, a narrow boat pulls away from the wharf with a mighty engine roar. The wake slops against the buildings and last-minute passengers leap the gap. I wince at the exertion in this heat. The roads above are close to gridlock but no horns sound. I sense a patience here, a gentleness, that I didn't find in China.

'Hello. Hello. Hello.'

The man's voice comes from a few yards behind me: a pedlar or a beggar.

'Hello. Hello' then a tap on the shoulder. I turn to meet a policeman. He's a foot shorter than I am, and dressed in black. His face has a greasy sheen. 'You come with me,' he says, and I feel the sudden birth of a worm in my gut, my old familiar fear of authority that springs from God knows where, that I've had and hated for as long as I can remember, and that is so deep-seated now it is effectively instinct. He beckons me to retrace my steps. I follow to near the bridge where a tree grows through the pavement. Around it there's a little square of baked earth with a sprinkling of cigarette butts. He points at the cigarette butts. One of them is mine. I had thought of tossing that butt in the canal,

161

decided against it, and discarded the butt by the tree, taking exaggerated care to grind it into extinction with my flip-flop.

The policeman has drawn a card from his breast pocket and is holding it for me to read. It says in English that there is a fine for littering of 2000 baht. 'You come with me,' he says again. I follow him up steps on to a covered footbridge above the road. It is deserted and surprisingly dark. He shows me the card again, stabbing his finger at the figure 2000. 'Pay now,' he says. 'Pay now, all over.'

The whole scenario is obvious to both of us. The white tourist won't want a fuss. He won't want to go to the police station. He is also rich. Two thousand baht is about NZ\$100, a neatly judged sum, affordable to the tourist but suggestive of a worryingly significant offence.

We both know that we both know that I will pay. And we both know that we both know that this sum will be trousered. Then I will be free to go and he will return to hunting tourists plump with cash.

I argue, briefly, but our lack of a common language works in his favour. He stabs the card again. 'You pay, all over.' He has his mantra, sees no need to go beyond it, because it works, it feeds his family. He checks repeatedly over his shoulder to see that we are alone. 'You pay, all over.'

I know people who would run at this point, and I admire them. They'd probably get away with it, too. Constable Thai would be unlikely to chase hard or summon assistance, because he's in the wrong. But I lack the balls to run. I pay. It is all over. He goes down one set of steps and I go down another.

As I walk away I catch myself trying to justify my cowardice. He could use the money. I could spare it. But I know I am lying to myself. I feel resentful and weak. It's a familiar feeling. I want to tell someone about it. There is no one to tell. Time will throw a scab over the tiny wound and eventually it will heal, but the morning feels sullied. And hotter than before.

I find Ploenchit Road without difficulty. The gentle and charming receptionist in a hotel thinks she may have heard of Mahatun Plaza and it may be along that way a bit. I go along that way a bit. Greased by a film of sweat my feet are sliding on my flip-flops.

The gentle and charming receptionist in a different hotel has definitely heard of Mahatun Plaza and she is sure it is back that way a bit. I go back that way a bit.

The gentle and charming proprietor of a stall selling fried bananas doesn't understand a word of English. But she recognizes the name Mahatun Plaza and grins and turns theatrically to the building behind her and smiles in a way that revives the morning a little. Until I look more closely at Mahatun Plaza.

The building is in the process of being gutted. It's clad in scaffolding. I clamber through the metal poles, rub dust from the window and peer inside. Inside is a bare concrete floor and a lot of rubble. The front doors to the building are chained and padlocked. My heart plummets, but at the same time I am tempted to laugh. It seems that I have flown a quarter of the way around the globe in order to be fined for littering. Ah well.

I buy a fried banana on a stick, and eat on the sweltering roadside uncertain what to do next. Beer seems the best answer. I remember not to toss the banana stick in the gutter. There are no bins. I pocket the stick.

The lane round the side of Mahatun Plaza does not seem to house a bar. But halfway along the building the scaffolding relents, and near the back there's a pair of glass doors. I pass through them and enter the air-conditioned relief of a lobby. The back end of the building it seems is still in use. On the far wall there's a pegboard list of resident enterprises. And I see the words Thai Filatex.

A uniformed commissionaire has joined me. 'Thai Filatex,' I say and he looks perplexed. I point at the name on the board and he says something that doesn't sound like Thai Filatex. But he ushers me into a lift, joins me, presses a floor button then nips out of the lift as the doors close. I feel vexed. I wanted time to compose myself. I wanted to wash the dirt from my hands, and to wait for the sweat to stop bubbling from my flesh. And I wanted to prepare a little speech.

The lift opens on an empty, silent corridor. All its doors are closed like eyes. Above a door at the end stand the words 'Thai Filatex'. I straighten my sodden shirt, knock, hear a voice and step into reception.

'My name's Joe Bennett,' I say slowly to the girl at the desk. I smile. She stares.

'I sent you an email.' I pause. Still she stares. She has good reason. I am sweating still and I feel puffy and strawberry red.

I have no idea what she is thinking or even whether she understands. Despite a sense of futility, I start again. I jab a finger in my own chest. 'My name's Joe Bennett. I sent you (and here I mime typing) an email.'

Nothing.

'I am researching a book about underpants.'

The girl flees into a back room without a word. She either knows who I am or is ringing the psych ward.

I hear a brief discussion in low voices. The girl comes back. She looks nervous. 'Thank you,' she says, and she invites me to follow her round a corner into a meeting room and to take a seat at a large polished table with perhaps twenty chairs pushed under it. The walls are business-pastel and free of decoration. The girl turns on the lights and leaves. I pull out the chair nearest the door and sit. My primary emotion is simply relief to be in air conditioning. The girl returns with a bottle of water, then leaves again. The water is wonderful.

A minute or two later a pregnant woman glides in. She is wearing a loose grey smock and a look of intense worry. Shaking her hand is like shaking a feather. She lowers herself on to a chair two away from mine, the corner of the table between us. I switch on what I hope is a reassuring nothing-to-hide, can't-you-see-I'm-friendly smile.

'My name's Joe Bennett,' I say. 'I'm from New Zealand. I emailed you. Several times.'

'We send you an email,' she says. The look on her face tells me immediately and conclusively that she's lying. And I think she knows I know. I feel sorry for her.

'I didn't get it,' I say. 'But it doesn't matter. I am here now.'

She greets this observation with a small but noticeable gulp. I sense that she has been told to get rid of me and the task appals her.

I explain my mission, that I am following a pair of underpants, that I am only here for three days, that I would like if possible to see the factory where they make rubber, because that rubber is sent to China and etc. etc. The woman listens and says nothing.

I stress that I am not in any way an industrial spy or a government agent, that I can confirm my story by telephoning my publisher or by showing her my books on the internet, and that if there is anything in their factory they don't want me to see then I don't want to see it, and that I haven't even got a camera, and that if they could just see their way to letting me . . .

'The factory is far away,' she says.

'That's not a problem,' I say, and I smile to prove it. My smile seems to have the opposite of the effect I was hoping for.

I explain that I'm happy to rent a car and drive anywhere in Thailand, although the notion of having to drive out through Bangkok gives me a lurch of dread.

'There is nobody at the factory. The factory is closed for repair.'

I don't believe her. But it seems best to pretend to believe her. 'Don't worry,' I say. 'I just want to see the building. I have to see it, for my book. Please.'

'It is national holiday tomorrow,' she says. 'Is nobody there.

The factory is closed.' The stress is hauling her features about. I feel like a shit for putting her through this, though at the same time I am wondering why I am being blocked. I change tack.

'What about the rubber trees?'

'You want to see rubber trees?'

'Yes.'

'Rubber trees are far away.'

'I would like to drive out and see your rubber trees.'

'It is national holiday tomorrow.'

'I know, but rubber trees don't have holidays.' I chuckle to indicate that I have made an attempt at a joke. She looks pained.

'Do you know where your rubber trees are?'

She pauses. I watch her trawling her mind for something to put me off with, and coming up with nothing. 'I talk to my boss,' she says.

'Can I come and talk to your boss?'

I would like to spare this woman from a mission that she is clearly hating, but she shakes her head with an urgency that implies horror. She disappears. I am alone for perhaps five minutes. Reaching into my pocket for my handkerchief I find my banana stick and put it in a bin.

'My boss go to lunch,' she says when she returns. It's 10.30 in the morning.

'When will he be back?'

'One hour, two hour. I don't know. She go for lunch. Maybe I telephone you at your hotel.'

'Why don't I telephone you?'

She senses victory or at least my departure, which is presumably what she was instructed to achieve. 'Yes, you telephone me.'

She gets up to leave.

'What's your number? And what time shall I phone?'

She writes the number, or a number, in my notebook.

'What time shall I phone?'

'This afternoon.'

'Two o'clock?'

She doesn't like my insistence. But she agrees to two o'clock.

As I am waiting for the lift, I turn to see the pregnant woman and the receptionist talking together and looking at me. I wave. They wave back with all the honest delight of girls in an Amsterdam window.

In air conditioning it is easy to forget that there is an equatorial world out there, a steamy aerial soup where you can watch the frond of a palm unfurl as you drink a single beer. The whole city needs refrigeration.

I have three hot hours to kill. I take the Sky Train to the only place I can name in Bangkok, Patpong Road.

Raised thirty feet above the streets the Sky Train is a boon. Air-conditioned and cheap – you can travel all day for 100 baht – it grants a view of the city that you are otherwise denied. From high above you look down into an intimacy of courtyard gardens, corrugated-iron hovels, hole-in-corner food markets, neglected canals, and the occasional villa built of teak, a remnant of the Bangkok that was. At ground level all this is hidden behind fences and commercial facades and the ever-swelling forest of shopping malls built to plunder the Western wallet. I glimpse a hospital solely for officers of the Royal Bangkok Constabulary and I mutter a silent prayer that it will shortly be admitting a particular patient suffering from a chronic infection of the colon. And then I feel shabby. He was feeding his family. Ah well, forget it, Joe.

I'd heard of Patpong Road before I was twenty, though without knowing then in which city or even which continent it lay. It was spoken of as the definition of the flesh-market, the platonic ideal of commercial sex, the place of no restraint, against which all similar places were measured. Even the sound of its name was evocative, implying a taut and bouncing deviance.

It's tiny. The famous Patpong Road, the cock-banging heart of

167

Bangkok, is little more than an alleyway. As you wriggle between the stalls on the thoroughfare of Sala Daeng, it's easy to miss. And at midday on a Thursday it's as dead as meat. The place seems barely even tawdry. Puddles, rubbish, stray dogs. Against the sky it is impossible to tell whether the neon signs – strip, sex, girls – are lit or not. Though the doors of the go-go bars are open, they are doing no business. In the interior gloom, janitors swirl at the floors with mops.

A battered woman calls to me from a bar where she sits alone with a beer and an ashtray. But she is as devoid of hope as I am of interest. I smile benignly as no customer would and she smiles back and lights a cigarette. A pimp levers himself from a low stool and falls into step with me, unfurling a concertina of postcards. It's a sexual menu, spelling out in English the services and shows available – blow job, pussy balloon, pussy rainbow, pussy ping pong. Prices are marked and every act is illustrated with an overlit snap.

'You want fucking? You want nooky? Sucky dick?' I shake him off without difficulty. He knows that his is not a daytime trade. For his appeal to work he needs the props of darkness, noise, excitement, fake glamour and probably booze. The sun's his enemy.

A minute's amble and I've done the whole of Patpong Road. Sin City is perhaps a hundred yards of tat. Like so many of the famous big things, the epitome things, the draw cards of the world, geographical, architectural, spiritual, sinful, their bigness rests in our imagination. Their magnitude has been swollen by words, words that doom the eventual visitor to a damning 'Is that it?' It's the tendency to mythologize that lurks at the heart of all religions, all advertising, that soars beyond the mundane and lures us forward.

The nearest Sky Train station to my hotel is Victory Monument. That monument wouldn't look out of place in central London. An obelisk of sorts is surrounded by statues of what appear to be Tommies loading shells, fixing bayonets, doing the stuff of war. Because the monument serves as a round-about and the roundabout is choked with traffic I can't get close enough to see if they are actually Tommies. But I don't want to anyway.

I know next to nothing of the history of Thailand but the only emotion this statue arouses is sympathy for the stone soldiers togged up in battledress, with jackets and straps and itchy woollen shirts. If they were indeed foreign, how must it have been to come here and fight for a cause that wasn't theirs, in clothes like that and in heat like this? And I recall a gravestone I saw set into a wall in similarly equatorial Singapore, com-memorating a sailor from the village of Telham in gently temperate Sussex. Here in the tropics he had contracted a fever, turned purple, swollen and died, aged twenty-one. His ship-mates had clubbed together to buy him a headstone.

Has anyone ever studied the effect of climate on a national psyche? It seems to me that few of the really hot countries, espe-cially those within a degree or two of the equator, have ever been prosperous. Does the heat sap the will? The notion makes sense to me.

At 2 p.m. precisely I pick up the phone then put it down. It may not help to seem keen. Furthermore, at smack on two they will be expecting to hear from me. I shall wait till ten past.

At five past, I ring. My pregnant friend answers immediately.

'Tomorrow is national holiday,' she says. 'Is no one to show you factory. Is no one to show you rubber trees.'

'But I don't need anyone to show me them. I just want to know where they are.'

'Rubber trees are in east of Thailand.'

'Where in the east of Thailand?'

She hesitates.

'I send you map,' she says.

'I can come and collect the map.'

'I send you map. By email.'

'When?'

'Soon.'

'Today?'

'Today.'

'Can I talk to your boss?'

'She is not available.'

I persist a bit but that is essentially that. I can get nowhere. My metaphorical forehead is bruised from banging against a gentle, frightened, pregnant wall. And I don't want to distress the woman more than I have already. She is only the mouthpiece. I do my best to thank her. And besides, it doesn't matter all that much.

I lie down on the bed, drained by jet lag and frustration and this vast and steamy city.

13

'Fun Time' It Said

When I wake the room is dark. The bedside clock says
10 p.m. I have hauled a New Zealand rhythm to the
equator and slept for eight hours. I am hungry and wide awake.
I head out into the night of Bangkok.

The hotel doorman greets me with his hundred-tooth smile.
Beside him now is a bruiser with an undershot jaw.

'Good evening sir how are you you want taxi?'

Then, Hollywood corny, he glances over his shoulder to check
that no one is watching at the reception desk, turns back and
whispers, 'You want girl?'

Before I can reply the bruiser takes over. He's bigger than I
am. In Bangkok he's Goliath. He ignites a smile like a Halloween
mask. 'I got good girls. Very clean girls. Very good. Very cheap.
I get you taxi.'

When I'm a hundred yards or more down the street I realize
who the bruiser reminded me of. He's a dead ringer for Jack
Bodell.

The number of people who remember Jack Bodell must be dwindling rapidly. When I was a child he was briefly the British heavyweight boxing champion but his career ended when he ran over his own toes with the lawnmower. How odd that such information should survive in my head. Lots of useful stuff has dissolved but somehow the image and a couple of details of the life of a man who meant nothing to me have become embedded. Maybe it's just that they entered early and got a good grip, so they've been able to cling on for forty years. Like Fred Trueman's middle name. It was Sewards.

And now those details will never leave my head. Stuff has accreted around them and over them but it has not erased them. And as the years pass, that more recent stuff will lose its hold and fall like dandruff, and when, perhaps twenty years hence, I lie burbling on some state-provided bed, it won't be of lovers that I shall burble or of deathless truths of experience, but of Jack bloody Bodell. And a nurse will stroke my hand because she is warm of heart and I shall try to make her understand and she'll say, 'Yes, dear, now don't you trouble yourself.'

Before my dog Jessie started to die, a neighbour used to take her every Sunday morning to visit the neighbour's elderly father in a dementia ward. The whole ward loved Jessie. As she cruised the bedsides of the senile, collecting pats, endearments and food, she'd be addressed by twenty different names. She wagged her tail to all of them, happy to be twenty different dogs, all fifty years or more dead.

Traffic moves freely now. In the comparative cool of the night, even insignificant streets have come alive. The numerous stray mongrels, all scabby and interbred, have risen from the shifting patches of shade in which they slept the heat away and are scavenging, scuffling, mating. Pavement stalls are open to feed me. I dine on kebabs of a sort and rice and a bag of sliced fruit that may be mango. I wander through streets of soupy air, where the lithe and little people pay me scant attention. The headquarters of the Girl Guides Association of Thailand has a tall spiked security wall and a guard snoozing in a watch house and in a corner of the courtyard a gaudy shrine to Buddha, which is not, I suspect, quite what Lady Baden-Powell intended. And I get a gust of difference, and simultaneously of intoxicating absurdity. For me such sensations are what make travelling worth doing. By midnight I am back in Patpong Road.

It thrums. The little street is barely passable. More than half its narrowness is occupied by a tat market, stalls offering the standard gaudy racks of sunglasses, cheap jewellery, hair clips, mobile phones, jeans, all brightly lit by arc lights fired from snakes of cable. People are fingering, bargaining, buying, all sorts of people, Thai and tourist, ordinary people, young and pretty, middle-aged and not.

As I shoulder through the throng my arm is repeatedly seized and my attention drawn to the pulsing bars. It doesn't need to be drawn. The noise is unignorable. The music is a primal, scudding, drumming thump, the heartbeat raised to shagging pitch and magnified and made external.

The hawkers who seize my arm in a parody of courtship are all young, both male and female, urging me in with an intense sales pitch. 'Come in, come on. Cost nothing. Just have look. Beer 100 baht. Pretty girl, pretty boy. Come in, come on.' They seem to mean it, squeezing the arm, the electricity of their touch a harbinger of flesh. They grin and look me in the eye and press. I am an obvious target by dint of age and sex and race. Why else would I be here? 'Nooky nooky, sir. Sucky dick.'

They know my upbringing is shouting no. People like me, people from Sussex, are scared to enter places like this. The moral policeman is installed young. But the hawkers know that if only they can help me through the door I'll need no further urging. Queer I may be, but still male and racked with lust, lust that sucks at the chest, that can drain the thighs of strength.

The hawkers, the street pimps, exude a commercial bon-homie, but their manner is without humour, without irony. Humour and irony are as inimical to this trade as midday sun-shine. They bespeak a detachment that sees lust as lust, as comic and futile.

Through a flicked curtain I glimpse a low stage and a parade of jigging girls in glowing white bikinis. The stage lighting is ultraviolet, electrifying the scraps of cloth, the crotch and breasts, the nubs of the matter. Each girl wears a number, like a cattle beast at auction. I glimpse tables and tiered seating and gawping men with beer. The image is seared into my retina in the two seconds or so that the curtain is open. The curtain drops and I move on. In another bar a thirty-something white man is dancing drunk, his hands above his head, a bottle of Heineken in one hand sending spume down his writhing arm. He's pulled the hem of his England football shirt up to his chest. His belly slops like a blancmange in a bag. On the stage behind him more girls are jigging with fixed implausible smiles.

In a bar at the end of the street, on a small veranda without overt sexual purpose, a husband and wife sit, middle-aged, white, and fiercely silent. She is wearing too much jewellery and a mask of controlled venom. Before her stands a glass of vermilion juice. Hubby has a beer. He is perhaps fifty, casually dressed, and so frantic in trying not to seem agog, so transparent in his dissimulation of interest, that I laugh.

My laugh must sound English, for the wife picks it out from the hubbub and her gaze locks on to me. I smile but she does not smile back. She knows I know. For me it's a release from the clamping walls of lust.

The little streets nearby have caught the same trade by conta-gion. In one of them I watch a man of fifteen stone and sixty years, dragged from in front by a laughing rent boy and pushed from behind by another. The man is pretending to resist, loving the parody of abduction. 'No, no, you naughty boys, no,' he moans, leaning back weakly against the pull and the push. 'I must go home.' The boys know him, it seems, and he them. He disappears up some shallow steps. Back down those steps he'll come alone, perhaps an hour from now, poorer and slaked.

The street twists and suddenly I'm back in ordinary hot nocturnal Bangkok. I install myself at a bar. It's little more than a booth, but a small netted goal, like an ice-hockey goal, has been pinned to the wall behind the proprietor and next to it a couple of badminton racquets. A sports bar, I suppose, in imitation of those Western establishments where fat men in football shirts drink beer and watch slim men play football in the same shirts.

The proprietor gives me a bowl of peanuts, a beer and a grin. 'Who you support?' he says.

'I'm sorry?'

'You England? Who you support?' and he nods at a muted TV in the corner. It is showing, inevitably, an English football match.

'No one,' I say, 'I support no one.'

He grins. 'Who you support?'

'Liverpool,' I say because it's easier.

'Liverpool, pah,' he says miming a happy spit. 'I support Man U', and he flexes his bicep like a snail in vellum and clutches it with his other hand. 'Man U very strong.'

'Have you been to Manchester?' I say, though I know it's a silly question. And besides, Manchester United has nothing to do with Manchester. It's a global brand, like Pooh or Rolex.

'Pah,' he says again, and rubs thumb and middle finger together in what may be the most universally understood gesture in the globe. 'No money. Baht no good. Very weak money. You dollar very strong', and again he flexes and clutches his bicep. I smile. He is delighted to have communicated enough to make me smile, so does it again. 'Dollar very strong. You rich man.'

And I am. In Thailand all Westerners are rich. They can and do buy what they like, safely on the far side of the world. From here it won't come chasing with recrimination. It can't afford to. Baht very weak.

And yet, with the exception of one policeman and a rubber company, how pleasant the Thais have been to me in the brief time I have been here, Thais who stood to gain nothing from me. Thais I have asked for directions, or for help with translation, small, gentle, almond-eyed people, whom you cannot imagine doing well in war.

I drink a few beers in the hot night. Language forbids much chat with the landlord but he is all attentive service, keeping the bar open for me alone, grinning, replenishing my bowl of peanuts. Before leaving I ask him what sport the goal on his wall belongs to. When he eventually understands the question, he shrugs. I pay, slide from my stool and as I walk away I hear him hauling down the shutters on his livelihood.

It's two in the morning. The tat market is closing but the flesh trade goes on. I have read that the Thai authorities recently imposed a curfew on places of entertainment. If so, Patpong Road is ignoring it. In the same publication I read that the commercial sex business of Bangkok served locals as much as foreigners. And it seems true. There are plenty of Thai men here, along with a lot of what I think are Japanese. But the only noticeably drunk ones, vociferously, unrestrainedly and unbeautifully drunk, are Westerners, Brits and Germans, in particular. The good old Protestant heritage. Press down on anything for long enough and it will curdle and squeeze out the sides.

The waiters and waitresses at breakfast are all tiny, svelte and long-fingered, like a fine-boned species of ape, lemurs perhaps. We tourists are less fine-boned. In front of my table, blinking, stands a great plump lump of a man, pale as a lily and six foot tall, dithering over the warmers of bacon and eggs.

He is still in his twenties but wider at the hip than the shoulder, his face a Billy Bunter oval, his straight dark hair gathered in a pony tail. His belly has begun its lifelong flop over his waistband. And what clothes he wears: a T-shirt promoting Hell's Canyon, Idaho, track pants that stop, intentionally, I can only presume, halfway down his pallid calves, grey business socks and a pair of branded black trainers the size of barges. Each of his legs weighs as much as a waitress.

A threesome from the English Midlands are waiting to be seated. The son is perhaps twelve years old. His T-shirt says, 'I'm with stupid.' Dad's in Marks & Spencer leisure wear. Mum's shorts were sewn from about an acre of cloth. Her backside juts like a shelf. You could rest a drink on it. Her sleeveless blouse exposes a sloppy wad of flesh pendent from the tendons of her shoulder.

And flitting in among us go the Thais, wriggling through gaps that we wouldn't consider gaps. It's hard to imagine that these specimens from East and West belong to the same species. Were there any aesthetic justice in the world, the Thais would be the lords of all things. I find myself wishing I were Thai.

Thai Filatex wishes I wasn't here. The pregnant woman has sent me an email.

Dear Mr. Bennett,

Attached pls find pix of Chonburi and Rayong which are the eastharn provinces of Thailand. The number shown on the map is highway code which you can drive to Chonburi or Rayong. It takes around 1–2 hours from BKK to there by car. I also attach some pix of rubber trees for you, just guideline. You can see the rubber trees along the road and you can take a pix or whatever you want, but do not slit the trees, otherwise your team and you will be killed by the owner. THIS IS SERIOUS!!!

Hope it would be useful for your writing.

So, Thai Filatex is clearly not going to tell me where their particular rubber trees grow or where their factory is. If I go back to their offices I doubt that they will even admit me.

The rubber trees in the pictures look like skinny silver birches. Their bark is whitish and their leaves, you'll be surprised to hear, are green. I dither. It seems pointless to have come this far to achieve nothing. But it seems equally pointless to rent a car and drive a couple of hours east to see some arbitrary specimens of a tree whose appearance is not going to surprise me. Still undecided I go walking to think. At home it's Good Friday. In Buddhist Bangkok it's just Friday. Every shop is open, every stall manned and every inch of tarmac is obscured by stationary traffic.

A woman is arranging five tangerines at the feet of Buddha. Three yards away a legless man in green shorts lies on a sort of skateboard. His only other visible possession is a begging bowl. It doesn't seem important to see rubber trees. But if you want to see some, there's a picture of quite a lot of them at http://www.worldofstock.com/closeups/TAT1017.php.

I take the Sky Train that terminates at the river on which Bangkok was founded. The train is sponsored by McDonald's. Its bodywork promotes the McRice Burger. 'I'm lovin' it,' says an idealized Asian youngster as his faultless teeth approach a glistening burger. As far as I can tell the burger consists of a bun of deep-fried rice enclosing a patty of deep-fried rice. Though there's also a sliver of lettuce.

Down by the wide slow river I amble the backstreets a while, just looking and sweating. I follow a moped through gates and find myself in something like a scruffy Oxbridge college, a sanctuary from the incessant traffic. The silence is a kindness. The courtyard is flanked by simple three-storey buildings of no great distinction. Look up, however, and each roof beam concludes in a needless gesture, a gilded timber extension that flexes towards the sky like a frozen elephant's trunk. The city centre is devoid of such gestures.

In the heart of the courtyard stands a temple of sorts, the size of a parish church. No one challenges my presence, but this place doesn't expect tourists. I feel like a tread-gently guest. A monk pads past with shaven head and sandals and the yellow-orange robe, like a sleeper who has woken in a strange house and wrapped his nakedness in a curtain.

A decade ago, an ex-pupil tried to teach me to meditate in what he said was the Buddhist manner. He said meditation gave him peace and distance. I wanted peace and distance. So each afternoon for a month or so I unhooked the phone and sat and closed my eyes and slowed my breathing and strove to concentrate on a blank inside my forehead. I fell asleep. Or else my mind just pecked at stuff that troubled me and nothing changed.

But of all the world's religions Buddhism seems the least preposterous. As far as I'm aware it invokes no heaven or hell or judgement, no Son-of-God hubris, indeed no God at all. 'Sort yourself out, be kind, and accept what happens' seems to be the nub of it and I find that wise.

The courtyard ends in a metal railing. Beyond it stretches the river, brown as chocolate and as wide as two football pitches. There's a feeble breeze. I sit on a low wall beneath a tree. On the other side of the tree but still in its shade a boy-sized statue of a standing Buddha is littered with floral tributes. At random interludes the tree drops seeds like flattened beans that land with a little skittery patter. They are pliant things in papery skin that peel apart lengthways into perfect halves. I nibble one but it is bitter.

To my right is a phone booth, in whose patch of shade a ginger dog lies furled and sleeping. A cat picks its way past me, all shoulder blades and skin, more leopard than Western pussycat. I like all this. Find me the parish church where the wild cats slink and stray dogs sleep in the shade. My feet are assailed by microscopic ants. Tiny buzzless flies perch momentarily on the hairs of my legs and tickle. Buddha let flies be, let everything be.

In a ground-floor veranda a dozen infants sit at desks, writing or drawing in remarkable silence. Above them a slow fan loops.

On the other side of the courtyard a more senior school is fronted by a basketball court. A boy and girl arrive on a whining Honda 50. The dog by the phone booth wakes and chases the bike across the courtyard barking. The bike stops, the dog falls silent, sniffs at the kids' ankles, returns to its booth and is asleep within seconds. This place has a feeling of sanctuary.

A Volvo with tinted windows glides quietly into the yard. A woman emerges in striped vest and shorts. She is so tiny it is hard to imagine her governing this half-ton car. When she sees me under the tree she freezes momentarily like a cat, assessing, alert, pricked. I smile. Her caution collapses and she steps delicately into the infant school, fanning herself with a scrap of yellow paper.

I sit perhaps an hour, watching the tiny events, the workmen arriving with a truck of sand then sitting to smoke, the brief flurry of noise in the senior school as the kids change classrooms, the occasional ambling monk. Is this a monastery? Some of the buildings look like dormitories. No matter. It's a quiet place in a frantic city, a place of teaching and sleeping, and its tree bombs me gently with beans. I feel at ease.

On the river behind me old wooden barges are rocked by the wash of freight vessels, tourist boats, and high-prowed painted gondolas driven by a diesel engine and a long metal pole that is both propshaft and rudder. A boat like a child's drawing of an ark says BENIHANA JAPANESE STEAK HOUSE on its roof.

I catch a boat like an aquatic bus. It has plastic seats and a plastic awning and a freight of tourists like me. As we cruise up the river a girl with a microphone bellows an incessant commentary in Thai and then in English. Both are deafening and neither is comprehensible. But the breeze is a blessing.

Large sections of riverbank are dressed in decorative poverty. Shacks of old timber and corrugated iron sit just above the water on piles like rotten teeth. Many of the shacks have slumped. In

places the piles have snapped or folded and a room has just collapsed into the river. In typical Bangkok contrast, right next
door there are walled and leafy gardens leading up to stately
embassies – French, Italian, Egyptian – the national flags flapping from poles. The gates are manned by security guards and
the walls topped with spikes.

The boat draws up at a dozen or more quays. Each is linked
with a designated attraction, a flower or jewellery market, the
royal barge museum, a wat or temple. From a vague sense of
touristic duty I disembark at the stop for the temple of the
Emerald Buddha. Ten yards from the riverside the breeze abates
and the sauna reasserts itself. The temple is easy to find but
impossible to get into because of my shorts. The Buddha, apparently, just can't abide the sight of my legs.

The temple looks vast, ornate and impressive but I don't much
mind having to stay outside. Like an animal scenting water I am
drawn back to the breeze, and another of the endless tourist
boats. Further up the river I goggle at the extraordinary Wat
Arun, shaped like the space shuttle at take-off and decorated
with shimmering multicoloured glaze, a glorious pointlessness,
a Buddhist Eiffel Tower. Yet I stay on the boat till the last quay
where I have no choice but to hop off.

In a sweltering backstreet a Belgian backpacker is twisting a
map round and trying to make sense of street signs. I try to help
and fail to help. But we fall into conversation and he asks if I'd
like to join him for a beer and we find a dark little bar. He's
young and cheerful, in cut-off jeans and a stained singlet. He has
a curtain ring in his eyebrow. The dimple created by the piercing
fills with sweat, bulges, then overflows with a droplet that traces
the arch of his eye socket before sliding down his cheek like a
tear. Fixed high on the wall a rotating fan swings its breeze our
way and I raise my face to meet it and I sway to follow it as it
moves past.

He has three and a half weeks in Thailand. His itinerary is as intricately planned as a bus tour for the elderly. He rattles off the places he means to visit. I recognize the names of none of them except Phuket, but I say that he must be having fun and he says yes, he is having fun.

'Are you travelling alone?' I ask.

'Yes,' he says, 'I am lonely.' He meant alone but I suspect that he inadvertently told the truth. When I say I must move on he urges me to have another beer. I recognize the symptoms from my own more itinerant days, days in my twenties when I would take off for somewhere whenever I could, hauled by the lure of elsewhere. That lure was as strong as sex for me. Names of distant places carried an intense exotic charge, South American places in particular, though I have still never been further south than Mexico. Even today I have only to see a passing reference to Quito or Lima or Caracas and I feel the ghost of my youth awaking and stretching its legs.

When I went, wherever I went, I mostly set off alone, and I always ended alone. And time after time I would find myself at a loss like this young Belgian, unable to grasp the romance, the heart, of the place I'd come to see, unable to find in the close-up spectacle of buildings, people and dust the long-range glory that had lured me. I hope he finds what he's looking for. I never did.

Nor, emphatically, has an American woman at the ferry terminal. She is sitting in a morose heap. Aged perhaps fifty she is wearing jeans as wide as they are tall, with roses embroidered round the hems. She has a bumbag on a very long belt. But the most obvious thing about her is her head. It is swathed in bandages, wrapping under her chin and over her hair in a loop, as if for a cartoon toothache. I can make out a little crust of blood behind her ear. She is engrossed by her suffering, breathing deeply, looking inward, not registering my presence. I find it hard to imagine what happened to her, though it doesn't look that serious. A fall perhaps, a nudge from a car? Her slick-haired husband doesn't sit with her but paces the quay, impatient for the ferry.

'It's coming,' he says. 'You OK?' His tone is less than caring.

'No,' she sighs. Her T-shirt is black with armpit sweat, drying at its edges to a rime of salt. And perched on the top of her bandaged head is a little denim cap with two words embroidered on the front in cursive script. 'Fun Time,' it says.

Tey approaches me shyly in a riverside restaurant and asks if he may join me. He wants to practise his English. I tell him his English is excellent and he thanks me and pulls up a chair. I've ordered a plate of river prawns.

Tey is twenty-something years old and an environmental officer. At the end of a day rendered gruelling by the heat his gentle seriousness is a tonic. He asks me, inevitably, what I'm doing in Bangkok and I tell him about my underpants, explaining that they are effectively a metaphor for commerce and industry and in particular the huge imbalance of trade between China and the West, and that on a tiny scale I am trying to understand one aspect of the way we live now, the way the globe has organized itself. At the same time I am testing my preconceptions of all things Asian, and in particular all things Chinese. Tey says nothing. I pause.

'And anyway,' I say, 'it's something to do.' We both laugh.

Tey, like pretty well everyone in Bangkok, is a Buddhist. All Buddhist men are supposed to become monks for a year or two, owning nothing but a robe and a begging bowl, and Tey is going to do so soon. He thinks that when he becomes a monk he may remain one.

I tell him I was forbidden entry to a temple because of my shorts. He shrugs.

'But isn't it a bit silly?' I say.

'Yes.'

'Would Buddha have objected to my shorts?'

'No.'

'Would Buddha be a Buddhist?'

He chuckles. 'The Buddha said it would be like this, that people would get his teaching wrong. He said that he was not a god but that people would make him a god. People want gods. They are all the same.'

'The people or the gods?'

'The people and the gods, I think.'

When I ask him whether he meditates, he says he does, but not as often as he should. 'I watch too many movies.'

We sit out till late on the restaurant veranda, nibbling prawns, drinking. I order a string of beers for myself, but Tey drinks only a single bottle of Spy, a red wine cooler that tastes of cherries.

Late that night I catch a motorbike taxi back to my hotel. It's a little Honda, like the one I had when I was seventeen. I drove it drunk a lot and I sang as I drove and I crashed often and I don't think I have ever known such freedom. It was my first ticket to go beyond, beyond home, beyond upbringing, beyond constraints. The police took it away in the end, and no vehicle since has matched it.

Helmetless now in the hot Bangkok night, clutching the leather jacket of my driver, swinging through traffic and up kerbs and round dogs I am invaded by a great gust of the past and I start to sing. My driver turns round and I grin and he grins back and he revs the engine up a notch. We pull in to the mock-posh forecourt of my hotel with a histrionic slide of the back wheel, alarming the toothy commissionaire and the bruiser who looks like Jack Bodell.

14

We Walked Around the World

A sort of shaking wakes me, a vague sense of violence and unfamiliar noise. I lie still a minute in the darkened room seeking to identify the source, then draw the curtains. The windows are like windows in a car wash. Through the slather of water I can see trees way down below, lashing. Though it's day time the cars have lights on, refracting like starbursts. I don't know whether I am imagining it but the tower of the hotel seems to be swaying, whoozing a fraction beneath my feet. I make coffee and sit as I sat on the first morning with my feet on the windowsill, to watch a tropical storm. But double glazing and air conditioning and insulation make it too televisual, too remote, and I shower quickly and head to the lobby. Perhaps reception will lend me an umbrella.

Reception doesn't do umbrellas. In flip-flops, shorts and shirt I head out the door and beyond the shelter of the canopy and I am instantly assaulted. The wind buffets me sideways. The rain on the side of my face hurts. Fifty yards down the road I dive into a doorway. Most cars are stationary, lights on and wipers frantic. Water leaps from the pavement and overwhelms the gutters. It's quite uninhabitable. I take off my flip-flops and in a lull between gusts I sprint barefoot back to the hotel. The commissionaire laughs then says sorry. I drip through the lobby, followed by a boy with a mop. When I come back down for breakfast in dry clothes the dining room is full. People are lingering at tables, sitting out the weather. I go to the business centre to check my emails and I learn that my dog is dead. Jessie is dead.

Yesterday afternoon she was lying outside. As the evening cooled she seemed unable to get up. The friends who are looking after my house carried her inside and laid her on the beanbag at the foot of my bed. She lapsed deeper and deeper into sleep and then she died.

The girl who runs the business centre is looking at me. When our eyes meet she turns and leaves. And I let myself cry for my dog.

I see her as I first saw her, caged in the municipal pound, curled on damp concrete. I see her running through the shallows on the south beach at New Brighton hopelessly barking at seagulls. I see her, well, it doesn't matter. To you or to her.

Mike buried her yesterday, Good Friday, while I drank with Tey. He carried her up the hill, laid dry straw in the grave, kissed her, told her I loved her, laid her on her side, furled her legs to look as though she were sleeping, closed her eyes, covered her with more straw and gently filled the grave. Last night as I sang on a motorbike Jessie was starting to rot. Gone to earth.

I leave money for my computer time on the unattended desk. 'Thank you' I write on the blotter beside it. I don't want breakfast. I don't want to see my fellow tourists eating breakfast. I don't know what I want.

The storm has gone. Bangkok is steaming. I wander at random, absorbing little, looking inwards. This evening I fly to

China. In a vast department store that I have entered without purpose, attracted only by the air conditioning, I thoughtlessly finger clothes and souvenirs and draw the attention of eager sales girls. They make some introductory remark and I look up at them and then they go away. I've hours to kill. I kill them with beer in a backstreet bar where men argue and women cook, and I kill them in unlovely streets and an area of wooden shacks full of dirty children with beautiful eyes. Another bar and beer and too much time to think.

I came here to see a rubber factory and rubber trees and I failed. I saw few of the regulation sights and I was bored by those I saw. I learned no more Thai than hello and goodbye. I was unjustly fined by a policeman and I did not put up a fight. I gawped at sex markets and poverty. I learned next to nothing of the city's past. I struggled with the heat. I made no friends that I'll see again. And on Good Friday while I drank and talked, my old dog died.

And yet, I realize now that I like the place, this dirty over-crowded city that is slowly sinking into its alluvial delta. It's the gentleness, I think, and the difference. In a dingy bookshop where I go to kill more time I buy a book called *Buddha*. It claims to be a simple factual biography.

At the hotel a throng of people is checking in and out. I take a seat on one of the sofas disposed in cosy groups about the lobby. Nearby sits a Welsh couple, perhaps sixty years old. The husband's struggling with a digital camera.

'When you do that it says flash,' he says.

'Press OK,' she says.

'OK?'

'Yes OK.'

'Nothing's happened.'

'Turn it off. When you turn it off does it come back on?'

'Ah that's got it. I've got them now.'

'That's nice. Have you got that one of the fruit?'

'The dorian?'

'Yeah, the dorian. Wasn't it ugly?'

A waitress brings tea on a tray. The woman pats the spot on the table where she wants the tray put. She doesn't say thank you.

'Ah good,' she says to her husband, 'the tea bag's in. Do you want it out?'

'Yes please. I've taken sixty-four.'

His wife extracts the tea bag by its string, then calls the waitress back.

'Have you got any tissues?' She speaks as one would to an idiot child, and she mimes the act of wiping. 'Tissues. Have you got any tissues?'

The waitress comes back with tissues, smiling.

'You see,' says the woman to the waitress, 'if you put the tea bag on the saucer it makes the saucer all wet. Then you put your cup on it and it drips, see.'

The waitress says nothing. She smiles and wipes the saucer and takes away the tea bag and the soiled tissue.

'You'd have thought,' says the woman to her husband, 'you'd have thought they'd have thought of that, wouldn't you?'

I get up, check out and leave Bangkok.

15

Gone West

Bangkok to Urumqi takes twenty-four hours. Less than half of that time is spent in the air. I kill the long hours by reading the Buddha book. Twice.

Buddha, it seems, saw life as suffering. Every pleasure, every love, every breath was entwined with loss. And the seat of all loss, all suffering, was desire. To escape suffering you had to escape desire. Desire included love, so Buddha walked out on his wife and child. Their suffering didn't seem to count.

Having become a solitary mendicant he subjected himself to a regime that trained his mind. Gradually he acquired a serenity that drew people to him. Beggars and kings alike took strength from him. His calmness made them want to confess, to fling themselves at his feet.

Just as Tey said, Buddha urged the beggars and the kings not to admire him or to make him a god. He explained how he had achieved his serenity, and he asked them to try it for themselves and to see if it worked. In other words he was a psychological empiricist. And all the rest of the stuff that has accreted in homage to him – the temples, the statues, the elaborate rituals, the textual exegesis – is flimflam.

You could argue that his sales pitch differs little from the full-page magazine ads for exercise equipment or super-memory courses – 'Do this and your life will become immeasurably better' – were it not for two details. First, he didn't ask for three easy payments of $39.99. He asked for nothing. Second, his snake oil is still selling briskly two and a half thousand years on. There has to be something in it.

I realize that I have been softened by my dog's death, that I am feeling raw, but I find myself warming to Buddha's simplicity. I can understand the urge that many felt to unburden themselves to him. Even though the biographical facts we know about him are sketchy, it seems that he radiated peace and sympathy, that he felt for others.

Landing at Shanghai we plunge amusingly through a smog that ends only feet above the runway. For my flight west I have to transfer to the domestic airport. On the shuttle bus the driver's enthusiasm with the horn is enough to tell me that I am no longer in gentle Bangkok.

In a queue for security screening a woman's bag splits. It disgorges clothes, cosmetics, a couple of wrapped presents. She is horribly flustered. I stop to help her regather her things, reassemble her baggage. Had I not been reading about Buddha, had my dog not died, I would still have helped her. But I feel a greater gentleness than usual. I doubt that it will last, especially in China. When all her possessions are finally resecured, we're twenty places back in the queue.

In the airport smoking lounge the air is ammoniac thick; it stings the eyes and rasps the mucous membranes. Two other men are in there, a Genghis Khan in jeans, haughty and Mongolian, and a dumpy businessman in a shiny suit, shouting down his phone. He spits the language out. In Bangkok the language seemed to run like water.

Six chrome rubbish bins stand about the lounge. Each is topped with an ashtray holding half an inch of water in which butts float and leach. A cleaner shuffles in. He's wearing slippers. He looks eighty, but drudgery may have battered his appearance beyond his years. He carries two buckets, one with a red plastic sieve set into it. With movements of astonishing slowness, as if death were only a nudge away, he removes one ashtray, swirls it to shift the sludge, then tips it into the bucket. The sieve catches the butts. Tobacco soup strains through. He dips the ashtray in the second bucket, collects half an inch of cleanish water and with aching weariness replaces the ashtray on the bin. He picks up the buckets, shoulders drooping like a bow. He moves to the next bin, head down, his slippers not leaving the tiles. What would Buddha do? I do nothing except feel sympathy, which must have done him enormous good.

Pronounced more or less Ooroomchi, Urumqi is the capital of Xinjiang, China's most western province where most of the country's long-staple cotton grows, the stuff that went into my pants. Strictly speaking, Xinjiang isn't a province. It's the Xinjiang Uighur Autonomous Region, but I'll come to that little fiction later.

Xinjiang comprises one sixth of China's land area but only one sixtieth of its population. In other words, it's big and it's empty.

As we descend towards Urumqi we don't fly over mountains. We fly beside them, a vast Himalayanish range, all snow and crag and dauntingness. It feels a very long way from Shanghai. Indeed, it is roughly twice the length of New Zealand from Shanghai.

The mountains drop abruptly to crumpled foothills, like a lion's paws planted on the edge of a plain. And the plain is the colour of a lion's pelt. A single road crosses it like a stretched black thread. It looks the sort of land the Taliban might fight over.

Stephen meets me at the airport. He's my hired driver, a four-square Chinaman, broad of shoulder, wide of grin and with only three words of English. He says 'No thank you' with joyous fluency.

With him is Ivy, my interpreter. I had tried to hire Stephen's wife to interpret, on the recommendation once again of Michael Gorman, but she has recently had a child. She passed me on to Ivy. When Ivy sent me an email I found it tricky to understand. When Ivy speaks at the airport I find it trickier. She has similar difficulties with me. But she seems good-natured and eager to please.

The drive into town takes us through an urban wasteland. Beside a military barracks painted the colour of cabbages stands a rusted forest of reinforcing steel, pointing at the sky, forgotten. The road shifts without warning from swishing tarmac to ruinous potholes. Rubble is everywhere, growth alongside decay. It's an imperfect, aesthetics-go-hang, urban landscape, a fringe world, a to-come world, aspirant and make-do, and very Chinese.

The centre of town is thrumming. It's ten o'clock at night but most of the shops are still open and it feels like early evening. That's because it is early evening. Though the plane flew through several time zones, we didn't adjust our watches. The whole of China operates on Beijing time. The withered hand of central control is far from dead.

Urumqi's main drag is lined with carts selling food. Jackhammers clang in a half-built apartment block. And twenty workers are doing something drastic to overhead cabling. The job involves an old truck, an older crane, a couple of men monkeying up a telegraph pole without safety gear, and a big black cable the width of a recently fed anaconda. The anaconda terminates in two lethal-looking prongs. It is being winched into the air by the crane and guided between the apparently live cables by the men up the pole and more men on the ground with sticks. Everyone involved is shouting. And thirty passers-by and I are enjoying the spectacle. I half hope that we will be asked to help.

Opposite my hotel the Blue Sky sea food restaurant is doing good trade. I am impressed. Because of all the cities in the world, every single one of them from Montevideo to Minsk, Urumqi is the one that is furthest from any sea. It's the bang centre of the bang centre of Asia, as central as central gets.

Reading clockwise from six o'clock Xinjiang borders on Tibet, India, Pakistan, Afghanistan, Tajikistan, Kyrgyzstan, Kazakhstan, Russia and Mongolia. It's a list to shiver the guts. And I may have left out a stan or two.

The province is ringed by mountains, serious mountains, rising to Everestish heights. The only gaps in the mountains, both lying to the east, are guarded by the crescent-shaped expanse of the Gobi desert.

At the heart of Xinjiang lies another desert, the Taklamakan, less famous but actually more desertish. The Gobi is pebbles and dust. The Taklamakan is every child's picture of a desert. It is shifting sand, hundreds of miles of dunes, dunes that march steadily south-west with the prevailing wind. If you want to cross it, you take a camel. But you still die.

To the south-east of the Taklamakan lies the salt plain of Lop Nur, where the Chinese banged away with their nuclear weapons at the same time as everyone else was banging away with theirs. And at least, unlike the French and British, the Chinese banged away more or less in their own backyard.

From there the Gobi loops away to the east and north. More directly north stand the Tian Shan mountains which I flew past, and beyond them the great grazing lands of the Dzungarian basin, exactly as one imagines Mongolia to be. That the Dzungarian basin isn't in Mongolia is merely an arbitrary consequence of human history. And Xinjiang's human history is a bloody mess.

Xinjiang means new territory or new frontier. And in the long and complex history of China, Xinjiang is almost as new to the Chinese as it is to me. Here's a potted history. Skip it and you'll miss the point of the place. If you want to know more, read the article on Eastern Turkestan in the 1966 edition of the *Encyclopaedia Britannica*, or *Wild West China* (London: John Murray, 2003) by Christian Tyler. That's where I got all this, though any inaccuracies are all my own.

One of the few certainties about Xinjiang is that its first human inhabitants were not Chinese. They were Indo-Europeans who came from the west during the Bronze Age. The Chinese arrived around the time of Christ during the expansion of the first great Chinese dynasty, the Han. (It is after this dynasty that all Chinese who consider themselves racially pure name themselves. Like all arguments of racial purity it's a pretty piece of mythological nonsense.)

At the same time as the Han Empire was expanding west, the Roman Empire was expanding east. There is reasonable historical evidence that the two peoples all but rubbed noses to the north-west of Xinjiang some time in the first or second century AD. But they recoiled as if stung and East stayed East and West stayed West for the next thousand years or so, until Marco Polo published his extraordinary adventures, many of which he probably didn't have.

The Chinese more or less held Xinjiang, or at least maintained garrisons here, until the Han dynasty disintegrated around 200 AD. They then, more or less, left. Assorted nomads and tribes took control. In the seventh century, under the Tang dynasty, the Chinese returned.

But all that is to oversimplify. By then the Turks had arrived. The Turks were not Turkish. They were a nomadic race originating from Siberia and Mongolia. They were close cousins to the Mongols, but the Turkic heyday was longer ago so few Westerners have heard of them. The Turks dominated and terrified central

Asia for the best part of a thousand years. Several tribes of Turks settled in Xinjiang.

Yet another element was a new mob called Muslims. In 750 a Chinese general found himself facing a Muslim army in Kazakhstan. The Chinese army consisted mainly of conscript Turks. Those Turks changed sides at the last minute, and the Chinese were routed.

Meanwhile, the Chinese were also doing battle with the surprisingly warlike Tibetans. The end result was that the Chinese were biffed out of Xinjiang again, this time for about a thousand years.

The various Turkic tribes were too numerous to count but the one that mattered was a tribe known as Uighurs. They gradually became the dominant force in Xinjiang. They achieved this mainly by just not going away. Eventually the term Uighur came to describe anyone living in the region who wasn't obviously something else, such as a Kazakh or a Han Chinese.

The Uighurs were Buddhists for a while, but by the eleventh century they had been converted to Islam. In the thirteenth century they were overrun, like everyone else, including the Chinese, by the Mongols. But they remained in Xinjiang and they remained Muslim and they remained Uighurs.

The history of the next few hundred years is even more chaotic. Every conqueror who felt like passing through, did. Allegiances switched and switched back, trade was conducted in every direction, but the Uighurs remained in Xinjiang, or Eastern Turkestan as they knew it and still know it, throughout. Indeed, they seem to have been the one constant in a place that has always been short on constants.

A thousand years after being biffed out by the Muslims and the Tibetans, the Chinese came back once more. They were now into the Qing dynasty, pronounced Ching. Strictly, the Qing rulers weren't Chinese. They were Manchus from, believe it or not, Manchuria. But even that is not the full story. The Manchus were actually more Mongolian than Manchurian. Indeed, if you trace them back far enough they were probably related to the Turks who became the Uighurs. So when the Chinese reconquered Xinjiang they were effectively fighting their own remote relatives. But that notion didn't cross their minds for one minute, and wouldn't have made any difference if it had, and eventually in the eighteenth century, as part of the expansion of the Qing dynasty, China retook this region, and named it Xinjiang for the first time.

In the nineteenth century things changed again. The Qing dynasty weakened largely because of what the Western powers were doing on the east coast, and other countries became interested in Xinjiang. It was just so central. Local warlords hoofed out or subdued the Chinese, and the British and the Russians sucked up to the local warlords. It was a mess and it remained a mess, the details of which won't concern us, until 1949 when Mao reannexed Xinjiang. It has been part of China since.

Mao gave the place the pleasant title of the Xinjiang Uighur Autonomous Region, but that fooled nobody. Because Xinjiang was strategically critical, and because it held oil, minerals and other good things, and because the Chinese have never much cared for their subject races, Mao set about making the place as Chinese as possible. In a classic tactic of colonization he flooded the place with immigrants, some of whom were given incentives, many of whom were given no choice.

Effectively Xinjiang is the Tibet that the West doesn't bother to protest about. This may be because the subject race is Muslim rather than Buddhist. The sort of people who protest a lot have always felt warm towards Buddhists.

This is not a history book and I have grossly simplified the story. But the one truth to be drawn from the whole elaborate and complex and internecine and tempestuous story of this region is that the people who have been in Xinjiang longest and who have never left it are the Uighurs. And in the part of Urumqi where I am staying there aren't any. In the busy late night streets, every face I see, apart from a few vendors with medieval wooden carts, is emphatically Chinese.

Before bed I eat a quick supper in my hotel. On the table next to me are a Geordie couple, part of a guided party travelling the Silk Road. I experience my usual difficulties with understanding Geordie, but I do catch one comment expressed, with some fervour, by the wife.

'Forty yuan for a yurt,' she says, 'that's a rip-off, that is. That's taking the piss.'

Forty yuan is about three pounds.

In Shanghai at eight in the morning, the streets are gridlocked. In Urumqi at eight in the morning, the only moving vehicle is a tanker playing a tune like an ice-cream van and spraying water to lay the dust. A child, apparently unaccompanied, dances in front of it. The dust blows in from the Gobi and settles everywhere. And although Urumqi is surrounded by several thousand miles of precious little it seems to be maintaining the Chinese talent for pollution. There's a pall in the air that is more than dust, that dulls the morning and masks from view the Tian Shan mountains.

Though Urumqi has been settled for a couple of thousand years, it has only grown to any size under Chinese rule in the last half century. The town centre could be any of the Chinese cities I've visited. I have described few buildings in China because few merit description. That's especially true here.

Under Mao, China was not known for its aesthetic building code. Somewhere in this country there had to be a factory that made sheets of badly glazed white ceramic tiles. They were used to clad buildings, especially municipal buildings such as schools. Somewhere else in this country there had to be a factory that made weak glue. The tiles fall away in chunks. I've not seen a chunk fall and I can't be bothered to wait by a school and watch, but everywhere I go I see tiled facades apparently attacked by a skin disease.

But now Urumqi is prospering. Skyscrapers are going up all over the town centre and they are not clad in ceramic tiles. Completed towers are crowned with some idiosyncratic design, in the manner, if not on the scale, of Pudong.

People's Square is precisely as anodyne as you would expect a People's Square to be: rectilinear raised flower beds, seating for a docile populace, a little kiddies' play area, an open paved area for the sort of edifying display that a docile populace needs to be edified by. And the place is surrounded by the blank walls and windows of administrative buildings. Administrative buildings are immediately recognizable everywhere in the world. I don't want to think why.

As the town wakes up and the morning gets under way I amble towards the southern end of the city. And gradually things change. I start to see Muslims. All the Muslim men wear hats, mostly pointy white pillboxes. The women wear headscarves. The head and shoulders of one woman are shrouded in a rug, heavy and woollen and brown, apparently opaque and without eye slits.

A Muslim baker flattens lumps of dough into rounds that he lays over a sort of cushion. The cushion is reverse printed with an abstract Islamic design. The baker leans forward and lays the dough inside a large cylindrical oven. Then with a devil's toasting fork he fishes out a cooked loaf, golden and fragrant and the size of a kid's tricycle wheel.

At a school gate the security guard sits in a sentry box with a screw-top jar of cold tea. The kids in the playground beyond him have been marshalled without difficulty into lines. They face the school. Over a PA system an anthem blares. You don't have to speak Chinese to guess the lyrics. 'O motherland, we will work hard for you. Duty, honour and obedience are pleasures. My country before my life. Long live whoever happens to be our current immortal leader.' The kids sing along and raise one arm in a Nuremberg salute. It's effective and ugly and transparently totalitarian. Though it should be remembered that schoolchildren do much the same every morning throughout the United States of America.

At the gates of the school a battered Uighur woman with a pan and brush sweeps up the kids' detritus. At her heels traipses a toddler. He is wearing a hooded sweatshirt with the words 'Mono Sports' across his tiny back. He seems inert.

A street market is opening. Here are mounds of walnuts and almonds and hazel nuts and dried apricots and raisins and spices that I cannot name, emitting a fragrance that is unmistakably the smell of the Middle East. I have never set foot in the Middle East and I don't know how I recognize this smell. Perhaps it is from occasional trips to Middle Eastern restaurants, but the fragrance is unChinese. And so are the faces. Increasingly I am seeing an array of racial types.

The food market morphs into a souvenir market, stall after stall offering daggers: daggers with curved blades and embellished handles, daggers with sheaths, daggers that fold like penknives, daggers forged to tuck into a sheikh's belt, daggers for sticking a back-alley victim between the short-ribs in a single mortal never-to-be-investigated thrust. Daggers for tribal feuds going back to the Old Testament. Yet I am in China.

Other stalls offer riding crops, fashioned from leather and knotted cord. They conjure an image of Mongol armies sweeping across a plain on tough little ponies. Incorporated into the grip of each crop is an animal's hoof, a cloven hoof, a deer or antelope's hoof, I think, topped with a decorative half inch of furry ankle. These goods may be tourist tat, but they are indicative tourist tat.

Two young men meet at a stall. Each wears a pillbox skullcap. Each says salaam. Then they shake and disengage their hands and move those hands up across the chest and lay them on their hearts. And I turn round reluctantly and head for a rendezvous with Stephen and Ivy because I have a cotton-packing factory to visit.

16

They Like Your Tractor

I have learned to expect certain qualities in a male Chinese driver and Stephen does not disappoint. He cedes nothing to anyone, exhibits no conscience, bullies the weak and uses the horn like an aural bulldozer. While doing his best to dislodge an old man from his tricycle, Stephen offers me a cigarette.

'Thank you,' I say.

He turns to beam at me. 'No thank you,' he says with triumph. He thinks it means 'not at all', or 'you're welcome', because that's how it works in Chinese. I haven't the heart to disabuse him.

The outermost edge of Urumqi consists of single-storey dwellings made of mud bricks. There is little to distinguish them from the ground they sit on, for the excellent reason that they are made of the ground they sit on. There is a look of desert poverty here, startling in its contrast with the department stores three miles away. The people I see are working with the implements of for ever, the rawest tools of our species, the ones that made agriculture and civilization possible – the spade, the grubbing mattock, the shoulder yoke with buckets and the two-wheeled wooden donkey cart. In our Nissan saloon we sweep on to a glistening bone-straight highway with toll booths. Apparently this road was built with money from the World Bank.

We travel through the comparatively fertile fringe of the great and empty plains, watered by the rain shadow of invisible mountains. The landscape is one vast horizontal, broken by lines of poplar trees that look as if they have been withered by a nuclear blast. The poplars stretch towards the horizon until their lines merge like railway tracks. Between them lie fields, with soil the colour of Jersey cattle. The fields have sides but no apparent ends. It's as if they started on the right of the highway, wrapped around the globe and reappeared 25,000 miles later on the left. Each has been ploughed, some by donkey, but most by squat little toytown tractors, like agricultural Trabants. The tractors cough a thick diesel smoke that, by a spectacular piece of what I can only presume is communist design, rises from the bonnet straight into the driver's face.

Each furrow is spread with a yard-wide strip of polythene that catches the light like a stream. Clods of earth have been turned on to the polythene at intervals to hold it down.

'Ivy,' I say, 'what are they growing in these fields?'

'Yes,' she says.

'No,' I say, speaking slowly and swivelling to face her in the back seat so that she can read my lips, 'what is the crop? In these fields. What,' I grope for accessible words, 'what grow?' I try to indicate the process of growth by unfurling my arms. As I do so I am assaulted by a memory of infant school where we were made to strip to our underpants, girls and boys alike, and curl ourselves into balls, and imagine we were seeds unfurling into spring and summer. All the underpants in the hall, every single pair, were white.

'Uh?' says Ivy.

'What are they planting here? The farms. What is the poly-thene, the plastic, for?' I point out of the window and try to mime a plastic strip with my hands, then point again. 'Is it vegetables? Or grapes? Or cotton? Or what?'

'Yes,' says Ivy and she smiles desperately.

I revert to looking at the landscape. But monoglot Stephen has watched my miming and he speaks to Ivy in Chinese. They have a brief fierce discussion that sounds close to a row.

Then, 'Is cotton in the field,' says Ivy.

'Cotton? Are you sure? Here?'

'Yes.'

I don't know whether to believe her.

Stephen speaks again, and again he and Ivy volley quick-fire Chinese between them.

'Is cotton for sure,' says Ivy.

'Thank you,' I say.

'No thank you,' says Stephen.

We speed past low hamlets of mud or concrete. In the sur-rounding fields a few starveling stock are tended by a child or a headscarved woman. The land rolls on interminably and if it's cotton they are growing, they are growing a lot of it. An hour north of Urumqi we drive into sudden surprising sunshine, hot on my flesh through the glass.

We turn off to Shihezi, pronounced, almost impossibly for a Western tongue, Tsuh-huh-tsuh. It's an unmistakably Chinese town, fast-built, ugly, practical, and with all decorations dom-inated by the colour red. Beyond it the road narrows to a lane and becomes integral with settlements, low-built squalid places of mud or brick or concrete with roofs of poplar branches and daub. Many houses look too low to stand upright in. All have walled enclosures for stock. We pass a cart drawn by three Alsatians. They strain against the harness, their vast tongues flapping like offal. Old men sit on steps in dark jackets and watch the world as old men do. Women grub at smallholdings in a manner that looks romantically earthy until one imagines having to do it. It's a place shorn of modern complexity, though over each settlement hang great droops and knots and bundles of black electric cable.

Our progress is slowed by a procession of ramshackle vehicles: motorbikes, a tractor, a motorized trike and trailer, several carts, all of them overburdened with people like an Indian train. Stephen blasts past them one at a time, not caring whether he passes to left or right. A bout of fierce acceleration startles a donkey.

At the head of the procession a Toyota Hi-ace van is decorated with white paper and flowers. I ask what's going on, though I think I know.

Stephen looks at me, and laughs, and mimes slitting his throat.

'Dead,' says Ivy.

'A funeral?'

'No, dead person,' says Ivy.

We overtake the makeshift hearse. On the roof of the Toyota, the principal mourners are wearing what look like white sacks.

At the entrance to the cotton-packing factory, a mural decorates the external wall, though since it shows the face of Hu Jintao, 'decorates' is the wrong verb. Behind him are some unconvincing pastel sunflowers, and where his body would be there's a list of characters, inevitably done in red. Ivy finds the written word easier than the spoken.

Love mother country
Together work
Be honest
Serve the peoples
Use science
Be discipline
Don't injury motherland

Don't discourage peoples
Don't ignorant
Don't selfish.

A man with a suede jacket, battered face, yellow teeth and a big grin greets us at the gate. The deal, set up by Stephen's wife, is that this man will show me the process of cleaning and packing cotton and then I will buy him lunch. It's a deal I approve of.

The yard is a Manhattan of cotton bales, all wrapped in bulging white canvas and stacked ten or fifteen high. I feel the urge to stab one of the great fat bales and see the cotton spurt.

The ground is littered with drifts of cotton bolls. I scoop a handful.

Each bunny-tail tuft of cotton, each boll, feels similar to cotton wool. I probably shouldn't be surprised by that, but I am. At the heart of each boll lies a seed about the size of an olive stone, detectable by touch but invisible in its cocoon of thin white fibres. Such fibres became my underpants. And I sense that I have got back to where I wanted to get to when I bought my underpants in Christchurch. Here in this yard is the raw material, the point where it all begins. I have worn cotton every day of my life and yet I have never seen the stuff like this. This boll in my palm is the stuff that some remote ancestor looked at, fingered and thought he could perhaps do something with. I'm holding a foundation stone of modern society. In common with many an ancient civilization that we like to patronize, we depend on vegetable fibres for clothing or for shelter. We haven't come as far as we'd like to think. One failed global cotton harvest and our world would start to fall apart.

The raw cotton arrives from the fields by truck or cart. Then a giant vacuum cleaner hose on a stand sucks it through overhead pipes two feet in diameter and into the processing part of the factory. But when I say factory, don't think factory. Picture a battered shed, perhaps thirty feet high, with tall doors of flexing corrugated iron.

The shed's security arrangements consist of a twist of wire through a hasp and shackle. Inside, cotton tufts pile up in every corner. We walk between drifts a foot deep. The place was built in 1953 and looks it. The concrete floor is crumbling.

This enterprise is ultimately owned by the government, which explains the effigy of Hu Jintao. But it is run as a co-operative by the cotton growers themselves, and they have made a success of it, to such an extent that it now operates on four sites. But none of those sites is operating at the moment because it is spring. The farmers who run them are out planting the next crop of underpants.

The manager explains to Ivy how the machines work and Ivy fails to explain it to me. But from the manager's gestures and from my own examination of the machinery the process is clear enough. Machines blow the cotton dry. At the same time they tumble it to separate it from the waste material, the leaves and twigs and morsels of soil.

Once it's been cleaned and dried, the cotton passes through machines with interlocking metal combs that catch the seed between their rows of teeth then close together and tear the seed from its fibrous womb. The seed goes one way to be pressed for oil (one of Ivy's rare linguistic successes), and the valuable floss goes another. It is blown into a hopper and compressed and wrapped in white canvas. The bale is stamped and taken out to the yard to be stacked.

I ask where the bales are sold to. According to Ivy, the manager has no idea.

We return to the car to drive, I presume, to lunch. But we draw up outside another factory. This one's more modern. The yard is blinding, the sunshine bouncing off polished concrete. The door has a real lock.

The old factory, apparently, can process only hand-picked

cotton, but this one is equipped to deal with the machine-picked stuff which comes with greater quantities of waste material. The machines are colossal and American. The manager leads me eagerly to a Scott Fetzer Co. Interchangeable Ignition Transformer, manufactured in Fairview, Tennessee. He opens the metal cover on the control panel and stabs a finger at the list of operating instructions, some of which are flanked by vivid danger signs. As far as I can tell he is asking me to show him how to operate the thing.

One button says 'ignition'. I mime the act of pressing it and then I say 'boom' and I fling my arms apart. The manager grins with delight and appears completely satisfied.

A channel in the concrete floor houses a murderous metal screw, like an auger. It would mince a human foot in a trice. It exists to shift the waste cotton seeds from the building. To ensure that workers don't accidentally feed it a limb, the channel is covered with heavy metal plates. About six of them are missing.

Lunch happens in the tumbledown village nearby. My arrival prompts dedicated staring from some old men seated outside, and giggles from a sprinkle of urchins. The restaurant is the standard-issue front room with soiled formica tables. Each table is set with a jar of cheap chopsticks in paper, toothpicks, a bottle of soy sauce and another of vinegar. When I step through the door the crowded room falls instantaneously silent, as if I were royalty or, perhaps more aptly, Martian. But our party is expected and we are ushered through to the back room where a single table is surrounded by a dozen chairs and topped with a glass lazy Susan. A standpipe tap drips in one corner and the air is stifling, heated by a cast-iron radiator the size of a small horse. It does not seem possible to turn the thing off. A dumpy woman comes round with a huge tin pot from which she pours weak and lukewarm tea into paper cups.

I light a cigarette and mime a request for an ashtray. The manager indicates the floor. Then two more men arrive, dressed in similar casual clothes to the manager. They shake my hand, softly, as all Chinese men seem to do, and sit down and talk to the manager. Two more men arrive. They shake my hand. Then two more. All are here for lunch on the foreigner. Nicely done, my Chinese friends. But I don't much mind. I just hope I've got enough cash.

One of the men is the resident clown, with a face like a balloon and a grin that would photograph poorly. Another, to my relief, is the intellectual. He professes himself incompetent in English, but isn't. Today, he tells me, he and the other recent arrivals are running a factory safety course.

The manager interrupts him. Mr Safety translates.

'Manager want to know you drink beer,' he says. All the men are looking at me.

'Of course,' I say with theatrical pomposity. 'I am English. The English are world champions at drinking beer.'

When Mr Safety renders this in Chinese, the table is suddenly all smiles.

'How many bottles you drink?'

'In England we drink ten bottles.'

This response proves very popular.

'For breakfast.'

They love this.

'For lunch, twenty bottles.'

'And dinner?'

'Dinner no bottles at all.'

When this is translated the men stare. I think they sense a joke coming.

'For dinner, we drink barrels.'

The line is a huge and farcical success.

Half a dozen litre bottles of Wusu beer appear on the lazy Susan. I seize them all and make a great show of guarding them.

The manager fetches more and pours himself a glass the size of a tea cup and another for me.

'*Kam pay*,' he says, which I haven't heard before but which requires no translation. '*Kam pay*,' I say. I down my tiny beer in a gulp, and upend the empty glass on top of my head. Then I strum my fingers on the tabletop and whistle while the manager finishes his glass. The crowd loves it.

'*Kam pay*,' exclaims the moon-faced clown. I thrash him too. In the hot room the beer is welcome. And food has begun to arrive. Plate after plate of fish and noodles and chicken, and vegetables that I've never seen before, and soup that no one touches.

'*Kam pay*,' says a man who has not previously spoken. A scar bisects his face horizontally, an engorged ravine passing between his top lip and his nose and curving slightly up around the hummock of each cheekbone. To imagine the accident that caused the scar would do no good for one's appetite.

'*Kam pay*!'

Another victory at a drinking canter, and general mirth. Though I can't help noticing that no one has been asked to *Kam pay* except me, and that I have drunk three glasses while no one else has drunk more than one. I don't care. I feel happy to be in Chinese central Asia, eating and drinking in a village I can't name with people I can't talk to and will never meet again. I am seized by a sense of the random, the arbitrary, of everything being just a fairgound ride and that all one can do is hold on and enjoy it. The intoxicating wind of freedom fans through the hair I haven't got. I giggle and stand.

'*Kam pay*,' I announce to the whole table and I down my glass and beam at them. But it seems there are rules to this game that I haven't yet grasped. Everyone smiles, but no one drinks. Until I put my glass down, that is.

'*Kam pay*,' says one of the safety managers. To me, of course. I refill my glass and beat him, but not by much. The whole table is enjoying the cultural exchange.

They are also enjoying my chopstick use. It is more deft than it was but sometimes my pincer grip is too strong. Greasy chicken bone encircled by greasy chicken skin is especially given to behaving like a squeezed lemon pip. But the nutritional loss is negligible, and the gain to the joy of nations substantial. I feel I am among friends.

One of the many pleasures of communal Chinese dining is that you have no idea how much you've eaten. When you've had enough you stop. When you realize you actually haven't had enough you start again. And at any time you can smoke.

When the first major bout of eating is done, the *Kam pays* resume. Each toast is one on one and I am invariably one of the ones. On perhaps the fifteenth toast I am at last defeated by the man with the scar. Now everyone is wanting to *Kam pay* me. And they do. More bottles keep appearing. I am conscious of grinning like a chimp. And then suddenly the meal is over. The intellectual explains, through a forest of empty Wusu bottles, that the men must now return to their factory safety course.

I reach for my wallet and am told in emphatic terms that I am their guest. I insist, with the intense sincerity of a lunchtime drunk. They won't hear of it. I tell Ivy to insist on my behalf. She does some impressive insisting. They do some equally impressive resisting.

'They want pay,' she says, 'they like your tcher actor.'

'My what? My tractor? They like my tractor?'

'Yes,' says Ivy. 'They like.'

'You are good Englishman,' says the intellectual and I only just resist the urge to hug him.

My bladder wakes me just as we are reaching Urumqi. I am prone in the back of the car. My cheek is stuck to the car seat with sweat and dribble. Stephen passes a bottle of water over the seat back.

'Thank you,' I say. My voice sounds like gravel in a pipe.

'No thank you,' says Stephen and in the rearview mirror I see the reflection of his big round smile.

When I'm undressing later in the hotel, it comes to me that it wasn't my tractor that endeared me to the cotton men. It was, though I'm not sure I'd displayed it to best effect, my character.

17

Faces

China does a distinctive line in civic bullshit, consisting mainly of romantic abstract nouns that bear little relation to reality. It is tempting to see it as simply the lies of a communist regime, but it is as old as Chinese civilization. Every dynasty wrote its own. You could call it mythologizing, or spin doctoring, but I prefer to think of it as merely lying. Emperors who had cheerfully tortured and slaughtered thousands, went down in the official records as 'The Breath of Universal Kindness' or some similar tosh. Tiananmen Square means 'gate of heavenly peace'.

At the entry to People's Park in central Urumqi there's a contemporary example: 'The long history and splendid culture of this park witnessed centuries of baptism and tremendous changes of the world and the traditional culture of primitive simplicity and elegance as well as scenery of enchanting beauty there attracts tourists from all over the world.'

The words glide smoothly over a brutal colonial history. And as so often in China they come to rest on scenic prettiness. Here the 'enchanting beauty' consists of a municipal park that would be unremarkable in Wigan.

By the park entrance is a little pleasure lake. According to the notice, the lake

> is as lucid as a mirror and is thus called Jian (meaning ancient bronze mirror) Lake. After liberation Jian Lake looked especially beautiful . . . The water is so clear that people can see their image clearly in the lake . . . Pavilions with the neighbouring long corridors attract the tourists to linger on with no thought of leaving. In midsummer it is pretty idyllic when the bright moon is high in the sky with sparkling moonlight on the tranquil lake surface.

On the tranquil lake surface at present are several newspapers, sodden and slowly sinking, numerous sweet wrappers, half a wooden paddle and a yoghurt carton. At the leeward end of the lake there's a two-yard curtain of scum. The water is the colour of civic-amenity water the world over. It resembles minestrone soup. The banks are of concrete-coloured concrete.

'In 1956 the Monument to the Revolutionary Martyrs was erected and has ever since become a shrine for people of all ethnic groups as well as students in college, middle school and primary school in Xinjiang to pay reverence to revolutionary martyrs and carry out revolutionary ideological education.' Whispering 'you betcha' to myself I set out to find the monument.

Concrete paths wind between trees. Some trees are sprouting the first pink blossom of spring, like wisps of candyfloss. In a concrete pagoda that would also be unremarkable in Wigan, a group of musicians has gathered, some old, some not. They are playing instruments that would be most remarkable in Wigan. One woman is blowing into a set of what look like wooden bagpipes, another runs a bow across what looks like a stringed chemical retort, and an effervescent oldster plays two blocks of wood. He does this by banging them together. The noise they make is quintessentially Chinese. I don't know whether the musicians are improvising or playing a score. I do know that they look engrossed and happy.

Here, as in Shanghai and Quanzhou, the Chinese exhibit their propensity for public pleasure-taking with the usual absence of self-consciousness. There is also an absence of Muslims. Every face I see is Chinese, but for two women in headscarves. Each of these women has a besom and a pan and a look of deep weariness. They move like prisoners of war.

It's only nine in the morning, but the Chinese are already dancing. Crones totter tiny waltz steps. They cling to other crones, or to nothing, their arms stretched out like winter branches. No one looks or cares. I see only smiles. A plump businessman in the regulation shiny suit and white shirt does a little solitary jig, a cigarette hanging Andy Cappishly from his lips. He breaks off to answer his mobile phone. He shouts his half of the dialogue, waving his free hand with unrestrained anger. Then he snaps the phone shut and dances again.

A troupe of middle-aged women swing swords very slowly indeed, under the instruction of a younger woman. The swords are curved, gleaming and a yard long, like the swords used for beheading on militant Islamic videos. The women sweep and stoop and bend and step. They are concentrating very hard. The instructor says stop and the concentration dissolves on the instant into gleeful chatter, giggles, little clappings of the hands.

A sign stuck into a flower bed says in English, 'See, the flower is smiling to you to say thanks.' The flower bed is bare soil.

Accompanied by two men on accordions, a woman sings. She doesn't sing to draw a crowd. She sings to sing. When a song ends no one applauds. Indeed no one pays her any attention. She riffles through the pages on the music stand to find another song to sing.

215

Signs to the Monument to the Revolutionary Martyrs have run out. I ought to just follow the people of all ethnic groups and the hordes of reverential students, but they seem to be paying reverence and practising ideological education somewhere else today. I give up on the monument. It isn't hard to imagine it. Besides, the museum should be open by now and I am keen to see Cherchen Man.

He was buried 3000 years ago in a simple poplar coffin. His grave lay a few hundred miles south-west of here on the edge of the Taklamakan desert in the virtually rainless Tarim basin. Time did all it could to him and it wasn't much. Judging by the photograph I've seen he looks little worse than some people I've drunk with. He's still got his clothes – a burgundy robe and deerskin boots. He's still got his skin, his hair and a moustache. The climate has mummified him.

But what matters about him, and what I want to see for myself, is his race. He is six foot six and is emphatically not Chinese. Here at the central point of the world's dominant land-mass, the place where East meets West, this man is a Westerner.

It's only a mile or so to the museum but that's enough distance for Urumqi to lose its commercial gloss and become any-city-in-China shabby. A wide road aspires to being a boulevard, but that aspiration is torpedoed by potholes and rubble-strewn buildings. It is hard to tell whether the buildings are half built or half demolished.

The museum looks recent and municipal grand. But it's shut. Half past ten on a weekday morning and there are no cars inside its gate, no people littering its imposing steps. By the gate is a little guardhouse. In the guardhouse is a little guard. He does not warm to me. I try a few hesitant words in Chinese – when, time, open – that get me nowhere. I resort to gesture. I point at my watch and perform an unmistakable mime of doors opening and a grateful tourist prancing through them to be delighted by exhibits both cultural and educational.

216

The guard shows little sign of enjoying the show then jabs a finger at a wall calendar. He is pointing at next month. Lacking the ability to question him further, I leave the guardhouse and start across the compound towards the imposing steps in the hope of finding some explanatory notice on the door. The little guard calls me back. He has laid a hand on the enforcement paraphernalia around his belt and lost any hint of affability. It doesn't look like I'll see Cherchen Man.

I stomp back down the ramshackle boulevard feeling thwarted. Through the railings of a locked park I peer at examples of the larger local mammals – antelope, a camel, wolves, a bizarre sort of tiger – all fashioned out of concrete. On the pathway in front of me less impressive creatures are offered for sale – goldfish, puppies, and rabbits in cages so small their fur is forced through the mesh in tufts. Newts squirm in a blue washing-up bowl and baby turtles in another. The sellers squat by their wares on blankets. Most are Muslim.

The Commercial and Construction Bank is bewildering. People throng the hall but without going to the counters. I indicate that I want to change traveller's cheques. The teller looks deeply puzzled, takes the cheques and my passport, consults a colleague, comes back, returns my property and points at the wall to my right. I shrug. She points again, vigorously, says 'Go' in a tone I am unsure of and returns to her mysterious work. When I turn I discover I have become the object of considerable interest. A security guard takes my arm and studies my documents, then leads me out of the building and round the corner and through a set of revolving doors into another banking hall indistinguishable from the first one. I choose a window at random. The young man takes my stuff, says nothing, goes to consult a colleague, returns and says, in English, 'three weeks'. In corroboration he ticks off three weeks on his desk calendar.

'Three weeks no good,' I say. 'Today? Possible?'

'China Bank,' he says and gestures along the street.

'Along there?'

'Yes,' he says.

'Is it far?'

'Yes.'

'How far?'

'Yes.'

'Five minutes? Ten minutes?'

'Yes.'

'Fifteen minutes?'

'Yes.'

'A couple of hundred miles through malarial swamps?'

The conversation is verbatim except for the last question. But it would have elicited the same answer. When China is confronted by an alien, yes seems to be the default response.

But, of course, I am in no position to complain that the Chinese haven't learned my language. I haven't learned theirs. I can reliably say only hello, goodbye, thank you, banana, postcard, how much, most of the numbers from one to ten, a few interrogative adverbs, and toilet. The word for toilet sounds like the act of flushing. I invariably have to repeat it half a dozen times. And occasionally I have had to resort to a mime that feels, but so far has not been seen as, sexually suggestive.

The language impasse can be frustrating. But I am also intrigued to learn where language matters and where it doesn't. The transactions of modern life, money, travel, services, are all linguistic. But beneath them lies the paralinguistic beast, who smiles and laughs, who fears or threatens, who breaks bread with others and drinks with them and is social and physical. To be shorn of language is not to be shorn of communication. Rather it is to become more aware of the human ape and his subtleties. I find myself paying far closer attention to faces, to gestures, to the very way the body is held, tapping into something that is universal and undimmed by the brief sway of linguistic civilization. I like all that. It underlines that we are more similar than we are different. And it gives travel an edge, a brightness, an aliveness.

China Bank, when I find it, is shut.

As I approach the Muslim quarter, poverty spills more obviously on to the pavement, along with black-eyed, rampant children, whose skin is the colour of fresh engine oil. They scuffle and play dice, and scamper fearlessly through traffic and are contagiously joyous.

In an open market, sides of mutton hang from a wheeled chrome rack. It's the sort of rack you see in Marks & Spencer holding a dozen frocks. A youth swats flies from a mutton haunch and urges me to feel the fatness of the meat. A gloom-laden man slumps staring at his mobile phone, his forearms resting on a tray of livers.

A grinding crunch of metal. I and everyone else turn to see a black saloon in the middle of an intersection with its nose wedged under a flatbed truck. The black bonnet is pinned and crumpled. Onlookers swarm on to the road, surrounding the vehicles like flies on mutton. On the fringes of the crowd there is tiptoeing and universal delight. Nearer the centre, more serious gawping faces, and at the heart of the drama voices raised in serious anger. I cannot see the drivers. Onlookers join the argument. Everyone shouts. No one hears. Horns blast. Vehicles force through the swarm. The argument falters then flares again. I stay five minutes on the kerb. The crowd does not shrink. No authorities arrive.

Lining the street are a hundred stalls selling identical clothes, their owners bellowing their individuality. For a few coins I buy half a dozen hot pastry parcels stuffed with mutton. I sit on a bollard, bite into the pastry and grease spurts over my chin, and I am assailed once again by the smell of spices that I cannot name but that could not be Chinese. I wipe my chin with my handkerchief, and sit like the prow of a boat around which the people flow like water. And what faces there are on the people.

If I had arrived in this street by parachute I would not believe I had landed in China.

A dumpy man in a suit and open-necked shirt has the round face of a Lebanese shopkeeper, his dark eyes set deep in the dough of his flesh, like currants thumbed into putty. Two paces behind him is a hook-nosed son of the desert, all haughty and Bedouin. Give him a white robe and a dagger in his belt and he would personify cruelty in the sort of comics I read as a kid. And I realize that it is from just such sources that I am recognizing these faces, characterizing them with the prejudices instilled in me by where and how I was brought up. I don't know exactly what Bedouin means; I haven't been to Lebanon; but these faces are indisputably Bedouin and Lebanese. And that one's Kazakh. I don't know how I know Kazakh. Until this week I couldn't have placed Kazakhstan on the map. But the round fur hat, the wide brow, a certain shape of the cheeks and lips that I can't define all say Kazakh, and the beard that is shaved from the face but that stretches under the chin like a wide and bushy strap is a Kazakh beard. Or rather it is the beard of a Kazakh herdsman who tends beasts on the high mountain slopes. I don't know how I know this, but I know this. Just as I know that that face there, with bulging cheekbones beneath narrow eyes, is the face of a Mongol, a Genghis, a descendant of the horde whose empire once stretched across the sweeping plains from Europe to the China Sea. Horsemen they were, and nomads, and they ruled the world. And in among these faces are a few that are simply startling. Startling because they are similar to mine. Across the way I keep catching glimpses of a lad selling pomegranate juice. He is squeezing the fruit in a silver press driven by a spoked thing like a ship's wheel. The juice is arterial purple. He sells it by the glass. The boy's hair is sandy. His face is freckled. Change his clothing and his language and he would go unremarked in Dublin. And he's not alone. There are other faces that you could only call northern European. Are they white

Russians? I don't know. But there is one type of face that is most noticeably not in evidence. Here, perhaps a mile from the centre of Urumqi, there are no Chinese faces at all.

I cross to the pomegranate stall, attract the lad's attention and say '*Zdrarstiche*', which is almost all that remains from two years of Russian at Brighton Grammar School thirty-five years ago. *Zdrarstiche* means hello. I think. I hope. The lad stares at me.

'*Zdrarstiche*', I say again. His face remains blank. I buy a glass of pomegranate juice to cover my embarrassment. It is astringent, and somehow manages to taste purple.

Round the next corner I meet a camel. I suppose I shouldn't be surprised. I am not the only tourist in these parts and nothing more exemplifies the local exoticism than a camel. Its keeper is done up in the sort of lurid uniform than one associates with whirling dervish dances as performed for heads of state or tourists or photographers from *National Geographic* magazine. He has breeches of red satin, a high-collared jacket of red satin with gold embellishments, a red satin hat as worn by American Rotary Club members and a bent cigarette. He looks morose. The camel looks morose, too. It has good reason. Not only is it tethered to a railing on a packed city pavement, but its dinner pail is heaped with a mess of swill that it has understandably ignored. Round its knowing-looking skull there's a decorative sash of red satin.

The camel is about half the size I'd have expected. At roughly the height of my shoulder, its humps flop like old women's breasts. Is it a juvenile, or perhaps a wild bactrian, the local variety, endangered now but uniquely capable of coping with the Taklamakan desert? I don't know and can't ask. The beast is available to ride, like a Blackpool donkey. I watch it kneel, though kneel is too smooth a verb. It collapses in stages. Its front legs buckle and crumple, then its back legs, then it settles into the ground like a broody hen. Its fur is surprisingly dense and shaggy. Its hooves are a foot across and its teeth are simply terrible.

I cross the road from the packed and higgledy-piggledy markets and find a deserted one. This is the International Grand Bazaar, purpose-built in 2002 to enshrine the ethnic variety and turn a profit from it. It includes a KFC, a Joy Square, a sightseeing tower, a bronze statue of a camel bearing little resemblance to the real thing over the road, and several three-storey halls selling indigenous stuff. The money that built it came from a property development company in Hong Kong. Judging from the paucity of shoppers the Hong Kongese will be fretting over their investment. But perhaps the tourist season has yet to get underway.

In Joy Square the riot squad is practising. Or rather a fledgling riot squad. They are about as menacing as Stan Laurel. Eight lads have been issued with uniforms, boots, shields, helmets and yard-long batons, but not with shirts or socks. Their shirts are all different colours. Their socks are mostly missing.

They have a commander who bristles like the standard sergeant major, and an instructor in civilian clothes. The instructor smokes as he instructs and sometimes stops to answer his mobile phone, leaving his charges frozen in some deeply unconvincing posture of defiance. The lads look at each other and giggle. The posture rapidly thaws.

The instructor snaps his phone shut and resumes instruction. 'All move one pace to the right – no the RIGHT – swivel, plant feet, position shield, raise baton.' The lads are hopelessly unsynchronized, floppy and weak, a rag-tag mob of school leavers. All are Chinese. This would appear to be their first lesson. Why is it going on in public?

If it is an attempt to intimidate, it's risible. Few locals bother to watch. Those that do, look on with a benign indifference, a sort of low-temperature curiosity. The spectacle is closer to clowning than policing.

And yet the authorities are very evident here. Recruitment posters abound for the armed forces and the police, posters in Chinese script, Arabic script and sometimes Russian.

I have already had abundant glimpses of the army and the police, more than enough to understand that authority here is different to authority in Sussex or Christchurch. It is less likely to be trustworthy. It is more likely to be corrupt. It is more likely to threaten or to employ violence. There has not been that long gradual acceptance that comes eventually with democracy, and that is the greatest achievement of a few bits of the West, an achievement that it is easy to lose sight of. In most of the world people think twice before ringing the police. China is by no means the worst. But nor is it the West.

Here in Xinjiang the Chinese authorities are clearly still nervous. They have reason to be. China has imposed its will on this Muslim land. When Mao annexed Xinjiang in 1949, the Uighurs made up about 90 per cent of the population. Now they're just under 50 per cent. And in Urumqi they are very much a minority, about one-eighth of the population. It's a classic colonial model. The development that is going on is Chinese development. The prosperity that is evolving is Chinese prosperity. You would have to be blind to walk this city and not notice.

The Uighurs have risen against the Chinese from time to time. Their protests have been quashed, ruthlessly. Ten years ago in Yining to the west of here there was a rebellion. Rebels broke into the police armoury and seized weapons and killed several policemen. Central government sent in the army, though they dressed them in police uniforms. There was a massacre, a bloodbath. The number of Uighur deaths has never been published. It almost certainly ran into thousands. Those thousands included unarmed women and children.

America's absurdly named 'War on Terror' has been a boon to the Chinese authorities. Under the guise of doing their bit to root out fundamentalism, they have crushed anything even remotely suggestive of Islamic protest against Chinese oppression. China does not mean to lose control of resource-rich Xinjiang.

An old man sits down beside me, a dead ringer for Ayatollah Khomeini, and watches me taking notes. He does not dissimulate his curiosity. He stares. I don't mind. I like the notion that to someone else's eyes I'm an exotic. As I write a script which he must find as opaque as I find Arabic, he mimes the movements sympathetically with his own hand and he laughs. 'English?' he says.

'Yes,' I say, looking up into his beard which has come rather closer than I might have wished.

That proves the end of communication, though not of conversation. He has plenty more to say. He may be calling me a colonial oppressor, or inviting me to his home, or trying to convert me to Islam, but I shall never know.

Then 'English?' he says again.

'Yes.'

He nods. We seem to have solved some problem. I solve it more radically by saying 'Goodbye' and entering the bazaar. It isn't busy. Nor is it the real thing. It's aimed at tourists. It's an example of that parody world that comes into being the moment tourism happens anywhere. The smell of money makes a place look at itself through a visitor's eyes, to see its own marketable bits and then to preen and plump them. And thus it becomes a self-conscious caricature of itself. It's like that moment when a crowd at a football match catches sight of itself on the big screen and stops being a crowd and becomes 'a crowd' performing the business of being a crowd. Or that dire day when a cute little girl learns that she is cute. She realizes that she can winkle anything out of daddy by curling her hair in her fingers and tucking her chin into her chest and looking up at him with panda eyes. From that moment she is never cute again, but only 'cute', a performer. It's just self-consciousness, otherwise known as the fall of man.

And the bazaar is stacked with an embryonic form of that self-consciousness. But it's young enough in its tourist tackiness for the objects still to have some interest, at least for me. I like the elaborate metal coffee-pots that may on reflection be teapots, the curved knives, the Islamic carpets, the vessels made of coiled wire, all manner of jewellery, and the bits of wild beasts. You can buy a five-yard python skin, a stuffed fawn sprinkled with glitter, Arctic fox pelts white as innocence, and massive wolf pelts, silver-grey and soft as down with head and paws intact and odourless. The death mask of the wolf is invariably set in a snarl. And I just love the ashtrays, cheap pewter things with the heads of prominent people stamped in the base. Here's a Lenin ashtray, a Brezhnev, a Nixon and a Pope John Paul. I buy a pope and ask for a Mao but I am told no.

I have the place almost to myself. As I idle past each stall the proprietor stands and follows me along its length. If I stop to finger anything it is instantly presented to me. Most of the vendors of these central Asian souvenirs in this synthetic cultural bazaar are, inevitably, Chinese. They are a mercantile race.

Across the road men are filing into a mosque. The step is littered with a silent scattering of shoes. Immediately outside the gates of the mosque a vendor with a clip-on microphone is hawking scarves, running the silk of his wares through crabbed and buckled fingers. A little alcove offers artefacts made of Xinjiang jade. I buy a Buddha carved in relief, fat, genial, cross-legged and half an inch tall and I string him round my neck. For Jessie, my dog, who upset a few people through excess of zest, but who never hurt a soul.

Invisible creatures will be at work on her flesh by now, on the silk of her ears, on those melancholic hopeful brown eyes. I bring the Buddha to my lips, murmur 'rest in peace', feel my throat choke up and snort at my own sentimentality. But I smile gently at all eyes that meet mine on the walk back to my hotel. And I give twenty yuan to a beggar whose withered, twisted leg is sheathed in a blanket but who waves a snap of it at passers-by to let them know exactly how withered and twisted it is.

I ask hotel reception whether the museum will reopen in time for me to see Cherchen Man. 'One moment,' says the delightful girl, 'I ring the government.'

I'm impressed by the optimism of 'one moment'. But she's back within a minute.

'Museum closed,' she says. 'Open next month.'

'But I won't be here next month.'

She shrugs.

Ivy meets me in the lobby. She asks me, more or less, where I spent the morning. I say I've been in the Uighur quarter. She gasps.

'So dangerous,' she says. 'Many bad people. Many dangerous people. Your money OK?'

This from an educated woman in her twenties who has lived her whole life in this city. There's something close to apartheid here.

18

Cart Meets Car

We're heading for a cotton farm run by one of Ivy's distant relatives. Or perhaps one of Stephen's. We are accompanied by a photographer who is also one of Ivy's distant relatives. Or perhaps Stephen's. The photographer is here at my request.

I have never owned a camera for reasons that seem obvious to me. But a few days ago the publishers emailed to ask whether I could get a snap of myself standing in a relevant cotton field in the relevant underpants. I said OK, though my email probably sounded a little keener than I felt.

I explained the request carefully to Ivy and she explained it to Stephen and they agreed it would be no problem and fixed it within the family. I was not surprised. Family remains the supreme social unit. It survived Mao's programme of collectivization. It survived the Cultural Revolution. It was just too ancient, too strong, too engrained. China is family. One reason, I suspect, is that in a world where officialdom has always been likely to be corrupt, the family is the one repository of trust.

The photographer relative is a softly spoken and gentle man with a metal camera case, a telescopic tripod and no English.

We turn off the highway and plunge into the timelessly rural. I am not tempted to romanticize it. Animals and men live side by side. Poverty is rife, goods primitive, and decent dentistry both a long way off and unaffordable. If you are born here, this is the world: cotton fields, mud, a few goats and a vast sky.

Arterial roads shrink to lanes like veins. The veins shrink to whatever you call very narrow veins. Then we stop. There is a vigorous discussion in Chinese. I don't understand a word but I am confident I understand the meaning. We are lost.

'Is good?' asks Ivy, gesturing at the landscape.

Ploughed fields and lines of poplars stretch to the horizon, under a sky made grey by a billion tons of cloud as thick as snot. Two fields away a group of human dots attend a yellow tractor.

'Is good,' I say.

The photographer and I walk to the heart of a vast field and then he gestures to me to stop. I start to undress. I hope that Ivy has explained to him the shot that the publisher wants. As I unzip my trousers, I hope this with some intensity.

The photographer looks up from fixing a lens to his substantial camera and doesn't seem alarmed by the sight of a 49-year-old wearing only Cambridge-blue underpants. He arranges me in various postures, then lies on his back in the crumbly soil to have me loom against the sky like a ravaged Charles Atlas.

Like most people, when a camera is pointed at me I turn spastic. I acquire a self-consciousness that makes me move like one of the Thunderbirds. If I smile it feels like trying to fold an oil painting.

And on this occasion the self-consciousness is intensified by a sense of guilt. I am standing in a field from which someone wrests a meagre living. I have just dropped by in a plush car to be photographed here, to spend ten ridiculous minutes posing before leaving again with a cameraful of glib images. Images that tell an untruth, images designed to amuse and deceive. I am acutely aware of being superficial and parasitic.

I am even more acutely aware of the yellow tractor. There is no doubt it is moving towards us. And the attendant dots are moving with it.

The photographer is taking his job very seriously. By gesture and example he indicates the poses he wants me to adopt, the thinker pose, the gaze-dreamily-beyond-the-horizon pose, the look-this-is-all-mine pose. The dots are becoming people.

I motion to the photographer that we are about to have visitors. He turns to look, then turns back and smiles. Now, would I move my arm a little to the left? And perhaps, yes, a tilt of the chin.

The tractor comes to a halt thirty yards away. Four men come to a halt beside it, long-handled spades slung over their shoulders. Three of the men are wearing Muslim skullcaps. Standing in their field in my underpants, I wave to them, wanting to appease them or amuse them, disarm them somehow. I want them to smile, to see me as a harmless buffoon who is aware of his own buffoonery. They stand impassively, staring. They don't smile. They don't speak.

I have lived for forty-nine years and it now turns out that every moment of those years has been tending inexorably towards this particular moment. I giggle.

'Good,' says the photographer and snaps a stream of pics. And we are done.

I pull on shirt and trousers and pad back to the car. As we drive away I swivel in the back seat. The men are still standing by the tractor, their faces registering nothing that I can interpret. We leave. And nothing, it seems to me, makes any sense at all. Between finger and thumb I rub the little jade Buddha that sits cool against my chest.

The photographer shows me how to look through the images on the camera. Most are ghastly. The remainder are worse.

Near a village a few miles further on, the remains of last year's cotton crop still stands, all brown and spiky. The photographer is keen to take more snaps. I am equally keen to keep my clothes on.

The desiccated cotton plants are only as tall as my thigh. Because these plants remain standing I presume that they were picked by hand. Each branch ends in a seed pod, wide open like a nestling's beak, and dried to snappability. It was from these seed pods that the mass of cotton fibres softly burst to bloom as a tuft of white that was picked by women with shoulder-slung baskets and sent by truck or cart to the factory.

A little mob of shaggy sheep, some grey, some brownish-black, grazes in the furrows between the dead plants. As far as I can tell they are nibbling at nothing at all.

The adjoining field has been ploughed and is now being sown. Last year's polythene strips have simply been ploughed in. The remnants litter the soil in greying shreds. Do they decompose? Judging by modern China's environmental record, I suspect not.

Attached to the tail of the tractor is a mechanism whose complexity surprises me. As the tractor moves, the polythene unwinds from a giant roll. A blade automatically slits it, and a seed drops from a hopper into the slit. At the same time little screws to either side flick loose soil up and over to settle in a mound that both holds the polythene in place and covers the seed. Men follow with shovels, tamping the mounds down or adding more clods.

The field is vast. The tractor travels one way for perhaps twenty minutes, till it is no more than a dot in a dust cloud, before it turns and slowly swells back to tractor size. It stops. Three men lean in to fiddle with the mechanism. All wear the work gear of the peasant the world over, and dirty skullcaps.

The photographer urges me closer to them for that authentic earthy shot. One of the workers turns, smiles, and hands me a spade. To my relief they all laugh.

The spade is a serious tool. It must weigh fifteen pounds or more. The ribbed handle is a yard and a half long, and a couple of inches thick. The bright and sharpened tip could slice off toes. Twenty minutes work with this thing and my urban hands would bubble with blisters. My back and thighs would scream.

The photographer poses me with one of the workers, the spade propped between us like a barrier. The man grins. His teeth are stubs. He looks about thirty. I am bigger framed than he is, but when the photographer makes us both grip the spade's shaft, his hand beside mine is a man's hand beside a boy's. I wouldn't want to swap lives. I don't know if he would. If my life were explained to him I suspect that he would see it as science fiction: the large house that I occupy alone; my sentimental affection for my dogs; my hectare of land on which I cultivate nothing; my absurd wealth; my supermarket shopping, my washing machine.

Mid-afternoon and we lunch in the nearest town. The restaurant is busy, dirty and Muslim. Kebabs smoulder on charcoal. Workers come in to be delivered a bowl of broth each and a mound of steaming bones – knuckle bones, femurs, whole sheep skulls. Each bone has been stripped of its muscle, but scraps still adhere to the shafts and crevices. With audible relish the men lift the bones to their mouths and rip, gnaw, suck.

We don't eat bones. We have beer and tea and broth and dumplings and a fistful of kebabs. The kebabs consist of alternating gobbets of mutton and fat on two-foot metal skewers as sharp as swords. I've rarely eaten better. The bill for four is about $10.

Early evening in central Urumqi. The streets are thronged and the stores open. The beautiful Chinese young are fingering racks of clothing that will make them look no more beautiful, and a hairdressing salon is dyeing hair in a way that will make them look rather less beautiful.

Food stalls, all run by Uighurs, offer fried corn cobs, steamed corn cobs, kebabs, a sort of nut brittle, a tray of sweetened bread cut into squares and sprinkled with herbs, rice and bright substances wrapped in a banana leaf. For a few yuan you can gorge yourself on surprises. At the fruit stalls men deftly carve pineapples into twists that look like helter-skelters on a stick. They drip such juice that they can be eaten only at a forward lean.

A VW Beetle is reversing along the pavement, honking its horn to shift the crowds. People casually sway like matadors to evade its bodywork by inches. The car swings backwards into an alcove. As it turns, the front bumper catches the wheel of a fruit stall, wrenches the cart a couple of metres and dislodges a heap of mangoes, a scatter of tangerines and a bowl of pineapple helter-skelters. The driver, middle aged, Chinese and furious, engages first gear and jolts the car forward twice, three times. But the bumper is hopelessly tangled with the cartwheel. He stops the car.

The stallholder is a dark-skinned Muslim woman. She stands and she stares, but she does and says nothing. I step in to help. I have to twist the chrome of the bumper a bit to disengage it from the crude wooden spokes of the cartwheel. A few more tangerines tumble. Numerous people pass by. No one else helps. The driver does not get out of the car. The stallholder shows signs of distress but still she does nothing. I have to lift one side of the cart to free it. When finally I separate the twentieth-century car from the medieval cart, the VW driver immediately revs the car and powers up the pavement, his horn blaring a path through the crowds.

I set the cart back level on its wheels and feet, noting the cumbrous weight of the timbers, polished smooth by years, perhaps generations, of hand grease. I collect fallen fruit. The pineapple helter-skelters are coated with grit and beyond salvage. But the tangerines and some of the mangoes seem OK.

Suddenly the woman shouts at me. I look up, thinking she is overdoing the thanks. I have done only what anyone would do, though I couldn't help noticing that no one else did. But she is not thanking me. She is rounding on me, delivering a fierce volley of what is unmistakably abuse. I am bewildered. Is she merely venting her rage by proxy? Her day's livelihood is half lost, and with the car gone she has nothing else to shout at, to express her sense of injustice. Or does she believe that in some way I am associated with the driver? I don't know.

Unlike the accident, the woman's tirade draws an immediate crowd. A dozen Chinese stop to gawp at me, and at the woman hectoring me, close to screaming at me. To them this is an enjoyable row. I sense they feel no sympathy for either of us. Here's a big-nose foreigner getting what for from a mere Muslim. We are spectacle. And I am immediately uneasy. For all the blamelessness of my actions, I feel like a guilty man. If the authorities were to pull up now I would be at a complete linguistic loss. And my presence would imply guilt. I place a final mango on the cart, turn and slither through the still gathering crowd, who part reluctantly at the last minute to let me through, putting an end to their fun.

I turn left and right at random to establish distance between there and me. Safely away I reflect that there is little to reflect on, that I don't know and will never know what the woman was thinking when she laid into me. But what I will remember is the utter lack of charity of the VW driver, and the implicit assumption of power of one race over another. And I will remember the faces of those who gathered to watch the row. They looked on the Uighur woman and me as children look on monkeys at the zoo.

I have stopped outside the Municipal National People's Congress. As with all structures erected in the name of the people, the people aren't allowed in. A tall wall and guards in guardhouses keep the people at an appropriate distance from this twenty-storey edifice. Within the wall the car park is empty but for a single limousine, sleek and reflective, its windows dark as secrecy.

A glassed notice board displays precisely the sort of propaganda you'd expect – a photographic record of a visit to the region by none other than old Hu Jintao, military salutes at a gleaming factory, a canal project with some excitingly computerized pumps, a group picture of a huge girls' choir – the same old tired stuff wheeled out by authorities of all stripes all over the world, and that no one ever quite believes, but that wears away at the subconscious.

I suspect I am the only person to have studied this board this month. The people pass by and life goes on, the life of the governed running parallel to but rarely intersecting with the life of those that govern. And both are generally happy to keep it that way. When the parallel lines intersect, then there can be trouble. And in times of trouble those who govern tend to be better armed.

19

Ozymandias in Mud

So, I have seen cotton seeds planted and the place where the cotton is cleaned and baled. I have seen cotton thread knitted into cloth, the cloth cut into pieces and my pants sewn from the pieces. I have seen how The Warehouse orders and procures those pants. I have seen containers packed and how their transport is arranged and I have seen the port my pants passed through on their way to New Zealand. Now I have only one gap in the chain to span, the gap between baled cotton and cotton thread. I need to see a spinning mill where perhaps I may discover whether the spinning jenny is, indeed, involved.

Such a mill is proving elusive. I have put Ivy on to it but I have also had the tenacious Ruth working the phone from Shanghai. Not to my great surprise it is Ruth who delivers. She rings to say that she has made an appointment for me at the Yida spinning mill in Urumqi in a couple of days. According to Ruth they are keen to see me.

Meanwhile, I want to go beyond Urumqi, to see a smidgen of

this vast and alien region. I am excited by its otherness, by its sheer difference from the life I lead.

Overnight a temporary wall of blue metal has risen around some roadworks, blocking access to the hotel. Stephen has to drive us down the footpath, which suits him just fine. The footpath is lined with vendors and their carts. As Stephen leans on the horn, I note with fresh eyes how swiftly the vendors shift. Their faces are taut, harried.

To drive south out of Urumqi is to drive straight into geographical remarkability. We skirt the flank of the Tian Shan mountains, seriously tall and snowy. The plain that they rise from is so bleak and arid that the mountains look somehow wrong, a giant topographical error.

The further we drive, the crueller the landscape. Dried watercourses scour through the sparse and withered scrub. We pass the eloquent remains of settlements that the terrain has seen off, the disintegrating shells of mud-built houses, of wattle-and-daub roofs. A railway runs parallel to the road. I imagine the men laying it, their bent backs and constant thirst. Here in the car we have nothing to drink. We trust a Japanese engine to get us through, to keep us insulated from the truth. Technology divorces man from the land. Life in London, in central Urumqi even, is barely touched by the elements.

On the plain I watch perhaps twenty smallish camels being herded by a motorcyclist. His rear wheel tows a plume of dust. When the camels break into a canter their necks stretch out ahead of them as though they were hauled by string. The camels and the earth are the same colour.

Plonked on the landscape without evident geographical reason is a chemical factory of some sort, like a boffin's lab made huge, breathing white smoke. The smoke streams horizontally with the wind as if the factory were a monstrous steam train. A few miles further on, the entire valley floor is filled by a wind farm. No people, only a field of turbines, their massive blades inanely spinning, sucking the strength of the wind into huge cables. There are too many turbines to count – five hundred of them, perhaps a thousand. Near where I live in Lyttelton there was a three-year row over the erection of a single turbine. Somehow I doubt that the engineers here had to bother too much with planning permission.

The turbines seem almost animate, stranded giants gesticulating to no one, like the NASA transmitter that endlessly sends a radio message into space, yearning for a reply it will never get.

We seem to be tending always down, like holidaymakers making for the sea. And that is apt, for the Tarim basin in which the Taklamakan desert sits was once, unthinkably long ago, a sea. Its heart is littered with million-year-old seashells.

The valley widens, the vistas stretch, then the walls close in again. On a hillside stands a nest of conical mounds, a graveyard. Each mound is shielded by a concrete slab to prevent the wind from scouring memory flat. There seems nowhere for the dead to have lived, but then the valley abruptly narrows to a gorge with trees and a sprinkle of houses beside a sparkling snowmelt river like a New Zealand trout stream. Momentarily I am surprised to see that the water flows and ripples here just as it does at home, building a bow wave before boulders and a glassy eye in their lee, slowing inside bends, bouncing and sparkling on the flats. On the far side of the river the railway clings to a perilous lip of rock.

The rocky range we're carving through is a ripple from the ancient collision of India into Asia. That collision slowly thrust the Himalayas to the sky, then, for reasons I can't begin to guess, left the Tarim basin unaffected, transmitting a huge shockwave far to the north, like a slow tsunami, to elevate the northern ranges. The notion is dwarfing.

The rock of the gorge gives way to spectacular sandstone ridges, sculpted by millennia of wind. Some are ribbed like washboards, others look as if they have been repeatedly scribbled on.

The patterns resemble snake tracks. Even inside the air-conditioned car it is apparent that we are driving into heat. The light is fierce. Far away to the east an oilfield is dotted with tireless nodding donkey pumps, their metal outlines flickering with heat haze. Mao had many good reasons to annexe Xinjiang.

High as a jet, it seems, an arrowhead of geese rows slowly across a colourless sky. The road splits. It's the first junction for a couple of hours. Korla is signposted 337 kilometres to the west. The first 20 kilometres of road are visible, spearing across arid nothing, the sand nibbling at its edges, then dissolving into vagueness. That route is more or less the northern Silk Road, skirting the upper edge of the Taklamakan desert. At its eventual end, way beyond the mountains, lay Rome.

As far as I'm aware, our destination is Turfan. I've read a bit about Turfan. It sits further below sea level than anywhere except the Dead Sea. Its average summer temperature is about 100 degrees Fahrenheit. And yet the place is apparently as green as a Sussex village, or greener. It grows figs, apricots, apples, melons and a hundred varieties of grape. The water to plump the fruit does not come from the sky. The annual rainfall is effectively nil and the potential annual evaporation is more than ten feet.

The place is a natural oasis but its water supply has been enhanced over the centuries by more than 3000 miles of canals and culverts, all enclosed beneath ground to prevent loss to the sun. Thus Turfan captures the springs and the snowmelt from the mountains and the result is bustling abundance amid nothing whatsoever.

Turfan is as old a place of human settlement as anywhere in Xinjiang. Its history is too complex to recite. It is enough to say that as an oasis on a trade route it has been prized and therefore fought over for several thousand years by every sect, tribe, marauder, caliph, emperor and khan who came this way. In the middle of the first millennium AD it changed hands every few decades. New Zealand, at the time, was governed by birds.

When we reach Turfan the police flag us down. The first thing I sensed about Stephen when I met him at the airport was that I wouldn't want to argue with him. He looks innately combative. But when the police invite him to join them in their little roadside caravan he goes like a lamb. They fine him for speeding between toll booths.

When he returns to the car Stephen is bristling with anger. He flings down the charge sheet. I pick it up, manage to decipher that the fine is 400 yuan and offer him the money. He refuses it, exploiting his full command of English.

'No thank you,' he says. For once, and quite by chance, his phrase makes sense. But I've got his linguistic measure.

'No, no thank YOU,' I say, and thrust the notes into his hand. He pauses, then turns to me and beams.

'No thank you,' he says, pocketing the cash.

Among conversations in the history of the English language, I suspect it's unique. And we understood each other perfectly.

Stephen then puts his foot to the floor and we drive past Turfan without stopping. I decide that it's best to say nothing

To our left run the Flaming mountains. They are among the hottest places on the planet, capable of generating temperatures of 80 degrees Celsius. In Fahrenheit that's a moderate one-day cricket score. At sunset the Flaming mountains are supposed to flame. Now, around midday, they look like what they are, which is pinkish sandstone.

We keep dropping. And the heat builds. Though this is only early spring, you can see the heat. It puddles on the land.

We pass through a little Uighur township that is built to defy that heat. The mud-brick houses enclose courtyards shaded by lattice roofs. And every roof has a lattice attic, where grapes are hung to shrivel to sultanas.

Here are biblical donkey carts, their drivers wielding whisks, a white mosque, little shops sunk below ground level, and children scattered on steps, in yards, on the road, roving as children rarely rove in the West because wealth brings fear.

A mile or two beyond the township we pull in under a sort of awning. We are the only car. A couple of Muslim men sit staring at us from the shade, chewing. Stephen directs me to a window where I buy an entry ticket for I don't know what, then steers me towards a gate in a tall mud wall. The woman who sold me the ticket scuttles from her ticket-seller's window to the ticket-checker's desk by the gate to check the ticket she sold me. It passes muster. I step through the gate and meet a dozen donkeys. Each is harnessed to a flatbed cart roofed with brightly coloured cloth to shade the passengers. There are no passengers.

'Taxi,' shout the donkey drivers, 'you want taxi?' I don't want a taxi. I want to know what this place is. Though in one sense it is obvious. It is a walled city. Or it was. Now it looks like a city of sandcastles after rain. All the usual buildings of a city – homes, storerooms, granaries, temples – have been reduced by time and wind to greyish humps and remnants. Erosion has softened every right angle.

The heat is relentless, brutal. I keep for a while to the narrow corridor of shade afforded by the city wall. That wall rises twenty feet or more and is built of mud. It forms a rough rectangle, each side perhaps half a mile long.

When I quit the shade, the sun hits my face like a slap. Sweat prickles my scalp. I follow a boardwalk towards the city's crumbling heart. Back at the gate a donkey brays. Other donkeys bray by contagion, the noise halfway between pain and mockery.

I duck under an arch, and enter what was once a living room. Alcoves are cut into the walls, alcoves that presumably held household artefacts however long ago. Low notches in the wall must once have supported the rails of a bed or some other furniture. My head brushes the ceiling. I scratch at a wall with a fingernail and the ancient mud comes away in a little talcum shower.

I lean on the door jamb as the ancient householder must once have done. Mud-dust drifts against every wall, like grey snow. Another thousand years and this place will be indistinguishable from what surrounds it. Here is Ozymandias in mud.

I see no one else. I am briefly the king of a ghost town. I climb an ancient stair and beneath my sole I can feel the mud powdering. But the heat bleaches me of energy. And to my ignorant eye one time-eroded mud structure is much like another. I return past the unemployed donkeys and out through the hole in the wall. Two sloe-eyed Uighur girls press me to buy key rings with miniature camel bells attached. They giggle and flirt. Stephen comes barrelling across and swats the girls away. Their eyes turn bitter. To judge by their tone, they curse him.

Dust has crusted on the information board, rendering most of it illegible. As I note down the few bits I can read, the tip of my ballpoint clogs. I have to lick it to write.

'Ancient city of Goacheng was founded in the 1st century BC in the Western Han Dynasty', and so on. The implication of all that I can decipher is that this place was a purely Chinese garrison town from its foundation until the invasion of the Mongols around the time of Chaucer. From what I've read elsewhere and from what I've seen of the region, this is a gross distortion. There is no doubt the Chinese were here around the time of Christ. But there is also no doubt that they left for long periods, and that when they were here they were often little more than vassals to a local king or khan, and that only intermittently did they ever have control of this alien province.

Confirmation of this history is written on the faces in the nearby village. As Stephen bullies his Nissan through the street market, they stare at us with something close to hatred. A man is wrestling a calf on to a cart. The man has a turban and a Taliban beard. Every woman is headscarved, every face central

Asian. This place is, and always has been, about as Chinese as Sussex.

I have no control over our expedition. It is clear that Stephen has decided what I need to see. Just beyond the village we pull in at a place whose function I can only guess at. The car park once again is deserted except for a builder's van. Two Chinese men are effecting repairs to the entrance. Once again Stephen urges me to buy a ticket of admission to a mystery. Once again the woman who sells me the ticket from a guichet, then goes to another guichet to inspect the ticket she sold me. On the other side of the gate an old man greets me.

'American?'

'New Zealand.'

He is puzzled. 'American?'

'English,' I say.

'England good.'

And that's our conversation done. We pass through a gate and into a field of nothing, scattered with mounds of dug soil and a boardwalk and heat. I am visited by a strong sense of absurdity. A hundred yards into the field we stop at the top of a shaft with cut steps leading underground. The man gestures me down but does not follow me. The steps end at the entrance to a black grotto and a light switch attached to some amateur wiring. I hold my breath, turn on the light, survive, and step into a coolness so delicious I want to drink it. I'm in, as I have already guessed, a tomb. And I am not alone. Mounted in dusty glass-topped cases are the long-term residents, a man and a woman. Of the two the man looks in better nick.

His feet are bare, his toes sexily long. Those toes have nails. His whole body has skin. His shirt has withered to rags exposing his sunken stomach and his thousand-year-old belly button. As far as I can judge, he's about as tall as I am. His teeth are goodish, but time has shrunk his lips and stretched his face to a grimace. I can't discern his race. His wife across the way has suffered more. One foot is still cased in a desiccated shoe. The other is a fan of dusty bones. Here's more or less what I failed to see in the shut museum.

These corpses were neither embalmed nor mummified. They were simply buried in poplar coffins. No rain fell, no moulds went to work, no rot set in. The earth just slowly leached them of their fluids. These people dried like sultanas. I like it here among the long-since dead.

The old man shows me to a couple more shafts. These tombs hold no bodies but are decorated in what are obviously Chinese motifs in obviously Chinese colours. One painting shows a moustachioed Chinese overlord with his foot on a chubby gut. Whoever the owner of the chubby gut is, the result is clearly a win for China.

Stephen and Ivy have not got out of the car.

'You like?' says Ivy.

'I like very much, thank you.'

'No thank you,' says Stephen inevitably and we're away again.

The Flaming mountains are riven by a valley like a bum-cleft. At its foot a stream glistens. Amid the sterility of hot bare rock the water is an apparent anomaly, an astonishment. We draw into yet another vast and almost empty car park. Half a dozen moody camels await the tourists that aren't here.

I am enjoying myself. The bass note of tourism is disappointment. Supposed attractions rarely meet the expectations they arouse. But because I have no idea where I am being taken, I am free of expectations.

What I find that I have been brought to see now are the Thousand-Buddha caves of Bezeklik. Arched and neat, the caves are dug into one side of a cliff. Each resembles the start of a narrow-gauge railway tunnel, abandoned after a few yards. Some of the caves are shuttered off. 'Keep off. Closed. Collapsing,' says a sign.

Each open cave is painted with images of kings and queens

who no doubt mattered in their day but whom time has now shrunk to mere stylized images, shorn of individuality. More interesting are the Buddhas. They swarm over walls and ceilings, painted or frescoed, endlessly replicating. Their presence demonstrates once again that not only goods were transported along this ancient trading route, but cultures and beliefs. Intense beliefs. Whoever dug these caves and then painted a ceiling with precisely one thousand identical images of Buddha was not someone of wavering faith.

Large chunks of friezes and frescoes are missing. A delightfully direct signboard announces that they were 'stolen by Stein in the winter of 1911'. Aurel Stein was a Hungarian-born archaeologist who spent years ripping ancient artefacts out of Xinjiang. Many are now in the British Museum.

In the last of the caves two pigeons broop gently at my intrusion, but don't shift from their perch on the rim of Buddha's halo.

At the foot of the valley, by a bend in the stream, a dwelling stands on a scrap of flat land. The house is mud-built, with a rough lean-to framework of poplar branches that the new season's vines have begun to smother. The upper storey of the house is a grape-drying room, and beyond it there's a gnarled and tiny orchard. But for the whisper of the stream the place is silent. Around it the sandstone gorge rises pink and barren and all enclosing. If ever I am to reach a hand into the dressing-up box of travel adjectives it must be now. This place is timeless.

In the late afternoon we head back towards Urumqi, stopping for lunch at a roadside restaurant. Four tables sit beneath a tattered awning. Two stout and merry women run the place, one evidently Chinese, the other with the lashed and wide black eyes of Persia. We have fresh-cooked Uighur breadsticks, noodles, beer and a plate of chicken bones relieved by chicken claws. Each of us is given a whole raw head of garlic. Stephen eats his then mine.

The toilet is on the far side of the baked backyard. It consists of an elevated hut with a floor of two concrete slabs set slightly apart. You squat or stand across that gap. Visible through it is an Etna of dried turds. And a pig.

The pig looks up at me, sniffs at my piss, then turns away in disappointment at the lack of substance.

Keeping to the shade as I return to the restaurant, I run my finger along the back wall of the house. A dog the size of a pony leaps through a barred window. It's black and keen to kill. I scream and jump backwards. The dog is brought up short by its chain. Its impetus is such that its back legs swing through and it falls in a heap. It is up again on the instant, barking maniacally until I am five yards away. Then it falls suddenly silent, turns, leaps gracefully back between the bars of the window and is gone.

I tell Ivy that on the way home I'd like to stop off at Turfan. Having come this far I feel I ought to see the irrigation system, the minaret that looks like an Islamic oast house, and the dusty streets of a settlement that comfortably predates Christ.

'Turfan?' says Stephen, making no effort to mask his surprise.

'Turfan,' I say decisively.

A quarter of an hour later we turn left off the highway and are driving up a main street of impeccable twenty-first-century urban China. Stephen looks across at me.

'Turfan,' he says.

I swivel to face Ivy. 'I'd like to see old Turfan,' I say.

'Old Turfan?'

'Yes. This is new Chinese Turfan. I want to see old Turfan.'

'Is not old,' says Ivy.

'No,' I say.

'We stop?' says Ivy.

'No,' I say. I can't be bothered and I've seen the photos and I've had three chunky bottles of afternoon beer.

'Urumqi?' says Stephen with a fat smile.

Yes,' I say, 'Urumqi.'

When we reach Urumqi in the early evening I discover that my hotel is holding an ethnic night. The hotel doors are opened for me by a boy and a girl dressed in traditional Uighur costume, all bright and shiny and flamboyant. Both the boy and the girl bow, smile and say 'Good evening, sir' in English. And they are both Chinese.

20

Stretching the Horse's Tail

Saturday, and I am due at the Yida spinning mill at 2 p.m. I spend the morning in People's Square where a low stage has been erected in front of rows of plastic seating. The seated area is roped off. The square has been decorated with red and gold lanterns, helium-filled and tethered to the ground by strings. When a breeze shifts through the square they dance like a field of giant tulips.

All this is in aid of recruitment to the authorities. An army officer in a booth is trying to interest youths in his promotional material. But he keeps glancing back at a little gas stove under his desk on which he's frying eggs.

I am given a leaflet that urges me to join the police. It has a few words in Chinese, Arabic and Russian, but consists mainly of cartoons. They depict policemen assisting the elderly, giving directions, rescuing the trapped, smiling like lottery-winners, and bearing no resemblance to any cop I've seen in China.

The fire brigade's here, too. Three fire engines have drawn a crowd of males, as big machines do everywhere. And other onlookers are staring up at the raised extension ladders in the hope that something will happen.

Music erupts from free-standing speakers, and dancers pour on to the stage. This is ethnic dancing for the people. The boys wear sky-blue jackets and tooled boots, the girls red satin dresses and dainty white shoes. The music is sinicized Muslim, racy, pulsing, exotic. The boys leap athletically to impress the girls, and the girls twirl coyly to seduce the boys. Or at least that's the idea. But it seems heartless stuff to me, a tamed exoticism, divorced from the way of life that gave it meaning. It reminds me of those national costume dolls in protective plastic sleeves that are inexplicably popular in the touristy bits of Europe.

(The only bit of Europe that doesn't seem to sell such dolls is England. England has no traditional national dress, unless one counts the uniform worn by Morris dancers, and most people are wise enough not to. If a doll were sold in true English national dress it would wear a skirt and blouse from M&S. And it would carry a plastic mac, because you just never know.)

The crowd in the seats has grown and I make to join it. A uniformed arm swings up in front of me and presses firmly against my chest. Its owner is not beaming like a lottery-winner. I don't argue.

The dancers are followed by an awards ceremony. A boisterous MC introduces a few uniformed dignitaries to the stage, men resembling the basilisk generals who stood behind Brezhnev at May Day parades. Then younger men come up to receive awards for I don't know what – firefighting, rescue, that sort of thing, I imagine – accompanied by half a dozen shoulder-toted television cameras. The cameramen are so keen that their viewers should see exactly what's going on that the live audience can't.

A hunched old man has been watching me make notes. When

our eyes meet he sidles across and addresses me in Russian. I manage to dredge up '*Rooski yazik ne zhnayoo*', meaning, I hope, 'I don't speak Russian.' Inevitably, I suppose, it convinces him that I do. He whispers fiercely to me and makes semi-covert gestures of dismissal at what's going on on the stage.

'*Rooski yazik ne zhnayoo*,' I say again, and he nods and keeps going. But it's clear what he isn't saying. He isn't saying how wonderful it is to see our young uniformed heroes honoured for their endeavours. When he eventually falls silent, I shrug.

'*Rooski yazik ne zhnayoo*,' I say once more.

'Ah,' he says with bitter disappointment, '*Rooski yazik ne zhnaetye*?' He spits and leaves.

The awards ceremony over, we are given a plump Chinese singer, then more dancing by a different ethnic group, then nothing. The seats empty and the crowd gathers round the military fire engines. Three youths in boiler suits and abseiling harnesses have climbed to the top of the extension ladders from which ropes are hanging. A countdown from ten and then the three lads leap from the gantries and slide to the ground, their arms and legs spread wide like falling stars. Two land deftly on the square and then turn to look up at the third who is spinning slowly at the midpoint of his rope, fiddling with a carabiner at his waist. TV cameras swing up to capture him. A brass hat looks down at his shoes and mutters darkly.

The woman who greets me at the Yida spinning mill is young, beautiful and impressively fluent in English. I tell her how impressively fluent in English she is.

'Thank you,' she says, blushing in textbook fashion, 'I spent three years at university in Melbourne. My degree was in financial studies. But when I finished I wanted to come home.'

She seems genuinely keen to show me the mill but we have to wait for a manager to join us. She gives me a light blue company cap and a set of earplugs.

'Do you keep in touch with your friends in Melbourne?'

'I have no friends in Melbourne. My friends are here.' Her tone is surprisingly emphatic. But then the manager arrives, jacketless, smiling, and we set off down corridors to the heart of the mill.

It occupies the site of a former government enterprise that went bust. The present owner is a private company, the Esquel Textile Co. Esquel began as a small outfit in Hong Kong in the late seventies. As China opened up, so Esquel flourished. The company moved into mainland Guangdong with the first wave of Western-style enterprises and simply grew.

Esquel makes shirts. It makes 60 million shirts a year. It makes shirts for Polo, Nike, Hugo Boss, Tommy Hilfiger and a trade-directoryful of other brands that you don't mentally associate with China. Two-thirds of those shirts go to the United States. Most of the rest go to Europe. If you're wearing a shirt from Marks & Spencer, Esquel probably made it.

The company grows, spins, weaves and knits its own cotton. A little of their thread goes on to the open market, but it is unlikely that it actually went into my pants. But, as my guide points out, cotton thread is pretty much cotton thread.

Esquel is in Urumqi because of the long-staple cotton. China just can't grow enough of that cotton to feed its clothing mills. Last year the country had to import 3 million tons of raw cotton, much of it from the United States. It then made that cotton into thread, made the thread into garments, sent the garments back to the United States and made a nice profit.

'In 2006,' says the girl matter-of-factly, 'the Chinese textile industry grew 50 per cent.'

You read a lot of figures like that in the newspapers. Some of them are probably trustworthy. They are the sort of figures that make Western investors' eyes water. They are the figures that have driven a tsunami of Western capital East, capital that has collided with China in much the same way as India once collided with Asia. Just as India pushed up the mountains that overlook this mill, so the impact of Western money pushed up the first skyscrapers of Pudong. But what is pushing them up now, in Pudong and in Urumqi, is increasingly Chinese capital.

Living in the West we are so familiar with private enterprise that we barely notice it. It's just a muted background hum. In China it is raw, new, dynamic and revving. You can hear its growl.

Sixty young men and women in face-masks sit in a very clean room. Beside each of them is an opened bale of cotton, like the bales I saw stacked at the co-operative. The youngsters are sifting the cotton by hand, grabbing a compressed wad from a bale and with intense attention ripping it tuft from tuft to check for impurities. Examples of impurities – feathers, hair, scraps of paper – are mounted on a wallchart for the benefit of visitors like myself. The young workers do not look up. With delicate Asian fingers they just tear apart cotton tufts under fluorescent lights. And this is all they do, for eight or more hours a day, and for six days a week.

I ask how long the average worker stays in this job and I am told that few last more than a month or two. 'Labour is becoming a problem,' says my guide.

In the best Western tradition the company has an official verbal view of itself: 'A company of fun people serving happy customers.' These words are posted on the wall outside the room where the cotton-sifters sit. I doubt that any irony is noticed.

Below the mantra are the articles of the company's mission statement.

Be a good citizen and a good employer.
Cherish the environment.
Explore and embrace innovative solution.
Reduce wastage through functional excellence.
Dare to err but quick to learn.

After the manual cleaning, the process of turning cotton into thread becomes entirely automated. A mesmeric Swiss-made machine sweeps endlessly back and forth over a compressed bale of cleaned cotton. The bale is the size of two cars. At each sweep the machine grazes a layer from the monstrous wad and sucks it into an air-drying duct where it is tossed and tumbled and fluffed and sent on its way to be carded.

Carding begins the process of straightening the cotton fibres, making them lie parallel to each other and overlapping. The carded cotton emerges like a fluffy horse's tail. The manager gives me a hank to toy with. It's sweetly tactile stuff. When I tease it apart it resists weakly.

'What holds the fibres together?' I ask.

Apparently every individual cotton fibre has a wall of cellulose. When the seed-head bursts open, the cellulose dries and shrinks and causes the fibre to twist into spirals, both clockwise and anti-clockwise. It's similar to the way a human hair curls when you draw it between clenched fingernails, or a ribbon furls when a scissor blade is run along it. These natural spirals make the cotton spinnable. Though the fibres are shorter than in, say, wool, the natural tendency of the spirals to intertwine and grip each other creates a strong thread.

After carding comes combing. The difference between the two processes, as far as I can gather, is one of degree. The long horse's tail feeds into another Swiss machine and emerges as an even longer horse's tail.

Each machine, whether it blows or cards or combs, has a host of identical siblings, thoughtless, obedient and quietly chuntering. These are the unpaid workers that create the world's wealth. A few slightly better paid workers tend the machines like stablehands, sweeping, feeding, nursing, cleaning.

After carding and combing the horse's tail is stretched again and twisted, gaining length and strength and beginning to look like rough thread. The largest room in the factory is the spinning hall, the size of a hockey pitch or two. I am reminded of my fifth-form history textbook and sepia photographs of cotton mills in Manchester, with women and children in rags and clogs tending clattering machines on which sat bobbins. Here are the same bobbins, thousands of them the shape of unopened pine cones. But the machines here don't clatter and most of the attendant slaves are gone. The hall is almost deserted.

I ask what these machines are called.

'Spinning machines,' says my guide.

'Have you heard of the spinning jenny?'

'No,' she says.

But effectively these machines are descended from the spinning jenny. And it in turn was descended from that most fundamental invention, the spinning wheel. It was the spinning wheel that enabled human beings to turn short fibres of either animal or vegetable origin into thread. From thread came cloth.

But the spinning wheel made only one thread at a time. As originally designed, the spinning jenny made eight threads at a time. These machines make hundreds of threads at a time.

Thread winds on and off the bobbins endlessly, passing through a series of eyes and guides to be stretched and twisted and improved and rewound. The autonomy of the machines is staggering. I watch as a machine halts at a fault in the thread, snips twice to excise the fault, reattaches the snipped ends with a multiple twist too swift to follow with the eye and chunters back into production. And everything is clean enough to eat off. The machines are so far beyond my capacity to design or build that I feel awed.

The final product of half a dozen industrial processes is a bobbin with the bulk of a melon and the shape of Mount Fuji. These bobbins are identical to the bobbins that I saw feeding the knitting machines at the Kingstar factory in Quanzhou. The bobbins are wrapped, stacked on pallets, and wheeled to railway carriages on the factory branch line. From here they cross China.

Most go to Guangdong and the Esquel shirt factory. From there the globe.

Every one of the million threads of cotton I am wearing at this moment passed through a factory like this and precisely this process, a process on which I am and always have been dependent but of which I knew nothing. It was this sense of industrial ignorance that launched this little quest. At the same time I realize that the process is essentially simple, a primitive discovery of an attribute of nature, refined to its essentials, then endlessly repeated.

An hour or so after we left it, we're back in a boardroom.

'So,' says Miss Lovely, 'any questions?'

I ask about the specific thread for underpants. The manager tells me it is single yarn for reasons of softness, 120-count or higher. Essentially the higher the count, the finer the thread. Shirt yarn has a count of between 40 and 80. Jeans yarn is 7 to 10. Shirt or jeans yarn is generally double yarn, which, as you may perhaps guess, is two single yarns twisted together for strength.

'And there are other mills in Urumqi?'

'Yes,' says the girl, 'several, but most are government mills. This is the best mill.'

I don't doubt her.

The cotton that Yida spins comes mainly from the Aksu region north-west of here. And it is all contracted direct from farmers.

'And those farmers,' I say, 'are they Chinese or Uighur or a mix of both, or don't you know?'

'They are all Chinese. We do not like Uighur people. They are lazy and they tell lies.'

21

I Spy Strangers

The plane climbs past the Tian Shan range, the snowy peaks blazing in the morning sun, and levels out over northern China on the long haul to Shanghai. I tilt back my seat and muse. I am glad that I visited the spinning mill at the end of my trip.

On the site of a failed communist co-operative here was a thriving modern business. Where once was low-tech here was high-tech. The machinery was imported and the style corporate. Yet the cotton-sifting room illustrated the way China can draw on the poor and rural young to be numbingly industrious.

The growth of the company paralleled the growth of China. It began in the halfway house of Hong Kong. When Deng Xiaoping made the first concessions to capitalism, Esquel made its first entry on to the mainland. The business now stretches from Guangdong in the south-east to Xinjiang in the north-west. And from the outset it has been dedicated to export. It has learned what the West wants and makes it more cheaply than the West can. It is, quite simply, the unfinished story of modern China.

And then there was the young woman who showed me round. She impressed me. It wasn't just her impeccable English. It was her twinkle, her sense of irony, her awareness. She will prosper. But there was also an emphatic Chineseness to her. In three years she made few if any friends in Melbourne. Her degree acquired, she returned without hesitation to the town of her upbringing in China's remotest province.

There is a famous Chinese folk tale of a princess who was captured by marauders and taken into exile. The nub of the tale is her inconsolable grief at being removed from home, from family, and above all from China.

It was obvious that the young woman at Yida was proud of her work and of her company. That, too, is typically Chinese. In China there is no stigma associated with industry or business. The truth is precisely the opposite. Chinese universities are chockful of engineers and scientists. When they graduate they flock to industry. It excites them.

When I was their age it didn't excite me. In common with many of my contemporaries, I disdained industry. I aspired to higher concerns and clean fingernails. It never occurred to me that the ease and privilege of my life rested on national wealth, and that wealth derived from inventing, making and selling things. Plus a fat historical dollop of conquest and theft. I was naive and I was decadent.

During a grim twentieth century, the Chinese had no chance to become decadent. They recognized the direct causal relationship between work and prosperity. And now that they've got the chance to have a go at putting it into practice, they're having a go and loving it. In the process, as they see it, they're returning China to its rightful position as the Middle Kingdom and leader of the world. They're loving that, too.

Everyone knows China invented paper, gunpowder, silk and

porcelain way before the West. But that is far from being all. China invented the magnetic compass before the West did, and the deep drill, and an efficient harness for draught animals, and lock gates and cast iron and the wheelbarrow and the suspension bridge and block printing and the loom and the use of water power and a winnowing machine and so on. Every one of these was in daily use in China at least a thousand years before it was thought of in the West. And each played its part in establishing a civilization that has a better claim than any other to have led the world. And now, after the worst couple of hundred years in its history, China is on the way back.

But to the Westerner, the most startling thing about the young woman at Yida was her disdain for the Uighurs. Despite having lived most of her life in Xinjiang, and despite being highly educated, and despite having spent time overseas, she dismissed the indigenous people en masse.

She is not alone. I heard the same sentiments from Ivy. I saw them enacted by Stephen at the wheel. I saw them embodied in events on the street and in the very layout of the city. The Uighurs are second-class citizens.

The term we reach for is racist. Racism sits near the top of our catalogue of sins. It is the indefensible position and I am not about to defend it. All I will say is that I, too, am racist. Before I came here I harboured a distrust of the Chinese. They looked different, they spoke a strange language, and they used chopsticks. I knew nothing of them, so the oldest part of my brain sounded an alert. Beware, beware, it bleeped, I spy strangers.

A couple of months in China and the bleep is silenced. Of course. People are people. That's all. That doesn't make me virtuous. I will fear other strangers. It's how we are. Racism is evolutionarily instinctive. It's the alarm call of the blackbird.

The young woman at Yida was sounding the alarm. She was also voicing official Chinese policy, though the government has never been as frank as she was. Beijing has done all it can to oppress Uighurs and other minorities. There's nothing new there. That oppression springs partly from a sense of Chinese racial superiority. It is indistinguishable from the British Empire's disdain for Johnny Foreigner, or the Roman Empire's disdain for barbarians. The word barbarian derives from barba, meaning beard. The further you went from Rome, the hairier and less civilized the people. The Chinese have always felt the same way. Unlike the smooth-skinned Han Chinese, the barbarian foreigner was bushily bearded.

And China has had good reason to distrust foreigners. Foreigners have always brought trouble. The Mongols did them over. The Manchus did them over. We did them over. The Japanese did them over. Their reaction, disastrous as it was, was isolationism. But as China trades more and more with the world, so it will become more trusting of strangers. It is happening already. Countless Chinese people have been good to this particular big-nose Westerner. They've made me smile. I like it here.

The following morning, I leave Shanghai on an absurdity. The Maglev is an elevated train. It has no wheels. It travels between the city centre and the international airport on a cushion of air sandwiched between magnets. Germans designed it, the Chinese built it and it runs at a monstrous loss. But you can't fail to be impressed by it. An LCD readout on the carriage wall tells you that somewhere around the middle of the eight-minute journey the train reaches a speed of 430 kmh, just for the hell of it. It's simply show-off stuff. 'Ooooh look at us,' says the Maglev to the foreign visitor, as down beneath him the Chinese shacks and huts and patches of cabbages dissolve into a blur, 'we can do *anything*. (Underpants included.)'

Acknowledgements

I'd like to thank The Warehouse Limited for letting me in, and especially Tony Pendleton of their Shanghai office. Also Kuehne and Nagel in Shanghai, Kingstar Light Industrial Products Ltd and Meida Elastic Fabric Co., both of Quanzhou, and the Yida spinning mill in Urumqi.

Michael Gorman was invaluable in giving me contacts in China. I'd like to thank Ruth for her industry and efficiency, Stephen for his driving and Ivy for trying very hard.

There's no point in thanking the hundreds of Chinese people who made me smile, but I do. I hadn't expected to smile that much.